Praise for *Michelle: A Biography*

"Liza Mundy's sane and realistic biography of Michelle
Obama implicitly acknowledges the new, more serious
status of a presidential spouse."

— *The Washington Post*

"[A] welcome primer . . . A quick read . . . so well-written
that you barely notice the length as you sprint toward
the end . . . 'Michelle's most important role is explaining
Barack Obama,' Mundy writes. 'She does this beautifully.
It is her crucial task to humanize him, to make sense of
him—to normalize him.' Mundy has done the same for
his wife."

— *USA Today*

"Mundy . . . offers delightful stories about the Obamas'
family life. Readers who want reassurance that Michelle
Obama is up to the job of First Lady and those who just
want to know more about her won't be disappointed."

— *Library Journal*

michelle

a biography

Liza Mundy

POCKET STAR BOOKS

New York   London   Toronto   Sydney

Pocket Star Books
A Division of Simon & Schuster, Inc.
1230 Avenue of the Americas
New York, NY 10020

First Pocket Star Books paperback edition May 2009

For information about special discounts for bulk purchases, please contact Simon & Schuster Special Sales at 1-866-506-1949 or business@simonandschuster.com.

The Simon & Schuster Speakers Bureau can bring authors to your live event. For more information or to book an event contact the Simon & Schuster Speakers Bureau at 1-866-248-3049 or visit our website at www.simonspeakers.com.

Designed by Suet Chong

Cover photograph © Timothy Greenfield-Sanders/Corbis/Outline

Manufactured in the United States of America

1 3 5 7 9 10 8 6 4 2

ISBN-13: 978-1-4391-5932-3
ISBN-10:   1-4391-5932-7

prologue

ON A SEASONALLY CHILLY DAY IN JANUARY 1964, a young Chicagoan named Fraser Robinson started his first day working for the city's water department. Robinson was twenty-eight years old, sturdy, athletic, bright, good-natured. The title of his job was "station laborer," but in truth, the term was a bureaucratic euphemism for janitor. In his new position, Fraser Robinson was expected to sweep, mop, and scrub floors and walkways at the city's water treatment plant; to polish fixtures, flush basins, empty garbage cans, pick up litter, load and unload trucks, clean up chemical spills. The only qualification for being hired, according to city records, was a "willingness to perform the job" and an ability to do strenuous labor. The salary was $479 a month, almost

$6,000 a year. It was not exalted work. Then again, it was better than many of the alternatives. Government work was usually a guaranteed tenure and came with a vacation and a pension. And at a time when job discrimination was routine and unremarkable, a young African American with a high school education could do worse than land a city job flushing basins and driving forklifts.

The job came at an opportune moment. Three days after Fraser Robinson started work, on January 17, 1964, his wife, Marian, gave birth to their second child, a girl. Their son, Craig, had been born a year and a half earlier. The couple named their daughter Michelle LaVaughn. LaVaughn was the first name of Fraser's mother. The Robinsons were a family who liked to name children after antecedents, a tradition that affirmed the importance of relationship and connection.

Fraser was perhaps the most common family name of all. Fraser Robinson was, formally, Fraser Robinson III. His father was Fraser Robinson II. His grandfather, a one-armed kiln laborer who died in 1936, had been Fraser Robinson Sr. That original Fraser had been born in Georgetown, South Carolina, in 1884, not quite a generation after the Civil War had ended and, with it, slavery. In the coastal community of Georgetown, most

African American families were descended from slaves who labored on the plantations that for many years provided the country with most of its rice, and the planters with their prosperity. At one time, 85 percent of the population of Georgetown County was enslaved. When the twentieth century was still young, that first Fraser Robinson had married a woman named Rosa Ella Cohen. They had at least four children: Zenobia, Verdelle, Thomas, and Fraser II. Some members of the Robinson family would stay in Georgetown, and many live there still, but sometime before 1934, Fraser Robinson II packed up his things and, in the midst of the nation's industrial transformation, joined the Great Migration northwest to Chicago. Fraser Robinson III, the newly minted city employee, had been born right here in Cook County, one of the nation's legendary incubators of political talent. He became a participant in the county's fabled political machine and a Midwesterner through and through.

The Great Migration was the vast exodus of American blacks out of Mississippi and Alabama and Georgia and the Carolinas, a massive stream of human movement that over fifty years would transform many Northern and Midwestern cities, Chicago among them, as seven million African Americans left their homes with the hope of reaching the post-agrarian promised land. The migration accelerated during World War I, when fewer Europeans were able to emigrate to an America of high-churning factories, creating a dearth of needed labor in steel mills, stockyards, railroads, and other industries. Before the war, many of these places had been unwilling to hire African Americans because their owners said that black men were unreliable and undisciplined. Now those same employers were eager to attract them. In Chicago, many jobs were located in or near the city's South Side, the sprawling area bordered by Lake Michigan on the east and downtown Chicago—the Loop—on the north. South Side provided proximity to the mills, rail yards, slaughterhouses, and meatpacking plants. It also contained working-class and even upper-middle-class residential areas. Already, on the South Side, there were distinct and cohesive settlements of Irish Catholics, German Jews, Poles, Lithuanians, Czechs, and Slovaks.

As African Americans poured in, these newly displaced Southerners found themselves channeled into a strip of land south of downtown, discrete and apart from the white areas. As the black population grew, some whites would flee South Side entirely, moving to the northern part of the city. Others would remain, in sections that were carefully demarcated. Throughout Chicago, a rigid pattern of residential segregation was perpetuated that would last for a very long time, enforced by a conspiracy of politicians, mortgage lenders, residents, and real estate agents. Chicago would be rightly described, even into the 1960s, as one of the most segregated cities in America, a distinction the city worked hard to earn.

But for an African American, Chicago still offered more economic opportunities and personal autonomy than the South, which surely was why Fraser Robinson II decided to move there. There was more work to be had than in South Carolina, and that work paid better. Urged on by the influential black newspaper the *Chicago Defender*, African Americans had continued the migration to Chicago for decades, sometimes following jobs, sometimes following relatives, sometimes following both. For example, Fraser Robinson II's sister Verdelle moved to Chicago because Fraser was there, according to her son, Capers Funnye Jr., who would grow up knowing his cousin Michelle Robinson. As she grew, Michelle would have family all over the city, from both her father's side and that of her mother, the former Marian Shields.

Ultimately a half million African Americans would

move from the South to Chicago, swelling the city's black population from 2 to 37 percent in 2000. The South Side would be where the majority would settle, though an African American section would grow up on the west side as well, and those two populations would expand toward each other and meet, making an *L* that forms one of the country's largest contiguous African American populations. Much of the world outside Chicago would assume the South Side was poor and black and criminal. In fact, the South Side has, for much of its history, been economically diverse and culturally vibrant. The South Side is home to the White Sox, to the prestigious University of Chicago, to Bridgeport, an Irish American neighborhood that was the residence of the late Richard J. Daley, mayor of Chicago and undisputed boss of the city from 1955 until his death in 1976. But as the African American population swelled, city fathers continued to do everything possible to keep black citizens packed into overcrowded schools and neighborhoods, at one point relocating the route of a new expressway, the Dan Ryan, in such a way that its asphalt and traffic temporarily kept black residents contained. Children were taught which sections were hospitable and which were not. It was an important thing to know. In 1919, a young black man swimming in Lake Michigan at a beach designated for African Americans had inadvertently drifted down until he was in waters off a white beach, and a race riot ensued in which nearly forty people, black and white, were killed.

Confined within their designated areas, Chicago's African Americans nevertheless developed a rich and internationally influential urban culture. The South Side would give the world the blues of Muddy Waters, the fiction of Richard Wright, the poetry of Gwendolyn Brooks, the presidential ambition of Jesse Jackson, distinctive contributions from people who were discriminated against, but who out of that experience created music and art and literature and politics, as well as a sense of solidarity and cohesion. Within the South Side a community grew up called Bronzeville; in the 1940s people liked to say that any African American Chicagoan standing at the corner of Forty-seventh and South Park (later changed to Martin Luther King, Jr., Drive) would within six minutes see someone he or she knew.

Six months after Michelle LaVaughn Robinson was born, the 1964 Civil Rights Act was signed into law by President Lyndon Johnson, prohibiting discrimination in public accommodations and government housing. Thanks to that and to subsequent measures, new residential opportunities would open up for families like

hers. Gradually. And not without turmoil. By the time
Michelle was a little girl, Fraser and Marian Robinson
were able to move into a neighborhood formerly open
only to white families. Over a few years that neighborhood would transform, becoming almost 100 percent
black as white families moved away. With that, they and
their children would embark on yet another chapter of
U.S. history and race relations, one defined by black advancement in jobs and housing, and white flight to the
suburbs.

So that January day when she was born in Chicago,
you could say that Michelle LaVaughn Robinson had already been through a lot. Her forebears had lived—and
fashioned—a multigenerational story of mistreatment
and endurance. They had made the journey through
slavery and out of it, migrated into a new landscape that
turned out to be a place of tarnished promise but one
they would remake and come to call home. The day she
was born, Michelle Robinson embodied the unique
combination of discrimination and opportunity, hardship and overcoming, of being acted upon and acting,
that would define much of black history in America. Of
history in America, period.

Growing up, she would continue to live the nation's
evolution.

And, as an adult, she would help to shape it.

Hers: an American story. One—as she likes to point out—that has too rarely been told.

"JAN ASKED ME TO SHARE A BRIEF UPDATE WITH YOU today on how the Obama family is holding up," says Michelle Obama, now forty-four, elegant and fit, speaking in a ballroom in the vast convention center that Mayor Daley built on Lake Michigan, a cavernous structure known as McCormick Place that rises beside expressways in a kind of no-man's-land south of downtown. Today's event is a women's fund-raising lunch for Congresswoman Jan Schakowsky, a Democrat who represents much of the city's North Side as well as some suburbs, including Evanston and Skokie. It is May 2008. Almost two thousand Chicagoans, most of them women, are here to support Schakowsky and to hear Michelle Obama speak. She starts out by filling in the crowd, Christmas-card style, on what's been going on in her household. Because they don't get to see her as much as they used to.

A graduate of Princeton University and Harvard Law School, Michelle Obama is now a lawyer, a mother, and a health-care executive. She is also the wife of U.S. Senator Barack Obama, who seemed to come out of nowhere to become the first African American with a real chance at the presidency. The women in this room are well groomed and affluent, multiracial, and some of them are part of Michelle Obama's now rather glittering social circle. Many live in the city, where working women support and sustain one another as part of a longtime network. Some live in Hyde Park, the prosperous and well-integrated South Side neighborhood where Michelle and Barack Obama have lived since they were married in 1992, and where they and their two daughters, Sasha and Malia, have become familiar and well-loved fixtures. Barack Obama is sometimes seen, for example, at the annual pancake breakfast held each spring at the Hyde Park Neighborhood Club, standing behind the griddle, wearing a cook's hat and making breakfast. The Obamas now live in a Georgian Revival mansion on a historic block at Fifty-first and Greenwood, where friends might drive by and spot Michelle out front, teaching one of her daughters to ride a bike. When they see her, they are likely to get out and hug her. If she says she hasn't had a home-cooked meal in days, they might run home and make her one. "They've got my back," she sometimes says about her tight group of friends and fellow parents. When parents at the University of Chicago Laboratory Schools are making assignments for potlucks, they know to make it easy on her by assigning the Obamas a ready-made contribution—but, still, a contribution—like "plates."

Michelle has come a long way from her ancestors' arduous journey to American shores, and even from her own upbringing in a semi-integrated Chicago. But she's come a long way in another sense. At the start of her husband's political career, Michelle was, she regularly points out, an ambivalent political partner. She once remarked that politics felt to her, sometimes, like "a waste of time." Now she is one of her husband's principal political surrogates. During speeches like this one, Michelle Obama talks feelingly and with authority about issues relating to women and children. She has said that "work-family balance" will be one of her signature issues if she becomes first lady: figuring out how to make things easier for working families, how to give them more parental leave, more sick days, time to attend a music recital or ballet performance. In every speech, she makes it clear that her husband's political career has meant considerable sacrifice for her own family, and talks about how hard it is for her, personally, to find equilibrium. In one little-noticed admission to an interviewer, Michelle Obama estimated that over the past year, her husband had been home with free time for a paltry total of *ten days*. That means 355 days in which Barack Obama was not home with free time, and it was Michelle who had to get up and get the girls ready for school and get through the day, somehow, herself, and try to preserve some semblance of a career and a life. She is not a martyr who endures this kind of thing silently. Today, she tells an anecdote about how the four of them—Michelle, Barack, Sasha, and Malia—traveled together recently, and "at one point someone asked Malia, our older daughter, what she enjoyed most about the weekend, and she said, 'Being with my dad.'

"And," she says, "it nearly broke my heart."

But she also talks about why she decided to give her husband the go-ahead to run. She feels that all children, not just hers, deserve "the resources they need to ensure a healthy future." She talks about the challenges faced by single mothers; about the lack of health-care coverage, and inflation, and the cost of gas, and the plight of military families. By dwelling on these issues, she gives her husband credibility with mothers and all women, assuring them that Obama shares their commitment to a life where they can have more time with the people who love and need them. "I wake up every morning wondering how on earth I am going to pull off that next minor miracle to get through the day," she often says.

She serves other critical political functions. Michelle's most important role is *explaining* Barack Obama. She does this beautifully. It is her crucial task to humanize him, to make sense of him—to normalize him. "Who is Barack Obama the man, the father?" she said in Nashua, New Hampshire, during the primary campaign. "What is his character? What are his values?"

It is the traditional duty of the political wife, of course, to reinforce her husband's virtues, channeling the audience's admiration through what has become known as the Adoring Gaze. But Michelle Obama's task is different, because Obama has such a complicated personal backstory. She often acknowledges to audiences that when she first heard about him, she assumed he would be strange. Born in Hawaii to an eighteen-year-old white woman from Kansas and an African exchange student in his early twenties who abandoned the family not long after Barack Obama's birth, Obama was raised in Hawaii and Indonesia, sometimes by his mother, but often by his Midwestern maternal grandparents. He is a biracial man, technically, who identifies himself, as he writes in his memoir, *Dreams from My Father,* as "a black American" and "a black man with a funny name." But when Michelle talks about him, he's just a regular guy who likes to go out for dinner and a movie and then come home to his girls.

"If he cares half as much about this country as he does about his own children, we're going to be just fine," she told a crowd in Butte, Montana.

"He was raised in his grandmother's home, and his grandmother is from Kansas, eating tuna with pickles in it" is how she put it to the *Chicago Sun-Times*. "The same conversations that we had around my kitchen table, we have at her house at Christmas. We are not that far apart."

And of course, she also likes to bring him down to size. At the beginning of the campaign, Michelle talked freely about how her husband forgets to put the butter away, or secure the bread, how he sometimes doesn't quite make the laundry hamper when he tosses his socks. "He's a gifted man, but in the end, he's just a man" is one of her other well-known lines. In 2005, after he won the U.S. Senate race, during which he was catapulted to celebrity after making the keynote speech at the 2004 Democratic convention, she accompanied him on his first walk through the U.S. Capitol. "Maybe one day, he will do something to warrant all this attention," she told a reporter. She's received criticism for sounding harsh, but defends herself by saying she wants people to have realistic expectations. "The only thing I'm telling people in Illinois is that 'Barack is not our savior,'" she said during the 2004 Senate race. "I want to tell it to the whole country and I will if I get the opportunity." It's a message that, reasonably or not, demands of voters the kind of loyalty she has had to deploy as a spouse. "There are many of us who want to lay all of our wishes, fears, and hopes at the feet of this young man, but life doesn't work that way and certainly politics doesn't work that way," she told the crowd. "You've got to be with him no matter what."

Her message is subtle: If I, as tough and demanding as I am, can identify and put up with his flaws, so can you. And if I can recognize and respect his diplomatic skills, then so can you. Her brother, Craig, often talks about how picky Michelle was about her boyfriends, and how, when he met Barack, Craig assumed that he would quickly join the ranks of cast-off suitors. That she did not cast him off, Craig said, was due to the fact that "[he] was a smart guy who didn't act like he was smarter than anybody else. That was the first thing. And he was tall and he knew how to manage my sister's personality." And that, Craig says, is a kind of qualification for president in and of itself: "All I can think about is him being in meetings with different kinds of egos and being able to bring them all together, including senators, including foreign officials, anybody. I don't want to trivialize the presidency, but a lot of it has to do with being a people person, being a diplomat."

Michelle is useful in other ways. When Barack was attacked as a cultural elitist, she was able to talk about her own working-class roots, which she does regularly. "We had four spoons," she deadpanned to a dazzled Stephen Colbert during an appearance she made on his show; Colbert had jokingly asked her how many silver spoons there were in her South Side home. "And then my father got a raise at the plant, and we had five spoons." She also enables Obama to talk about family values even as he has put such strains on his own household. More than once, in high-profile Father's Day speeches, Barack Obama has exhorted young black men to take better care of their families, deploring what he describes as a culture in which too many father children and abandon them. And one of the reasons he can sound plausible on the subject is that, despite his own absences, the demands of her job and the pressures of public life, he and Michelle have kept their household stable and intact.

And she enhances his appeal to black audiences, because hers, not his, is the classical African American dream story. In a 2007 speech in South Carolina, she talked about "that veil of impossibility that keeps us down and keeps our children down—keeps us waiting and hoping for a turn that may never come. It's the bitter legacy of racism and discrimination and oppression in this country. A legacy that hurts us all."

What's striking about Michelle Obama is how much adoration she inspires in a ballroom like this one in Chicago, and how controversial she has become in the world beyond. She is a woman whose friends, and they are many, love and passionately defend her, in part because she is herself such a loyal and committed friend to them. But there is some disparity between how she is viewed in her relatively private realm and how the public at large sees her. According to an Associated Press–Yahoo! poll released in July 2008, 30 percent of the public viewed her favorably, while 35 percent viewed her unfavorably. Both her negatives and her positives were higher than those of Cindy McCain, wife of John McCain, the Republican nominee. The poll found that she is much better known than Cindy McCain, which is no surprise, because she gets much more coverage. In June 2008, the Pew Research Center for the People and the Press published a report showing that Michelle Obama had received four times the media coverage of Cindy McCain.

Michelle tends to be polarizing. The Pew report showed that Republicans dislike her more than Democrats dislike McCain, and that Democrats like her more than Republicans like McCain. In short, she inspires both strong enthusiasm and strong skepticism.

Certainly, hard-line right-wing opponents of Obama have singled Michelle out as a ready target. If politics were a military battle, you could say that she is seen by antagonists as the equivalent of Obama's weak left flank. "The gift that keeps on giving," one right-wing blogger called her. Early on, critics bored into her Princeton thesis, a paper she wrote, on assignment, in her very early twenties. The thesis explores race and identity on an Ivy League campus in the 1970s and 1980s and meditates on why campus culture seemed to drive black students to socialize with one another. It was attacked as a work of racial separatism—an oversimplification. In February 2008, she made the mistake of saying, "For the first time in my adult life, I am proud of my country because it feels like hope is finally making a comeback." She has called America a "mean nation," and one that is "guided by fear."

Yet critics have pointed out that Michelle Obama is a living example of what America has to offer—a testament to its kindness, its boundless opportunity. They point out that she has graduated from not one but two Ivy League universities, has worked at a big corporate law firm, and went on to make hundreds of thousands of dollars a year helping the University of Chicago hospitals upgrade their relationship with the community. So what, exactly, has the country given her to be ashamed of? "America's unhappiest millionaire," one critic called her. "Mrs. Grievance," said the conservative *National Review*.

Around the same time that the opponents were reaching full cry, Obama was obliged to break with Jeremiah Wright, the pastor who married Michelle and Barack and baptized their daughters, after Wright was shown in video clips saying "God damn America!" and conjecturing that the government deliberately spread HIV in the black community. Seeking to use both Wright and Michelle to impugn Obama's patriotism, some critics speculated, without proof, that Obama belonged to Wright's church because angry Michelle brought him there. Others said that it was sensible, no-nonsense Michelle who had had the strength of mind to say it was time to cut ties with Wright. In May 2008, a malevolent collection of attackers fanned a rumor, which had no evidence behind it, that there was some tape, somewhere, of Michelle Obama using the word *whitey*. Or maybe it was *why'd he*. Who knew? Who cared? Barack Obama was asked about it, and the tale was angrily refuted. Some of the media attacks have been grossly and unapologetically racist. Fox News referred to her, unbelievably, as "Obama's Baby Mama," a term for a casual girlfriend of easy virtue.

But the questions raised about her lack of appreciation for her own very American success have been legitimate. In speeches, she brings out example after example of people who are not doing well in America, rarely making reference to her own great history of both opportunity and achievement. It's as if her own life is the American aberration. "The life that I am talking about that most people are living has gotten progressively worse since I was a little girl. And this is through Republican and Democratic administrations. It doesn't matter who was in the White House," she has said. "So if you want to pretend there was some point over the last couple of decades when your lives were easy, I wanna meet you!" But no one is arguing that moving up is easy, only that it is possible.

Today, for example, she tells one of her signature anecdotes about her own sense of having been discouraged: the story of a "ten-year-old girl in South Carolina" who singled her out on a street corner to point out that if Obama wins the presidency, it will "be historical." When Michelle Obama asked the girl what that meant to her, the girl said, "It means I can imagine anything for myself," and started to cry. Whenever she tells this story, Michelle projects a host of emotions onto the little ten-year-old girl, conjecturing that the girl knows what it feels like to "attend underfunded schools" and to be neglected and discouraged. "You know why I know what that little girl is feeling?" she asked a crowd in Rhode Island in early 2008. "Because she was me. See, because I am *not supposed to be here*."

In her zeal to reach out to the middle class, she sometimes projects her own experience onto the lives of voters whose working-class circumstances don't come close to matching hers. In April 2008, in Indiana, Michelle sympathized with Cheryl and Mike Fischer, who talked about layoffs pending at Amtrak, where he works as a machinist. The Fischers told her that if Mike's job was cut, they had the option of moving to Chicago, but had rejected that option because they wanted to stay close to their families. Michelle answered that the same impulse kept her from moving to Washington when Barack was elected to the U.S. Senate. "A lot of people said you are going to move to Washington. I was like, 'No.' All my support is the support you build up over the years. It is

my mom, girlfriends—you move away from everything."
In her mind, to move to the capital because her husband
had just been elected to the U.S. Senate was akin to a
laid-off machinist relocating to find work. In 2007, the
Obamas brought in $4.2 million. Yet she complains to
audiences about the price of ballet lessons and summer
camps. She can sound haughty and put upon. She once
said about her husband's career: "Who in their right
mind would want this? Barack could live an easier life, a
criticism-free, wealthy life," she has said. "Sometimes
I'm like, 'What's wrong with you?' that he didn't do
that."

The Obama campaign has tried to manage her multi-
layered political personality by, among other things, setting up interviews with friendly magazines like *Us Weekly*
and *People,* and television shows like *The View* and *Access
Hollywood.* In those settings, she has shown off the quick
sense of humor her girlfriends know well, and the justified confidence she has in her own beauty. (She gets a
manicure and her hair done every Friday.) One commentator astutely pointed out that, in attempting to
make her seem less outspoken and threatening, the
campaign has endeavored to make Michelle Obama
seem more girlie and conventionally feminine. "It's fun
to look pretty," she told her admiring interlocutors on

The View, a comment that's indisputable, and a lot more anodyne than saying, "Politics is a waste of time." In one sense, that appearance achieved its intended purpose: Thousands of American women scrambled to buy the leaf-print dress she wore on the show. A black-and-white dress, in case you were wondering. The Internet was all abuzz: Was Michelle Obama saying something about integration?

Throughout the campaign, Michelle Obama has claimed to be frustrated by the public misunderstanding of her. "I will walk anyone through my life," she told the *New York Times* in June 2008, saying that anybody who talked to her for five minutes would see she was a person who would never say "whitey." But voters have often been left on their own to piece together an understanding of who Michelle really is. That's partly because, ever since she became controversial, the campaign has controlled even more tightly what she says and where she says it. In the summer of 2007, for example, when I was working on a *Washington Post* analysis of Barack Obama's swift political rise, the campaign provided access to Michelle, who talked revealingly about her decision to give him the go-ahead to run for president and made some keen observations about the factors that propelled him to fame. I also interviewed her brother, Craig Robinson;

Barack Obama himself; their friends; and members of his political team. In 2008, I approached the campaign about a book on Michelle, saying that Michelle is a compelling figure, a woman whose life story represents a key American narrative, and that, given her newcomer status to public life, the electorate has a real curiosity about her. This time, the campaign declined to provide access to her and discouraged those who know the Obamas from talking. Fortunately, enough of those who knew her were willing to be interviewed that it was possible to write what is, I hope, a full and satisfying portrait.

So, who is Michelle Obama? She is, in many ways, an old-fashioned person, a woman who longs for a traditional, intact family around the table and sees herself as a mother first and foremost. She has a quick and wicked sense of humor. Her favorite part of campaigning is reading to young children, which she does vividly and with gusto. But she is determined to play a major role in her husband's campaign and has traveled incessantly as his senior adviser and stand-in since the early days of Iowa. Before agreeing to her husband's presidential run, she insisted upon—and got—a series of meetings with his closest advisers, during which she sought assurance that the campaign was plausible and that it would be well run.

She is said, by those who know her, to be as smart as her husband. Some say she is smarter. Unlike her husband, who in his early twenties spent a great deal of time by himself, reading, she seems more of a doer, an extrovert, a list maker, not ruminative. She does not like to cook. She is almost heroically well organized.

She is a better boss than an employee; she likes to be in charge and does not like her time to be wasted. She is forceful and can be intimidating. Her husband says she is "a little meaner than I am." Her brother says even family members are scared of her. He may or may not be joking. She is the person her husband trusts to be his radar about people; she is seen as more skeptical than he is. He calls her "the boss." She is said to be an extremely loyal friend, and funny. She loves reruns of *The Brady Bunch* and *The Dick Van Dyke Show.*

She is indeed a proud product of the South Side, a working-class girl who has moved up in life in part because of her country's post–World War II mobility and civil rights movement, but also thanks to her own initiative and intelligence. She retains a commitment to those in her community who have not done as well as she has. She is ambitious like her husband—more driven than many people realize. She was the one, for instance, who actively introduced him to much of Chicago's black political royalty and business class when he was contemplating his run for the Illinois senate. While she has been ambitious on his behalf, she has not been shrunk by his ambition—and that may be partly because it has yielded so much so fast.

But in temperament, Michelle will always be the Cassandra to her husband's Candide. That more pessimistic instinct is best understood in the context of the larger African American experience. Eugene Y. Lowe Jr., a historian of religion who is assistant to the president at Northwestern University, and who was dean of students at Princeton University when Michelle was an undergraduate there, calls to mind the classic double consciousness lodged in the black psyche, one articulated over a century ago by W. E. B. Du Bois in *The Souls of Black Folk*. "You know, there's—in the black experience, there's abundant reason to be angry, and also I think abundant reason to be hopeful," he said.

Abundant reason to be angry, abundant reason to be hopeful. It's an oversimplification, but it could be argued that, in their public rhetoric at least, Barack Obama represents the expression of hope and Michelle, sometimes, the expression of anger, or maybe just dismay, and that together the two of them make for a real and important dialogue about race and life in America. Have things gotten better, or have they not? Yes, and yes. This also explains why Michelle has drawn more of the attacks from people who don't want to hear the anger or who think anger should be a thing of the past. Race is by no means the only way to understand or think about Michelle Obama, but still, it's unavoidably true that Michelle, even more than her husband, is a product of the broader African American community and is inextricably tied to its narrative and its fate. Her public comments are characteristic of those who benefited from the social changes of the 1970s and 1980s but remain acutely aware that others did not.

"African Americans have far more of a collective shared perspective on the last twenty-five or thirty years than whites," says Ronald Walters, a political scientist at the University of Maryland. By the last twenty-five years, he means the period after the civil rights movement, when changes were set in motion that would transform many lives, but which also saw a backlash against affirmative action as well as a vilification of the lower-income black community as pathological and responsible for its own problems. Walters is not convinced white Americans can ever understand the extent to which many black Americans feel themselves part of, responsible for, and beholden to their community.

"When the public policy dialogue issues out a number of subtexts which say in effect, these people are responsible—communities filled with drugs, don't go to school, they are in fact responsible for the social disorganization and incarceration rates—that's not something that simply is absorbed by a lower-income group. That's a collective thing," says Walters. "There is a group feeling in the black community that has always felt the sting of that inferiority as a collective sting, and victories as collective victories."

So, Michelle Obama is many things: a woman of great accomplishment, certainly, she has gone beyond the twenty-one-year-old who wrote a Princeton thesis expressing apprehension at the realization that the future held, for her, further assimilation. She lives in a multi-racial community; her mother-in-law was white, and so is a sister-in-law. But she remains a product of the community where she grew up and identifies deeply with it and with anybody whose life has been hard and full of obstacles. When people ask whether America is ready for a black president, that question in some ways is caught up in their reaction to Michelle. Barack Obama may be postracial, but Michelle Obama is not. There are those who think her presence in the White House would be more significant than his. Meg Hirshberg, an influential political donor in New Hampshire, remembers watching Obama perform in a debate and seeing him turn to greet Michelle. The image transfixed her.

"I really thought his election would do so much to restore people's faith and belief in the U.S. around the world. And also our belief in ourselves," she said. "I got a tingle down my spine to see them. The thought flashed through my mind: Can you imagine them being the president and first lady? Can you imagine? It knocked me out, as far as what we would be saying to ourselves and the world. He's not a descendant of slaves, but she is." By this, she meant that having Michelle Obama in the White House would transform our country's image and self-image. Michelle herself often says she hopes she and Barack can present to the world a different image of African Americans.

"As we've all said in the black community, we don't see all of who we are in the media," she told *Good Morning America*. "We see snippets of our community and distortions of our community. So the world has this perspective that somehow Barack and Michelle Obama are different, that we're unique. And we're not. You just haven't seen us before."

It's true that Michelle Obama's experience was different from an earlier generation of African Americans who grew up in the 1940s and 1950s in the segregated South. But it is still a classic narrative, the one that came after that. More urban, more modern. Rather than being explicitly shut out or regularly and unapologetically discriminated against, during her lifetime Michelle Obama was granted admission to privileged quarters that only recently had become open and that were still uneasy about her presence, or, at best, unprepared. She has lived and worked in a series of transitional landscapes. One way to understand Michelle Obama is as a person who has lived much of her life on contested terrain.

Now, perhaps, more than ever.

1

LIKE HER HUSBAND, WHOSE FIRST BOOK, *DREAMS from My Father,* was an extended meditation on his father and the impact of his absence, Michelle Obama also inherited dreams from her father. Michelle was fortunate in that her own father was present for her when she was a child—in fact, the signal influence of her life. In virtually every speech, Michelle invokes the image of Fraser Robinson III, that Chicago city worker who labored every day in a job that was almost certainly not a match for his abilities, driven by his commitment to providing a stable and happy home for his family. A vigorous man who was crippled by multiple sclerosis, a progressive disease that set in when he was just in his thirties, Fraser through his congenial presence defined the home she grew up in. Michelle invariably describes herself as the product of Fraser's unflinching work ethic, his deep commitment to family, his view that who you are is defined not only by how you behave in public, but what you do in the shadows, when nobody is watching.

Understand her father, and the community that he raised her in, she implies, and you will understand her.

"Deep down inside, I'm still that little girl who grew up on the South Side of Chicago," she told an audience in New Hampshire in January 2008, in what is a characteristic remark. "Everything that I think about and do is shaped around the life that I lived in that little apartment in that bungalow that my father worked so hard to provide for us." Invoking her father and the working-class community he represented, she shows audiences a different image of African American family life than they tend to get from the media; establishes herself as a middle American, not an elitist; and illustrates her view that American life used to be more congenial for families. In speeches, she often talks about how much more arduous family life has become, nostalgically recalling how it once was feasible for one middle-class parent to work and the other parent to stay home. The happiness of her own family is the source of her oft-expressed view that, nowadays, life for families has gotten harder.

In fact, the reality of her upbringing is more complex. While there were many pleasures in Michelle's childhood—bikes could be left on sidewalks and moms could stay home and children could roam more freely than they do now—it's also indisputable that the Chicago she grew up in was not entirely hospitable to citizens like Fraser Robinson and his aspirations to move his family forward. Her dad and her community may well explain her own grounded and hard-working nature, as well as her commitment to her children, but Chicago in the 1960s was almost certainly the source of her oft-expressed skepticism about politics. It was not only a racist and highly segregated city, but one with a complex and ambiguous political system, a system that Fraser Robinson participated in, either because he enjoyed politics or because it was one of the few paths open to an ambitious black man.

In fact, Barack Obama would himself get a primer in the old Chicago when he moved to the city in 1985 to work as a community organizer in the very neighborhoods with which Michelle was familiar. At that time, Barack knew little about the city and set out to learn it better by getting into his beat-up Honda and driving from the northernmost tip of Martin Luther King, Jr., Drive, a major thoroughfare that runs through the South Side, down to its southern end point. In so doing, he must have unknowingly passed the apartment where Michelle spent her toddler years. According to Marian Robinson's voting registration, in the 1960s the Robinsons lived in an apartment on South Park, a street that would later be named after King, in one of the city's traditionally black, working-class neighborhoods, the area where, for decades, black residents had been forcibly channeled.

Obama also got a primer on the political system that operated in the city under Richard J. Daley, a system in which a few African Americans were favored and thereby made complicit in the segregation and mistreatment of the rest. He received this lesson from a Hyde Park barber, "Smitty," who explained why so many South Side establishments displayed a photo of Harold Washington, the city's first African American mayor. "Before Harold, seemed like we'd always be second-class citizens," Smitty told Obama as he was giving him a haircut. "Black people in the worst jobs. The worst housing. Police brutality rampant. But when the so-called black committeeman came around election time, we'd all line up and vote the straight Democratic ticket. Sell our soul for a Christmas turkey. White folks spitting in our faces, and we'd reward 'em with the vote." The name for this, Smitty and another patron told the listening Barack, was "plantation politics."

All of which Michelle's father could surely have told him. In addition to his paid work, Fraser Robinson was a volunteer precinct captain for the Democratic Party, an essential member of the powerful political machine run by Daley, who, in addition to being mayor, was the chairman of the Cook County Democratic Central Committee, meaning he controlled both the government and the political party, and could use one to do the other's bidding. Chicago is divided into fifty wards, and each ward has an alderman—an elected official who sits on the city council and passes laws—as well as two committeemen, one Democratic, one Republican, who run the party in that ward. Assisting the committeeman was the precinct captain, a locally powerful neighborhood leader whose job was to get people out to the polls on election day, and, ideally, make sure they voted the way Daley wanted them to.

By all accounts, being a precinct captain was a good job for a convivial person. Fraser Robinson was said by his neighbors to be a "joking man"—a characteristic he also bequeathed to his good-humored, swift-quipping daughter—and grassroots political work may well have been something he relished in his healthier and more mobile years: going out, distributing literature, knocking on doors, chatting with neighbors, visiting households for weddings and funerals. The precinct captain was someone people turned to when they needed services like snow removal or a dead tree cut down. In most cities, taxpayers can expect these services to be performed as a matter of course, but in Chicago, citizens often were obliged to ask, as a way of making them feel grateful and beholden. The precinct captain thereby enjoyed authority and status.

"The precinct captain kept constant contact with his voters" is how John Stroger, an African American who started out as a South Side precinct captain in the 1950s and later rose to become the first African American president of the Cook County Board of Commissioners, put it. "It was a ritual to see them all the time, be with them, commiserate with them when they had problems, and celebrate with them when things were going good." In Daley's Chicago, politics was local in part because it had to be. You stayed in your own neighborhood because it could be dangerous to venture out of it. "The whole life of the community revolved around the church and the political establishment," Stroger said. The point of all this neighborly love was to create a sense of indebtedness, the better to get the voters to vote the way they were supposed to. People came to trust the precinct captain and would often follow his instructions when it came to candidates for local office. Folks might know whom they wanted to elect president, but when it came to the head of mosquito abatement, they would take their cue from the captain. "They vote for [the precinct captain] who is there with them on a daily basis, who is trying to help them with services that they rightfully deserve," said James Taylor, an Arkansas native who started out in Chicago as a precinct captain and garbage collector and eventually became a powerful committeeman.

"I was there, I was talking to them about how much it would help me if they voted for our particular candidates . . . They came out and they voted well . . . I eventually became the best precinct captain in the ward."

Voting "well," that was the goal. Voting for the machine. Voting for Daley. But by working as a precinct captain, Robinson was participating in a larger political system that was, at best, a mixed blessing for blacks. The Chicago Michelle was born into was a city where the power structure conspired to keep its African American citizens bottled up—what Don Rose, a longtime Chicago political consultant and historian of city government, calls a "massive incremental conspiracy to keep [blacks] in their place." Certainly, Chicago had been a segregated city before Daley took office, but he ensured that it stayed that way. "Containing the Negro was unspoken city policy" is how newspaper columnist Mike Royko put it in *Boss,* his exposé of the Daley years. During his tenure, segregation persisted in schools and neighborhoods. Mortgage lenders refused to lend money to blacks who had the temerity to want to purchase homes in white neighborhoods. Real estate agents did the same. The unspoken rule was that blacks could move no more than one block outside a traditionally black area. "Blacks could walk through a white neighborhood, but only if they looked like they were going to the nearest bus stop or a restaurant to wash dishes," as Royko put it. "During the 1950s, most restaurants wouldn't seat blacks, most hotels wouldn't accommodate them, and the Loop was considered off limits."

And prejudice did not die off with the passage of the 1964 Civil Rights Act. To the contrary: In the mid-1960s, Martin Luther King Jr. attempted to bring the civil rights movement north to Chicago, moving his family into a ghetto apartment in order to end slums, protest housing conditions for blacks, and open up the segregated housing system. On one of two marches into all-white neighborhoods, King was hit in the head with a brick thrown by one of the white demonstrators who lined the streets shouting racial epithets. The animosity in the city defeated him, leading him to declare, famously, that the only place he ever feared for his life was Chicago.

Chicago was different from the South. Here, racist tensions evolved in part because the city contained so many immigrant populations, people who often had been born in other countries and who settled in neighborhoods that tended to be cohesive but intensely xenophobic. "As a rule, South Side whites hated blacks more than North Side whites did, because the blacks were closer," Royko writes.

The way Daley preserved this state of affairs was through a political system in which a handful of African Americans were rewarded for helping to keep the others subjugated. Daley held power, and preserved segregated schools and housing, thanks in part to the self-interest of six African American aldermen—the Silent Six, they were called—who were willing to do the mayor's bidding when it came to perpetuating de facto segregation. Daley gave these aldermen plenty of jobs to dole out to constituents, and the Silent Six used these and other perks to manipulate their voters to keep Daley and his people in power. The precinct captains were a key part of this enforcement. Of course, this was true around the city—precinct captains were hard at work in all wards, black and white—but African American voters were more vulnerable to pressure, because they were much less enfranchised. In some cases, the machine would threaten constituents with loss of services. "Negroes were warned that they would lose their welfare check, their public housing apartment, their menial job, if they didn't vote Democratic," says Royko.

As a precinct captain, you could expect, in return for this political policing, a city job. In fact, doing "volunteer" work was almost the only way you could get one. "To get a city job, you'd have to have some kind of recommendation from your ward committeeman," says Don Rose, describing a system in which it was crucial to have a recommender, somebody watching out for you—your patron. Daley kept a file cabinet with a list of jobs in it, and was said to know the names of everybody who held them. A city job was particularly valuable to an African American in that it insulated him somewhat from the capriciousness and racism of the open job market. "This was in the fifties and early sixties. Before affirmative action, patronage was as close as you could get to affirmative action, and if you didn't get rich, at least it was a steady job," says Rose.

"We had some volunteers, but the majority of people were [serving as precinct captains] because their jobs depended on it," says Cliff Kelley, a former South Side alderman who was not one of the Silent Six, but was familiar with machine culture. Most of the time, Kelley says, a person's political activism, and the job he held, were inseparably linked.

In view of this tradition it's also likely that Fraser Robinson's water department job was a reward for political service. "He was [almost certainly] a patronage employee," says Leon Despres, who for years was the alderman for the Fifth Ward, and, though white, became known as the "only Negro on the city council" because he opposed the Daley Machine and spoke out against segregation. Knowing how things worked in other wards, Despres finds it overwhelmingly likely that Robinson "was a solid political appointee, and by his loyalty he was advanced to this splendid position." The water department, where Fraser Robinson worked, was a renowned repository of patronage jobs.

Robinson stayed in the water department all his life and was rewarded with early advancement. In 1968, after starting out as a station laborer, he was now "foreman of laborers," a supervisory position that came with a raise of almost $200 a month, according to city records of his employment history. That same year, he was promoted to "stationary fireman," a job that entailed tending the water department's boilers. In 1969, he was promoted again, to "operating engineer," tending boilers as well as steam turbines, pumps, and heating and air-conditioning units, work that required real skill. Thus in five years he received three promotions, so that by 1969 he was making $858 a month, about $10,000 a year, which was a respectable salary, almost double what he started out making. Toward the end of his career, he would be making more than $40,000 a year.

Michelle Obama talks often, and movingly, about how important the job was to her father. She and her brother, Craig, describe what an inspiration it was to both of them, seeing Fraser Robinson get up to go to work every day, something that became increasingly difficult after his disease set in. Despite the fact that he needed a cane—and, later, crutches and eventually a motorized cart—he never stopped working.

"My father had M.S. and worked every day and rarely complained," Michelle told an interviewer in 2007, describing the man from whom she and Craig got their own work ethic. "He died on his way to work," she added, describing his premature death in early 1991, when he was just in his fifties. He had recently been in the hospital for a kidney operation, and afterward died unexpectedly of complications. "He wasn't feeling well, but he was going to get in that car and go."

But it's also likely that for all the pride Michelle took in her father's professional dedication, she also drew a lesson about politics. Part of Michelle's skepticism about it comes from the version she saw up close as a little girl: how the system bought you and protected you, but also controlled you. "If you didn't do this, didn't behave in a certain way," says Rose, "you could lose your pay, [the Machine could] demote you, fire you." People who underperformed in their political work were susceptible to being "vised," or summarily fired. That was politics in Chicago. "Some of [Michelle's] subconscious—some of her disdain as to politics could have to do with how [her father] was treated, and what he had to go through," says Al Kindle, a political consultant who grew up on the South Side.

And that, Kindle says, is why the black community was ambivalent about patronage and about Daley: the Machine lifted you up—got you services and perks—at the same time that it kept you down. "It was clear that you didn't get access to certain services unless you were a friend to the power structure. That spigot could be cut off. As a young African American with a family, you had to think about that with a jaundiced eye. Just as it helped you, it restricted your choice." So it could be that Robinson's son and daughter developed a dislike for politics even as they developed a deep, deep love for him. "We as a family were extremely cynical about politics and politicians" is how Craig puts it. That started to change when they met Barack, whose political career was pushed in part by a coalition of people who had grown up in opposition to Daley and whose goal was breaking the Machine.

2

DURING THE LATE 1960S AND EARLY 1970S, THE horizons for African American families in Chicago began to lift, and the fortunes of the Robinson family kept pace during a remarkable period of transition and opportunity. Their family, and many others, began to see their lives transformed from a forcibly segregated existence to one with more freedom to live where they chose; from a culture in which blue collars were all that most people they knew could hope for, to one in which those collars began to have white specks; from being consigned to overcrowded and ill-serviced schools, to greater educational opportunity. Around 1970, according to Marian's voting registration, the Robinson family was sufficiently well-positioned, financially, that they were able to move away from what was known as the "black belt" and into the better-supported neighborhood of South Shore, which, until recently, had been exclusively white. It was a period of expanded opportunity and also one of some upheaval, during which her family would continue to serve as a stabilizing presence.

Their new home was on the 7400 block of Euclid Avenue, in the middle of a lovely street of landscaped red-brick homes and small, elegant apartment buildings. This was a particularly desirable block. Euclid is a street that runs north and south, but at the north end of the 7400 block, it dead-ends into Seventy-fourth and then picks up slightly to the west on its way up to Seventy-third. At its south end, Euclid stops at Seventy-fifth, a busy commercial thoroughfare, on the other side of which is a large park. The result is a self-contained one-block neighborhood, the ideal place for a child to grow up, play, scooter, bike ride.

The house where she spent her formative years is a bungalow, one of Chicago's most traditional dwellings. Families would often redo the attic or basement of these compact houses to get another floor of living space. The Robinsons rented the top floor of the bungalow owned by Michelle's aunt, who was a piano teacher. According to her mother, Marian, Michelle, who from an early age was a hard worker and a driven and focused child, would practice the piano endlessly, unbidden. The four-person family lived for years on the upper floor, until, according to city records, the house was bequeathed to the Robinsons in 1980. Michelle and Craig slept in the living room, which was divided by a partition. One of Michelle's friends remembers playing with Barbies in her bedroom—she had the African American Barbie, the Ken, a toy house, and cars—a room that seemed impossibly small, little more than a closet, though Michelle also wedged in an Easy-Bake Oven. But while they may have been cramped, the family was comfortable enough to live on a single salary. There is a long tradition in the black community of women working—black women rarely have had the option of staying home as full-time wives and mothers—but thanks to the city job, Marian Robinson could stay home, and did. She tutored both children well enough that both were able to read before they started school, though Craig was more tractable than his younger sister. The Robinson family has never made a secret of the fact that Michelle could be independent-minded, even hard-headed; it's a family joke. "Both my kids were reading at much higher levels when they were young because they liked reading," Marian has said. "I taught my son to read, but when I went to show Michelle how to read she wasn't ready so she just ignored me. I guess she figured she could figure out how to read on her own, but she was too young to say that."

The neighborhood of South Shore, where Marian Robinson still lives today, was an enviable one overall. Bordered by Seventy-first Street to the North and Seventy-ninth Street to the south, South Shore is located along the scenic southern lakefront of Lake Michigan—hence the name—and continues west for about thirty blocks. To the north it's bordered by Woodlawn, a less affluent neighborhood that underwent a racial transformation from white to black in the 1950s and saw a decline, as stores and businesses fled and city services declined, contributing to the myth that a neighborhood "went down" when black families moved into it. In fact, it was the city government itself that often prompted the decline by intentionally abandoning neighborhoods—as did banks, grocery stores, and other businesses—after whites moved out. At the northern tip of South Shore is the greensward of Jackson Park, where in 1893 the Columbian Exposition was held, an event that first led to parcels of land being sold for development in the South Shore area. Slightly farther north is

Hyde Park, the leafy neighborhood that surrounds the University of Chicago. The university over the years has not enjoyed good relations with the neighborhoods to its south; in the 1950s and 1960s, the University of Chicago was in regular conflict with Woodlawn. There, residents, many of whom were poor and often lived in substandard housing and projects, were especially vulnerable to displacement whenever the university attempted to expand into the area, as it regularly did. From this uneasy relationship, The Woodlawn Organization was founded by Saul Alinsky, with the aim of resisting the university's incursions and protecting poorer citizens from being displaced. Michelle would deal with remnants of that town-gown hostility much later, when she would take over community relations for the University of Chicago hospitals.

Back when Chicago was first incorporated, the South Shore area was swampland and forest. German truck farmers began moving in during the 1860s and 1870s, and in the 1880s, the Illinois Central Railroad built a station at Seventy-first Street and Jeffery Boulevard, about five blocks from where the Robinson family would settle, an area that would develop as a commercial enclave. In the 1920s, the area boomed; English and Swedish residents gave way to Irish Catholics, who gave way to Jews. Those two groups had tensions of their own: the neighborhood boasted the exclusive South Shore Country Club, built on the lake near the public beach at Rainbow Park. Irish Chicagoans could join the club, but Jewish ones could not. Neither—it went without saying—could blacks. Residents were middle- and upper-middle-class, skilled, and educated. In the 1950s, the area had a black population of 1 percent.

But during the 1960s, things had begun to change. It's hard to overstate the scale of this transition, a time when the center no longer held and it was no longer clear which neighborhoods belonged to whom. Chicago is often referred to as a city of neighborhoods, which, those who live there say, is one reason it functions so well. "Chicago still works better than most big cities in the country," says Abner Mikva, a former federal judge and member of the U.S. Congress who lives in Hyde Park and was instrumental in furthering the career of Barack Obama. The city, he points out, "really has emphasized neighborhoods more than any other town in this country." But the downside, particularly back then, was that people became intensely attached to their home turf, which often was ethnically homogeneous and hostile to outsiders.

For black citizens, this had long meant that many parts of the city were off-limits. "All my life—I was born in this city—as far back as I can remember, there was always some consternation, some hesitation, as to where I should go to feel safe," recalls Bishop Arthur Brazier, the former pastor of the Apostolic Church of God, founding president of The Woodlawn Organization, and a some-time tennis opponent, in doubles games, of Barack and Michelle Obama. His son agrees. "There were racial boundaries, and you knew where those boundaries were," says Dr. Byron Brazier, who has recently taken over his father's post at the Apostolic Church of God, and is a decade or so older than Michelle.

"I can remember when South Shore changed over," says Stephan Garnett, an African American Chicagoan who grew up in a different part of South Side, but who as a child would visit relatives in Woodlawn. "I remember my aunt and uncle told me: 'Don't cross Stony Island [the street that demarks one border of South Shore]' because I would be in physical danger." He remembers that he and his cousins "would go anyway when they weren't looking—it was the only way to get to the Jackson Park lagoon," a part of the park where they liked to go fishing.

Now all that was changing.

"It was," recalls Arthur Brazier, "a period of extreme turmoil."

The transition was fueled by many things: the passage—and, finally, the enforcement—of fair housing laws. The expansion and increased affluence of the African American population. And the energetic fear-mongering of banks and real estate agents. The real estate lobby fomented relocation through what was known as block-busting or panic-peddling, a corrupt and manipulative technique whereby an enterprising rogue agent would deliberately sell a house to a black family, then trot the family out and publicize what had just happened. This would cause white home owners to panic and try to sell their own houses before prices started plummeting, banks started redlining—denying loans to entire neighborhoods—and city services deserted the neighborhood. The same agent would then approach these white families about selling their homes, maybe offer to find them another one in the suburbs, making money on both sides of the transaction. So it was a combination of affluence, expanded opportunity, fear, greed, and racism that drove black advancement and white flight, as people like the Robinsons chased the same American dream as people who had lived in South Shore before them. "We wanted to bring up our two children, ages 5 and 4, in a world that would be far more pleasant than it had been to us," a Mrs. Leonard Jewell told the *Chicago Tribune* in 1967. She and her husband, both African American, had just moved into a house on Euclid Avenue two blocks from the Robinsons.

It's possible to see the changes by looking at copies of the *South Shore Scene,* the newspaper published by the South Shore Commission, which was formed in 1953 as a civic organization. In the 1960s, the group was trying to keep white families in Michelle's neighborhood—or, some might say, it was trying to limit and control the influx of blacks. "Non-white families are now living in South Shore, both as owners and tenants. They are here. This is a fact," a community leader named Robert Shapiro wrote in 1963, exhorting residents not to flee their homes just because black families were moving in beside them. The new goal of the community, Shapiro said, should be "having the white and non-white families learn to live and work with each other." Shapiro was president of the South Shore Commission. At the time, the proffered solution was something called "managed integration." Managed integration involved a combination of pleading with whites to stay and persuading landlords to reject "undesirable" black families from rental housing. So incoming African Americans were hearing two messages: You are welcome to move in, but not too many of you and just the respectable ones.

In 1963 and 1964, the *South Shore Scene* ran articles reporting that the commission had filed suit against realty companies for panic-peddling. But the paper also carried ads for the "Tenant Referral Service," an organization that tended to refer only white families to landlords, with the hope that some whites would stay and that blacks would be kept out of rental housing. In 1965, the paper carried its first photograph of a black person: a student who was being presented an arm patch by a school principal, for excellence in volunteering. That year it also profiled a black family moving in to South Shore: a chemist and his wife, who was a teacher. And it publicized a South Shore Commission effort to organize home visits, whereby "Whites and Negroes in South Shore will get together for coffee and conversation," encounters that usually involved white families visiting the households of their new black neighbors to assure themselves these households were as orderly and well run as their own. "We hope the people making the visits will be having a new experience," one of the organizers told the paper. In 1967, the *Scene* carried its first advertisement with a black person in it. But it also carried subtle reminders of how black in-migration was viewed negatively almost as a matter of course. In the late 1960s, the commission recommended busing some black children away from the area, to ensure that the majority of children in the neighborhood schools would be white. An article in the *South Shore Scene* stated that the goal was to avoid "resegregation" in schools, which is to say, a situation in which the school became mostly black. The term for this was *inundation*.

By the 1970s, the president of the South Shore Commission was African American, signaling that the transformation was complete. By 1980, when Michelle Robinson was sixteen, the neighborhood was 96 percent African American. A complete racial transition had taken just two decades.

But while the effort to keep the neighborhood integrated did not succeed, the effort to keep it middle-class and well equipped did. In 1967, Bryn Mawr, the elementary school Michelle attended through the eighth grade, received city money to start a gifted program. She was selected to participate in it in the sixth grade, and in eighth grade graduated as class salutatorian. As part of the gifted class, she was able to take biology classes at Kennedy-King, a local community college. She was also able to take French. It's safe to say the schools in South Shore were better equipped than the schools in the neighborhood the Robinsons had departed, and that one key benefit Fraser's city job had won his children was better schooling. In the early 1970s, the local A&P tried to move out of South Shore, but the Concerned Citizens for Action to Save the South Shore Shopping Area kept it in place. Even more significantly, after white families moved out, the South Shore Bank tried to abandon South Shore and move to the Loop, which would have made it difficult for many local businesses to obtain loans—"If you'll show me a slum, I'll show you a black community without a bank," the head of the South Shore Commission told the *Chicago Tribune* in 1984—and home owners as well. But the commission fought the move, and the federal comptroller of the currency forced the bank to stay in the neighborhood for which it was named. So while whites did leave, the neighborhood itself, through community activism, was not abandoned by stores and services as acutely as some newly black neighborhoods had been.

"The area, with 80,000 residents, has not gone the way of Woodlawn," the editor of the *South Shore Scene* noted, with satisfaction, in 1978. "The area has survived the damaging radical turnover through the determined efforts of its residents, financial and community institutions who were and are committed to restoring and upgrading the community."

Still, the fact of flight meant that one of the hard truths Michelle Robinson was introduced to, as a young girl, was that advancement for blacks meant confronting a repudiation by whites. Langston Hughes wrote in 1949: "When I move/Into a neighborhood/Folks fly./Even every foreigner/That can move, moves./Why?" The socioeconomic advance of the Robinsons was accompanied by physical evidence that white people did not want to live near her and felt the neighborhood would decline as a result of her family's presence. Her brother, Craig, would later tell the *Providence Journal* that in family discussions, their parents told them not to be crippled or cast down by the racial prejudice visible all around them. Craig, who recalls the last white family moving out when he and Michelle were children, said their parents spoke to them frequently about race relations and racial discrimination. Their parents assured them "they were as good as anyone else, and that it was ultimately about hard work and achievement," Craig remembered. Fraser and Marian would talk to them about prejudice by pointing out that "life's not fair. It's not. And you don't always get what you deserve, but you have to work hard to get what you want. And then sometimes you don't get it; even if you work hard and do all the right things, sometimes you don't get it."

"That always seemed so unfair to me," Craig reflected. "Yet it prepared me for handling life." The power of their parents' message overpowered the message the world was sending them. "When you grow up as a black kid in a white world, so many times people are telling you, sometimes not maliciously, sometimes maliciously, you're not good enough," Craig also pointed out. "To have a family, which we did, who constantly reminded you how smart you were, how good you were, how pleasant it was to be around you, how successful you could be, it's hard to combat. Our parents gave us a little head start by making us feel confident."

The Robinsons also gave their children a head start by telling them that, sometimes, the way around prejudice is education. "The academic part came first and early in our house," Craig Robinson told the *Hartford Courant*. "Our parents emphasized hard work and doing your best and once you get trained like that, then you get used to it and you don't want to get anything but As and Bs." Fraser Robinson, Craig said, was "smart, he was hardworking, he raised two bright kids, great family atmosphere, and he did that on a laborer's salary."

Nevertheless, it seems safe to say that even a child could hardly remain unaware of what was happening. "It's difficult to miss," ventures Jesse Jackson Sr., who also has a home in South Shore. In 1968, the area "was becoming a sea of for-sale signs," recalls political consultant Al Kindle. He remembers people setting fire to businesses to collect on the insurance before the property value plummeted. "Conversations were always: We were the first black family," Kindle recalls. "It would be understood within your family that as you became the first, whites were moving out. Conversations were going on all along. The ramifications and dynamics were clearly around you."

Stephan Garnett recalls attending a South Side public elementary school at a time when white flight was under way, but some white children still remained. One day, he came home and started talking to his parents about "niggers" and how dirty they were and what bad habits they had. He had learned the word from schoolmates but did not know what it meant. His parents sat him down and, as gently as possible, explained that the white children had been talking about him. Garnett, now a distinguished journalist who teaches at Northwestern University's Medill School of Journalism, recalls, "I burst into tears." As he grew, his mother told him that if racism "doesn't kill you, it makes you stronger." His father told him to think of himself as a "citizen of the world."

Certainly, people on Euclid Avenue knew what was going on. One of the first African Americans on the 7400 block of Euclid was Terrance Thompson, a musician who upon returning from Vietnam decided, with his parents, to buy a three-flat apartment building located across from the bungalow the Robinsons would move into. Another thing South Shore is known for is "flat mansions": stately two- and three-story apartment buildings where each roomy apartment takes up an entire floor. Thompson says he and his parents had previously lived in a two-flat building along with his grandparents, but the family had outgrown it and decided to move. Thompson, an affable, gregarious man, is a drummer, born into a family of accomplished musicians who were an integral part of the city's jazz scene.

"My mom and dad were kind of famous," he said modestly one afternoon, standing outside the apartment building. His father, the late Marshall Thompson, was a tap dancer and house drummer at the London House jazz club, a world-renowned restaurant and nightclub until it closed in the 1970s, where he played with the likes of Oscar Peterson. His mother, Earma Thompson, is a jazz pianist who has made several recordings and has accompanied many of the greats. She and Terrance were invited to play at the wedding reception of Barack and

Michelle Obama, which shows how close Michelle has remained to her childhood neighborhood.

Terry Thompson says that he and his parents went in on the property together. The white owner was glad to sell it to them, Thompson recalls, even though the building had a restrictive covenant—a common means of preserving segregation for many decades—that forbade the sale to blacks. The owner ignored the covenant—possibly because he wanted to get out, possibly because he had forgotten about it, possibly because he disagreed with it, possibly because it was illegal now, anyway. Thompson kept the deed "as a reminder." After that, "We tried to make [neighbors] comfortable," says Thompson, who would shovel the snow for his older, white neighbors. Even so, white families started vanishing. "We didn't know exactly the reason why they moved out," he says. "There weren't any harsh words, not any harsh attitudes."

Earma Thompson remembers that after buying the apartment building and becoming its landlord, the Thompsons "had white families on the third floor and second floor, and they let us know they weren't going to stay. They weren't rude."

That was also the experience of Ola Credit, who lives behind the Robinson bungalow. Hers, she says, was about the fifth black family that moved onto the block, in the mid-1960s. For a while, there was a period of amity and coexistence. "Basically everybody else here was white, and [her children] played with the neighbors, they would get on their bicycles, everybody was friendly and with a smile and said hello." At that time, the 7400 block of Euclid had a strong "block club," which in Chicago is a grassroots community group that gets together to discuss everything from the theme of Christmas decorations to the question of what to do about a neighbor who doesn't mow his grass. There were a few years when the block club included white families. And then, all at once, it didn't. "When they got ready to move, they said, 'We'll be moving,' " says Credit. "I think one time we even gave a little party."

And once the whites did move out, there was some justifiable satisfaction that the neighborhood had stayed intact and there was no deterioration. "Oftentimes blacks moved in and the property values went up, not down," points out Jesse Jackson. "Blacks moved in, were upwardly mobile, everyday working kind of people, and the neighborhood began to restabilize." Like a palimpsest, South Shore now retains remnants of many pasts, some immediate and some older. Black churches now hold services in buildings that once were synagogues or Greek Orthodox churches, and some churches also maintain relationships with a corresponding church in the South, which for many Chicagoans is their "old country."

And the new residents, by and large, were simply glad to have such a commodious neighborhood to live in, better, in most cases, than the one they had moved away from. "My kids were glad to have a nice place to live where they didn't have to bring their bikes in, and could leave them out at night," says Sammie Jackson, who also lives behind the Robinsons.

So by the time Michelle was ten or so, in 1974, the neighborhood had a sense of warmth and safety, even as other parts of the city may not have been welcoming. "When you grow up in a black community with a warm black family, you are aware of the fact that you are black, but you don't feel it," adds Stephan Garnett. "You feel accepted, you feel comfortable in your own neighborhood." Growing up, as he also did, in a stable middle-class black neighborhood, "I felt secure, I felt insulated. Your parents also did what they could to basically keep the slings and arrows away from you. They protected you. After a certain point you do just kind of think you're in your own world, and you become very comfortable in that world, and to this day there are African Americans who feel very uncomfortable when they step out of it, and would only think of going to a historically black college." That's because, he says, once you leave your neighborhood, "This is a society that never lets you forget that you are black."

And the Robinson family clearly functioned like a protective seal. "We learned from the best how a happy home should operate," says Craig. Fraser Robinson was home for dinner; Marian Robinson shared her children's outspokenness but also their love of home and hearth. Fraser, who before his disease set in was an accomplished boxer and swimmer, loved sports, and Craig was a gifted basketball player. The two used to joke about how you could tell a lot about a man's character by the way he played basketball, a theory Craig would eventually try out on Barack Obama. The children had chores: They traded washing dishes every other day, and, on Saturdays, Michelle had to clean the bathroom. In addition to the nuclear family members, Michelle had, in her words, "lots of aunts, uncles, cousins, second cousins, third cousins" who came around. Another neighbor, Johnie Kolheim, used to see the Robinson kids out the window of her own flat-mansion building, directly across the street. She remembers Craig as tall and good-looking, usually wearing basketball clothes. Michelle was "very personable, and down to earth. She never impressed me as one who would go with a group," but, rather, as a child who knew her own mind.

Her mother also paints that portrait of Michelle, a focused, determined child with a strong sense of self. "I always say Michelle raised herself from about 9 years old," she told the *Chicago Tribune*. "She had her head on straight very early." Craig likes to joke that they would play "office," and Michelle would be the secretary, and he would be the boss, and he wouldn't have anything to do because she would insist upon doing everything. He also recalls that she hated to lose at board games and had trouble watching sports because she couldn't bear to see her team lose. Later, she would walk out of Craig's basketball games if they were too close. She was tall, like her brother, and lovely. "She always had poise," says backdoor neighbor Credit. Credit says that Michelle played with her daughter, who was one day older than she was, and that when Michelle was in high school, a younger relative of Credit's took her to the prom. Credit says she always expected Michelle to be a model—she was graceful and self-contained.

"She was always a good person, and she was very respectful to the elder people, she was always speaking with a smile, she was well mannered, and she was always quiet. I have a son who was younger, and Craig was his role model." Both the Robinson children, she says, were examples for other children.

Credit also remembers Fraser Robinson as a man with a ready smile, even as his disease progressed. "He had those crutches, and it was sad to see him like that. He walked and he always had a smile on his face, always joking. A joking man—he could always find humor." No matter how high in the world Michelle and Craig rose, the Robinsons remained tied to longtime neighbors. "They are just like family to me: I have gone through the sickness, the death, the graduations, the weddings," says Credit, who would later attend Michelle and Barack's wedding at Trinity United Church of Christ. There, Credit enjoyed seeing socialites, the glitterati of Chicago, among whose ranks Michelle was now moving.

All in all, it was a comfortable working-class existence. Marian Robinson would later tell *The New Yorker* that they never felt deprived. "If the TV broke and we didn't have any money to have it fixed, we could go out and buy another one on a charge card, as long as we paid the bills on time." On Saturday nights, the family played Chinese checkers, Monopoly, and other board games. Once a year they might drive to Dukes Happy Holiday Resort, an African American–friendly resort in White Cloud, Michigan, for a vacation. Barack Obama would later describe the Robinsons as something out of *Leave It to Beaver,* a functional nuclear family where the parents got along and the children were loved and nurtured even as it was made clear that they were expected to study and succeed, and where relatives were always coming around to eat a meal or play jazz or trade anecdotes. Michelle's mother, Marian, was "salt of the earth," according to a family friend, as well as being no-nonsense and firm. And the children respected their father so much that their greatest terror was to disappoint him. Their mother sometimes administered corporal punishment, but their father simply . . . looked. "You never wanted to disappoint him," Michelle would tell *Newsweek.* "We would be bawling."

Growing up, however, Michelle also would have been aware that not all members of the community were doing as well as she was. "You're not raised on the South Side without knowing that there are poor communities. Even if you don't live in a poor neighborhood, you're not far from one," says Stephan Garnett. The city made sure that the vast majority of Chicago public housing projects were constructed in African American neighborhoods, not white ones; and even within South Shore, there were rental properties that housed families with lower incomes than those who lived on Michelle's street.

In that era, some pockets of South Shore had a median income as high as $23,000, while other pockets had a median income of under $9,000.

During the 1970s, a split began to take place in South Shore and throughout the city. Some members of the African American community would continue to experience even greater prosperity, enhanced by affirmative action and other measures taken to offer advancement and make up for past discrimination, while others would be left behind, falling victim to gun violence, climbing crime rates, drugs, and all the afflictions that came with working-class jobs drying up in urban areas. The trend began in the 1950s when meatpacking plants began closing. In the 1960s, the stockyards and steel mills followed suit, and the gap between the poor and the more well-off would become wider and more apparent. This decline of the working-class sector is something Michelle Obama talks about frequently—it was a decline she personally witnessed. When Barack Obama came to Chicago in 1985, his job was to help the community find a way forward despite the disappearance of the industries that had given the South Side its character. It was his job—a hard uphill battle—to work with community leaders and pastors, to seek a new way out.

Michelle was living in the heart of the community

while the closures were happening, and the gap is something that preys on her mind and affects her sense of self. Around this time, Michelle has said, she learned how to perform the trick of being a smart kid who doesn't stand out on the street, a technique she referred to as "speaking two languages." As she put it, "What I learned growing up is that if I'm not going to get my butt kicked every day after school, I can't flaunt my intelligence in front of peers who are struggling with a whole range of things." The trick, she has said, is that "you've got to be smart without acting smart." Critics charge her with being downbeat and insufficiently grateful for her own prosperity, but she is clearly speaking about inequity she has seen up close. "We have become a nation of struggling folks who are barely making it every day," she said at a South Carolina church in January 2008. "Folks are just jammed up, and it's gotten worse over my lifetime."

This sensibility—an acute awareness of people for whom life has not gotten better, even as it has gotten better for her—has been with her for quite some time. In her senior thesis, "Princeton-Educated Blacks and the Black Community," the question of what upper-income blacks owe to the less fortunate was a major preoccupation. For her thesis, she mailed questionnaires to black Princeton alumni, asking whether they were more comfortable spending time with blacks or whites, and how they felt about African Americans who weren't doing as well as they were. "Feelings of obligation to improve the life of the Black lower class, feelings of guilt for betraying the Black lower class, as well as feelings of shame or envy toward the Black lower class are investigated in this study," she noted. In one question, she asked alumni about "their personal attitudes towards lower-class Black Americans."

"When you think of lower-class Black Americans and the life they lead, how true for you personally are the following statements?" she asked. Among the answers she offered as possibilities were, "I feel proud that I have been strong enough to avoid remaining in, or falling into, that life," and "I feel lucky that I was given opportunities that they are not given," and "I feel guilty that I may be betraying them in some way," as well as "I feel ashamed of them," and "Their situation is hopeless."

The point is that Michelle's world saw people facing starkly different prospects. The area where she grew up provided a home to African American families like hers that were on the way up and to those that were languishing. The division would be exacerbated by affirmative action, which, for all its advantages, would propel many socioeconomically successful African Americans out of their home neighborhoods. People moved away. As a result, even South Shore would see some decline. When the city began demolishing some of the more notorious high-rise public housing projects in the 1990s, the people who lived in them had few places to go, and since most were African American, they tended to move into black neighborhoods nearby or to some black suburbs. While the more upscale areas of South Shore near the lake have remained unchanged, some areas have seen crime go up. Along a commercial corridor not far from Michelle's mother's house, the parade of small businesses—wig shops, hair salons, Laundromats—includes the occasional shuttered storefront. The parking lot of a now-defunct muffler shop is empty and strewn with glass. Though residents still try to police a block they continue to be proud of, Terry Thompson says, "The kind of crime that we have at this moment never existed before."

For Michelle, the development that would take her out of the neighborhood was the city's launching of magnet high schools. Next to housing, segregated schools had long been a blight on the city's reputation and a major sore point with African American citizens.

For good reason. "The summer of 1963 saw massive protests against school segregation, which culminated later that fall with a massive school boycott," notes Don Rose. Black schools were overcrowded and had far fewer services than white ones, and the city had gone to great lengths to make sure black children stayed in them. In the 1960s, the city employed the notorious "Willis wagons" to keep black children in their own schools. They were called that because under the tenure of school superintendent Benjamin Willis, as black schools became packed and white schools emptied out, the city brought in "portable classrooms"—aluminum trailers—to house the overflow students and to try and keep them there. Even so, white students were draining out of the school system as their families moved to the suburbs.

Many cities at this time were under scrutiny by the federal courts to ensure that they took measures to encourage desegregation. By the 1970s, Chicago wanted to reverse or even just abate white flight, and it wanted to provide high-achieving black students with schools that were well equipped and offered the advanced classes they deserved and needed. So, just as Michelle was moving into her teenage years, the city created a school that took her beyond her own neighborhood to a place where children of different races were officially encouraged to bond. By the accounts of many classmates, Michelle adjusted to the change gracefully. Friendly like her dad, never a snob, she developed into a much-liked young woman who could move easily among students of all races.

3

THEY STOOD ON RISERS, THIRTY-THREE OF THE highest-achieving students at a school of high achievers. It was 1981 now, and those members of the senior class at Whitney M. Young Magnet High School who had been admitted to the National Honor Society were gathered for a yearbook photo. They'd been inducted at the end of junior year, obliged during a week of initiation to do silly things like wear a dunce cap, or stand in the lunchroom and recite nonsense poetry. They'd kept their grades up and survived senior year, or almost. In a few months they would go their separate ways, but for now they were to-gether, black and white, male and female, kids from all parts of Chicago, in a moment of solidarity and justifiable pride. In the front row was that year's Honor Society president, Santita Jackson, daughter of the Reverend Jesse Jackson, smiling and demure in a plaid skirt and turtleneck sweater. To one side was their sponsor, the science teacher, Ms. Takekawa, in a plaid jacket and glasses. In the back row was Christy McNulty, wearing a light button-down shirt with stripes, her hair loose around her shoulders. And next to her, looking pleased and confident and wearing a V-neck sweater, was her friend and erstwhile political rival, Michelle Robinson.

Christy McNulty, like Michelle Robinson, lived in South Shore. Hers was one of the few white families that had stayed in the neighborhood, and she had gotten used to the attention she attracted, a lone white girl walking down the street, people sometimes calling out to her "Snow White!" She, like Michelle, applied to Whitney Young and was accepted. She, like Michelle, took a bus and an el train to get to school, a trip that took anywhere from thirty minutes to two hours, depending on the trains and the weather, which in the winter was vicious, with cold and snow and wind that made you stagger. She, like Michelle, had run for senior-class treasurer, and Michelle had beaten her by, she recalls, something like one vote.

Christy didn't hold it against her. She and Michelle got along well, as did most students at Whitney Young. So well that, just before the camera shutter closed, Michelle reached out and draped her arm around Christy, her palm resting lightly on Christy's left shoulder. "It was just spontaneous," Christy, whose last name is now Niezgodzki, recalls. Christy lives in Phoenix. All these years later, she can still remember the moment when Michelle Robinson reached out to embrace her. It was characteristic. "She was always a very positive person, very friendly, open—I never saw her discriminate."

And really, the entire high school was like that. To the other side of Michelle, another white girl, curly-haired Julie Wachowski, was putting one arm around Michelle and another around Alexandra Petrilli, who was white, who in turn was putting an arm around Angelique De-Vold, who was black. The result was a multiracial group of smart, smiling students standing on the back riser with arms interlaced. Despite Chicago's history of racial tension, in the late 1970s and early 1980s, Whitney Young by all accounts was its own little biosphere of amity and inclusiveness, a place where students so valued one another that they titled their yearbook *Circle of Friends*. For the photo on the front page of the 1981 *Whitney Young Dolphin,* fifteen students of different races and ethnicities lay down together in a giggling circle, holding hands, heads pointed inward, grinning up at the camera. Judging from the memories of those who went there, Whitney Young was an experiment in diversity that worked. The school provided what was, in America, an unusual educational setting: Though it was racially integrated, African American students were in the majority. For them, Whitney Young made for a reasonably gentle bridge to a multiracial environment, a safe place where they could branch out socially and yet enjoy strength in numbers. It was a privilege that at many high school and college campuses is reserved for white students, who rarely reflect upon it.

At Whitney Young and other magnet schools, the aim was to bring students of all races and neighborhoods together and to provide them with superior facilities and high-level honors and AP classes, especially in the arts and sciences. Students could also take college-level courses at a nearby University of Illinois campus. The school was named for the late Whitney Moore Young Jr., a Kentucky-born African American civil rights leader who had served as executive director of the Urban League, a post from which he fought for equal opportunity for blacks in schools and workplaces. The school was constructed in the west part of downtown, in a neighborhood where a number of freeways converged, on land available in part because nobody else seemed to want it.

Actually, the area around Whitney Young hardly merited the term *neighborhood*. Though it's gentrifying now, in the 1970s when Michelle first began to pick her way from the el station toward the school, she would walk through a gritty postindustrial landscape that consisted of factories, trade-union headquarters, and town houses, some abandoned. Some still showed the devastation from the rioting and fires that followed Martin Luther King's assassination. In 1968, after the death of the country's foremost civil rights leader, the city's racial strife had come to a head, as it had in a number of other U.S. cities, when residents rioted and set fire to buildings. This did not happen in South Shore, or even much in South Side, where local leaders were able to quell the unrest. But it exploded in other sections, including this one. During the King riots, Mayor Daley finally and inescapably alienated a large part of the African American population—and many whites, too—by issuing his infamous "shoot to kill" directive to the police force, ordering them to use guns against any arsonists. Just a few months later, the 1968 Democratic convention again brought rioting to Chicago, to a part of the city not far from Whitney Young. Following both of these events, black residents began to reassess their view of the mayor. An independent coalition of blacks and progressive whites began to come together with the intention of breaking the Machine, forming an independent movement that in 1983 would result in the election of Harold Washington. Similarly, from the ashes of strife and anger rose Whitney Young.

The school opened in 1975. Not long after, Michelle Robinson enrolled in ninth grade, the first person in her family to attend. "My parents weren't college-educated folks, so they didn't have a notion of what we should want," Michelle would later tell an interviewer. But they clearly were motivated to give their children the best possible educational opportunity. The local public high school was just a block from their home, but Craig already had been sent by his parents to Mt. Carmel High School, a parochial school that produced a number of excellent basketball players, of whom Craig was one. The decision to leave the neighborhood for school represented a new chapter both for Michelle and for Chicago. For someone like thirteen-year-old Michelle, it took an adventurous spirit to travel to a school that was miles from her home.

"When she applied and came here, the tradition of leaving one's neighborhood to go to high school was very new, and a person had to be gutsy to do it. For most kids who came here in those times, the idea that you would take two or three buses and a train to come here was a very new idea," says Dagny Bloland, an English teacher who came to the school in the 1980s. "It was an industrial neighborhood, with factories, sometimes abandoned. The stores weren't here yet, and the churches were not thriving. It was a real experiment to come here. I think you had to be the sort of person and the sort of family that would put education above everything else."

It also showed her parents' commitment to upward mobility. Whatever they did or did not know about life outside the working class, Marian and Fraser Robinson recognized that education was the path that would lead their children into a world where they might enjoy more autonomy, more say over what they chose as a profession, more control over whom they socialized with and where they shopped and ate and lived and raised their own children. They recognized that, in schools and in workplaces, new opportunities had begun opening for African Americans, opportunities that far exceeded those that had been available to their generation.

Byron Brazier, the pastor of the Apostolic Church of God, describes this period, the 1970s, as having a powerful psychological impact on many young African Americans. In the mid-1960s, after the passage of the Civil Rights Act, Lyndon Johnson encouraged the nation to take "affirmative action" to do away with discrimination in workplaces. The term and the changes that would result had a profound effect on Brazier and others who, like him, benefited from inclusion into white-collar workplaces. Brazier—who enjoyed a successful corporate career before taking the cloth—recalls that the 1970s saw a "transformation of thinking" among many young African Americans, "a sense of possibility, accessibility, things being open." Similarly, the opportunity to attend Whitney Young opened up prospects for an intelligent, driven, and high-achieving student like Michelle, even as it could be criticized for draining talented students like her from neighborhood schools.

"It was a school that some of the best and brightest African Americans went to," says the political consultant Al Kindle.

And in fact, classmates recall, it was harder for a black student to get into Whitney Young than for a white student. That's because at the outset, the goal for Whitney Young was that it should be racially balanced, consisting of 40 percent white students and 40 percent black students, with 10 percent Spanish-speaking, 5 percent other races, and 5 percent students admitted at the principal's discretion, often in response to a call from this or that influential alderman. The idea was to draw from all neighborhoods, select students who were exceptionally able, and achieve racial balance.

It was a losing battle at that time, however, to try to attract a sizable complement of whites. In 1974, the city's overall high school population was about 52 percent black, 38 percent white, and 9 percent Spanish-speaking, meaning that to make its quota of 40 percent white students Whitney Young would have to attract a disproportionate number of the city's white students, despite the fact that students often had well-equipped high schools in their own neighborhoods. "They were really trying to [pull white students] in so they could make it integrated," remembers Christy Niezgodzki. They did not succeed. In 1987, a team of outside assessors found that at Whitney Young, "the white population has declined from approximately 34.2 percent in 1980 to 18 percent in 1986." Michelle's time marked a high-water mark of white enrollment, after which it would decline before bottoming out and then rising in more recent years.

"A major problem exists with the declining white enrollment," the 1987 study noted, pointing out that many white students had good neighborhood schools with competitive programs, and many lived far away from Whitney Young. True, the school had a radio station, an Olympic-size swimming pool, and honors classes, but those amenities weren't enough for some families. Recognizing the racial prejudice that still existed, the report added, "The fact that Young is a predominantly black school is viewed as a limitation for the recruitment of whites from many south-west and north-west areas." The report further noted that "there is a declining white population living in the city of Chicago and a large percentage of city whites send their children to Catholic or other non-public schools," and that most neighborhood schools were fighting hard to keep their existing white students. It also noted that Young, "in an effort to maintain its white percentage, may accept marginally qualified white students who may not be successful in the long run."

Essentially, the report acknowledged that a kind of affirmative action was being applied to whites, who faced less rigorous academic standards for admission. This is important; it shows that the high-achieving black students going to Whitney Young, such as Michelle, did *not* have to confront the resentment that some of them would later run into on college campuses, where they had to withstand accusations that they had received a special break. To the contrary, blacks were the ones who had to fly over the high bar to be accepted, while whites could get in under more lenient requirements. (Whitney Young would later abandon racial quotas and use testing only as a criterion. The school is now considered so desirable that students of all ethnicities are clamoring to get in. No surprise: According to the assistant principal, Mark Grishaber, every student in the class of 2008 was admitted to the college of his or her choice.)

But while all this tense racial calibration was going on outside the school doors, a very exceptional racial détente was taking place inside. As the 1987 report noted, the school itself worked wonderfully. Students were "being challenged to think and to respond to higher-order inferential questions." There were many clubs and leadership opportunities; college-bound students were particularly well served by the courses offered; the entire school community was committed to academic excellence; and "there appear[ed] to be a genuine love of and concern for students" on the part of teachers and administrators, something students noted and appreciated, according to the bureaucrats who prepared the document.

There was also an air of tolerance and unity. The

school contained a program for the deaf and hearing impaired, which helped make some students sensitive to the needs of others with disabilities. Moreover, even though white students were not as numerous as the school system wished, those white students who chose to attend Whitney Young were a self-selected group. With so many incentives for staying in their neighborhood schools—or fleeing the city—those who did make the commitment tended to come from progressive and open-minded families. It took a certain adventurousness on the part of white students, too, to try Whitney Young. As the English teacher Dagny Bloland recalled, white students who attended Young by and large came from families, like those of Christy Niezgodzki, who remained committed to the public school system and the city of Chicago, and who were committed to their children learning in a diverse environment. "This is a unique situation in which it isn't just a bunch of kids that come here from different neighborhoods; it's a real shared commitment [and] I think parents know, 'My child is going to have a wider world,' " says Bloland.

Many of Michelle's classmates agree. "It was racially diverse, it was ethnically diverse; it had great school spirit. It was pretty new, and it was fantastic," recalls Robert Mayfield, who is African American and served as president of the senior class in 1980–1981. Tall and genial and outgoing, Mayfield now works doing public relations in Washington, D.C. Mayfield's fellow officers were his friend Leon Wilson, vice president, who would go on to become an actor in Los Angeles; Michelle Ealey, class secretary, who would become a pharmaceutical representative; and Michelle Robinson, the class treasurer, who did the math and kept the budget straight. All four senior-class officers were African American, but that didn't mean white students were excluded from clubs and leadership. Christy Niezgodzki remembers very little typecasting or self-segregation; while it's true, she recalls, that the swim team was stereotypically white and the dance team was mostly black, most clubs and teams were mixed. Their senior year, the school play was *Arsenic and Old Lace,* and the yearbook shows students black and white playing leads. The school was designed to promote racial mingling. Like Hogwarts in the *Harry Potter* series, it was divided into four "houses," the idea being that smaller units would give students a sense of belonging, and each house was designed to reflect the racial makeup of the school. The yearbook shows no clubs based on gender or racial identity.

"There were some students who would just keep to their comfort level, and to their groups, and there were

other students who ventured out, and I would say most
students ventured out. It was sort of funny—going back
into your neighborhood you would stick to your groups,
but in school you would learn about each other," Niezgodzki recalls.

The class secretary, now Michelle Ealey Toliver,
agrees. "Although it was racially diverse, the school was
not racially divided. It was a melting pot. Our home-
coming court was black and white, there was no racial
undertone. Everything was just, I don't know, harmoni-
ous. Sports and everything. We had two Chinese guys
who were phenomenal basketball players."

Her classmates remember Michelle Robinson as
friendly, focused, and more quiet than you'd expect,
given her outspokenness on the campaign trail. Niezgodzki remembers that when they were running for
treasurer, both of them had to make a speech to the entire class. She had the sense that for Michelle, speaking
in public before hundreds of students was "a big step,"
not something that came easily. Mayfield recalls her as
unpretentious and a steadying presence; as a colleague
on the student council, she had the kind of personality
that helped him stay calm in the midst of academic and
extracurricular pressures, and he figures she does the
same now for Barack. The school did have some cliques,

based on test scores and interests and athletic ability, but he and others recall that Michelle could "float gracefully" between social groups in the school.

And she was not easily distracted from her studies. "It was obvious that she had goals and she was going places," says Toliver. "She didn't goof off like some other students. She was in a lot of honors classes . . . she was on a very advanced, focused track." Overall, the entire school seems to have been focused; Niezgodzki recalls little illicit partying, saying she saw more drugs and alcohol at a private school she and her parents visited in the suburbs. In his autobiography, *Dreams from My Father*, Barack Obama admits to drinking and doing cocaine with his buddies at the exclusive Punahou School in Hawaii. It would seem that Michelle led a more straitlaced existence, in a less privileged public school environment where fun consisted of fashion shows and sock hops. Another classmate, Ava Griffin, recalls that the high jinks that did go on tended to be reasonably wholesome, like the day a group of students were dissecting pig uteruses in biology class, and somehow pig embryos ended up in the cafeteria condiments, and a memorable food fight ensued. "She stayed away from that kind of stuff," says Griffin.

But she was also, even then, quick to assert herself

when she felt wronged. "Michelle's always been very vocal about anything," her mother, Marian Robinson, told *The New Yorker*. "If it's not right, she's going to say so." When a typing teacher did not give her the A she deserved according to a words-per-minute chart, Michelle objected vehemently. "She badgered and badgered that teacher," Marian Robinson said. "I finally called her and told her, 'Michelle is not going to let this go.' " Later, at Princeton, Craig would remember Michelle's complaining that the university was teaching French wrong, and that classes were not conversational. Her mother's advice to Craig, who was sharing a campus with his sister? "Just pretend you don't know her," Craig recalls. This also seems characteristic; throughout her life, Michelle has been unwilling to accept what she perceives as an injustice.

During this time, she was able to make friends with children of prominent families. One of her close friends was Santita Jackson, who lived in another, more upscale part of South Shore. "It was clear that they had a certain spiritual kinship," recalls Jesse Jackson Sr., describing Michelle as "an odds buster, and an overcomer. She always had her eye on the north star, so to speak."

Like any high school, it also had cliques based on what part of town you came from. Toliver remembers that kids from Michelle Robinson's South Side made up one clique, while those from the city's other sizable historical African American community, on the West Side, made up another. "There was a whole West Side versus the South Side friendly rivalry." She remembers that the "South Side was probably the higher socioeconomic group, a lot of the South Siders were children of politicians or children of very important people, like Jesse Jackson, and a lot of aldermen's kids went there." The funny thing, she says, is that the politically more powerful, socioeconomically more affluent South Siders dressed more casually—kids from Michelle's group "wore Levi's blue jeans, while we dressed up." Sure enough, Michelle's junior-class student-government photo shows her dressed in jeans and a button-down shirt, one hand on her hip, smiling easily. But even at that time she liked the finer things. Her mother laughs about how she bought a Coach bag with babysitting money, and when Marian marveled at the price tag, Michelle pointed out that while her mother might buy ten cheaper pocketbooks, she would need only one.

The fact that she qualified for the National Honor Society shows that she had high grades; to be admitted, students had to have a 3.0 grade point average or higher—a B average—and they had to perform community service. In a speech in New Lenox, Illinois, during her husband's Senate race, Michelle told a group of middle school students that she ranked thirty-second in her high school class. According to her mother and brother, this did not come without effort; she was the kind of student who excelled in part because she worked tremendously hard. Craig has often told how he would go off to play basketball, and she would be studying. When he would come home and watch TV, she would still be studying. Tests came easily to Craig but presented more of a hurdle for Michelle. "She was disappointed in herself," her mother has said. "She used to have a little bit of trouble with tests, so she did whatever she had to do to make up for that. I'm sure it was psychological because she was hardworking and she had a brother who could pass a test just by carrying a book under his arm. When you are around someone like that, even if you are okay, you want to be as good or better." Michelle frequently deplores the modern reliance on test scores, describing herself as a person who did not test well.

Today, the memory she shares most often about her education is one of being discouraged. "Not many people believed in the possibility of me," she told a Chicago group in 2006, speaking at a lunch for a program called

High Jump that supports academically gifted children of limited means. "I beat the odds," she told them, saying, "The world tells us not to search too high, it puts up all kinds of barriers for kids saying, 'You can't do this' and 'you can't do that.'" In speeches she habitually describes herself as a person who was not supposed to get where she did. "All my life I have confronted people who had a certain expectation of me," she said in Madison, Wisconsin. "Every step of the way, there was somebody there telling me what I couldn't do. I applied to Princeton. 'You can't go there, your test scores aren't high enough.' I went. I graduated with departmental honors. And then I wanted to go to Harvard. And that was 'probably a little too tough for me.' I didn't even know why they said that."

It's hard to know how this view applies to her high school years; assistant principal Grishaber says most teachers who were at the school when Michelle was a student, and are there now, do not remember her. In her Chicago speech, she commented that when she was applying to college, she applied to Ivy League universities and to backups—Princeton, Harvard, and the Universities of Wisconsin and Illinois—because she was advised to play it safe. "I listened to all the limitations I was told I had." But at the talk in New Lenox, Illinois, she said that, basically, no one gave her any advice at all. "No one talked to me about Princeton or Harvard . . . or even going to college." What does not change is the memory of being discouraged or ignored. According to Mayfield, in general the college counseling was good: "I think they gave most of us very good advice to encourage us to go on, and most of us did." However, he says there was one counselor, a white woman, who was rumored to be less supportive of the African American students. "It was that generational thing," he said—someone who had not changed with the times. "Maybe the one [Michelle] got was one that a lot of people did not like." If so, it made a lasting impression: In speeches she often describes herself as the product of neighborhood schools, dismissing magnet schools as an undesirable outgrowth of a failed public school system, the kind of place you have to "finagle" to get into.

According to Michelle, she applied to Princeton because Craig went there first. He had heard about Princeton from the director of a summer basketball camp, was accepted in part because of his basketball talent, and would become one of the school's all-time leading scorers and two-time Ivy League player of the year. Initially, Craig has recalled, he was inclined to go to the University of Washington, where he had been offered a full scholarship. But Fraser Robinson well knew the value of a Princeton degree and urged him not to take the tuition into account. "If you pick your school based on how much you have to pay, I'll be very disappointed," his father said. "My parents were always clear," said Michelle. "They always told us that you go to the best school and don't worry about money." Marian went to work as a secretary in part to help pay for their education. The family knew that a school like Princeton could lift you into a new socioeconomic category. "No disrespect to the other schools that were recruiting me, but Wall Street doesn't happen if I'm not at Princeton, sorry," Craig would later say. He has also talked about how daunting the place was at first. He took a bus from New York City to Princeton, carrying a suitcase and a duffel bag, and recalls classmates pulling up in cars and unloading more stuff.

"I was overwhelmed by Princeton," he would later say. "I was so far behind, and I didn't even have a fan." His first semester, he felt he was struggling and called his father. "He told me that you're not going to be number one at Princeton, but you're not going to be last either. That kind of put it all in perspective for me. After that, I was all right."

Both of the children would clearly agonize over whether it made sense to use their Ivy League degrees to pursue a lucrative corporate career, or to do work they loved and found more gratifying. Craig, after playing professional basketball in Europe, would get an MBA at the University of Chicago and go to work for Morgan Stanley Dean Witter, and then a boutique investment firm, Loop Capital Markets. For a while he enjoyed his wealth, but he eventually realized that the job wasn't making him happy. "I'm so embarrassed to admit it," Craig later told the *New York Times*. "I had a Porsche 944 Turbo. I had a BMW station wagon. Who gets a BMW station wagon? It's the dumbest car in the world. Why would you buy a $75,000 station wagon?" Concluding that "I've got all this stuff, and it hasn't made my life any better," Craig at age thirty-seven left the world of investment banking and took a job that he loves, coaching basketball. He recently left his position as head coach at Brown University to become head coach at Oregon State. But the fact that he spent time on Wall Street first gives some inkling of the pressure, for children who went to school on scholarships, to enter a remunerative profession, pressure that Michelle would feel as well.

Michelle, who visited him at Princeton, says she figured if Craig could get in, so could she. "I knew him, and I knew his study habits, and I was like, 'I can do that too.'"

Doing so would propel her into a markedly different environment, one that was even more high-achieving than Whitney Young, but not nearly so inclusive. "A lot of the African American students that I was good friends with in high school, once they went to college, they realized, I think, that there was a lot more separation out in the world and discrimination," says Niezgodzki. "At [Whitney Young], they could run for student government, there were no boundaries and really no limits. And once they went into college, I think they had more of a culture shock, especially if they went to the Ivy League."

As Byron Brazier puts it, more generally: "The seventies were a growth period for America, especially in relation to the population of African Americans. It was a growth period in that we all learned a lot about each other."

The eighties would be a little different.

4

IN THE LATE SUMMER OF 1981, WHEN MICHELLE arrived at Princeton's suburban New Jersey campus, with its gray neo-Gothic towers and athletic fields exuding that sweet, late-summer, mowed-grass smell, African Americans made up less than 10 percent of the student body. There were 94 African Americans in her freshman class, out of more than 1,100 students. The school had never been a pioneer of racial advancement, to put it nicely. In 1904, Woodrow Wilson, who was president of the university, notoriously noted that "the whole temper and tradition of the place are such that no negro has ever applied for admission, and it seems extremely unlikely that the question will ever assume a practical form." In 1936, Bruce M. Wright, an African American, was admitted by mistake, and, when he got to campus, was asked to leave. As the historian James Axtell noted in *The Making of Princeton University,* "When he summoned the courage three years later to ask [a dean] for an explanation, the dean drew attention to the number of Southern students at the college and suggested that 'a member of your race might feel very much alone.'" The dean of the chapel told him, later, "The race problem is beyond solution in America. Don't waste your time fighting the system here."

The school has always been an exclusive, clubby place, something that could be said of all the Ivy League schools, and probably most private colleges. But the description has a literal truth at Princeton, where social life traditionally has been dominated by a row of "eating clubs," capacious houses of different architectural styles lining a broad street called Prospect Avenue. The clubs acted like fraternities: Upperclassmen—and, eventually, upperclasswomen—were selected through an exhausting and often overwrought rushlike process known as "bicker," in which applicants were grilled by members who afterward would discuss their social merits during long, emotional sessions. If admitted, students would socialize mostly at the clubs. They would also take their meals there. For upperclassmen, there weren't many other eating options, so not getting into an eating club had real consequences. And not getting in was a fact of life, for some more than others: In the 1950s, many eating clubs were notorious for their unwillingness to admit Jews. Into the 1980s, three declined to admit women.

On the other hand, by the 1980s a majority of the eating clubs had abandoned bicker entirely, and opened up to the point where they admitted students by lottery. A dogged undergraduate, Sally Frank, initiated a sex-discrimination complaint that would result in the acceptance of women into the three remaining all-male clubs. One capitulated in 1986 and two hung on until 1990. At the same time, the university was constructing a set of residential colleges that would give students a place to live and eat, and reduce the clubs' dominance over university social life.

The campus was in a state of change, then, when Michelle matriculated, something that's always true of college campuses but was especially so in the 1980s: The now-ascendant forces of 1960s liberalism and the changes brought on by the civil rights era were coming into collision with the nascent conservatism of the Reagan era, not to mention the reactionary inclinations of some alumni. At Princeton, African American enrollment had begun to climb under the tenure of President Robert Goheen, who had appointed an African American administrator, Carl Fields, to help students of color get acclimated. By the time Michelle entered, Princeton had a president, William Bowen, who was an architect and outspoken proponent of affirmative action.

At that time, a debate was under way around the country about just what "affirmative action" could mean when it came to education. The extent to which schools could take race into account when admitting students was unclear and much contested. The argument in favor of affirmative action was that it constituted restorative justice, a way of making up for discrimination, past and present, that denied blacks not only equal work opportunities but, often, equal classroom resources. All sorts of ancillary arguments were taking place, meanwhile, about race and test scores, with some social scientists arguing that African Americans on average score lower on standardized testing because of innate differences, while others located the cause in external factors like poverty, discrimination, disadvantaged classrooms, and biased tests. The era also saw some of the most intense skirmishes in the campus culture wars, as a number of conservative scholars wrote high-profile books deploring the broadening of the literary canon to include more women and minority writers. It was a time of real acrimony, real resentment, and real entrenchment.

Princeton, as it happened, held an influential place in the affirmative action debate. In 1978, just three years before Michelle started, the U.S. Supreme Court ruled on a landmark case brought by Allan Bakke, a white man who applied to medical school at the University of California at Davis, which reserved sixteen of its one hundred slots for minorities. Bakke had been rejected, while minority students with lower test scores were admitted. Bakke, whose objection could be said to crystallize the resentment of whites who felt the gains of minorities had been their own personal loss, argued that the school's racial quota system violated his constitutional right to equal protection. In a narrow, 5–4 ruling in *Regents of the University of California v. Bakke,* the U.S. Supreme Court ruled that he was correct, and that strict racial quotas for admission were unconstitutional. But at the same time, the court said a different kind of affirmative action *was* acceptable, in which institutions could consider race as one criterion among others.

In its opinion, the court was influenced in part by the writings of Princeton's Bowen, who advocated a "holistic approach" to college admissions. By this, he meant an approach whereby a student's race might be considered along with other qualities, some more concrete than others. They could include a student's performance in the classroom, on athletic fields, or as a leader, but also, of course, a family connection to the school. It is this vague form of affirmative action that was upheld by the court in *Bakke* and subsequent decisions. So as it happened, Michelle Robinson ended up on the very campus where theories of affirmative action were being developed, during an era when the discussion had special urgency. The battle wasn't just being waged at Princeton. It was being incubated and planned there.

The central justification for what Princeton called its "race-sensitive" admissions policy is that diversity in and of itself serves an educational goal. The idea is that students of different races and genders and backgrounds, converging on campus and pinging against one another like molecules, serve to educate one another and teach one another how to better live in a pluralistic society. Seen this way, racial preferences help universities fulfill their educational mission. As Supreme Court Justice Lewis Powell wrote in the *Bakke* case, "People do not learn very much when they are surrounded only by the likes of themselves." The defense amounts to an academic freedom argument, that universities should be able to determine whom they want to admit and why. For the students who were doing the educating of one another, the process was perhaps more difficult than for those who were formulating the theory.

It goes without saying that some alumni leaped to the battlements and loaded their crossbows with flaming arrows. In 1972, the same year Bowen took over as president, a group emerged calling itself Concerned Alumni of Princeton. CAP, which grew out of a group that had opposed coeducation in 1969, took it upon itself to fight a spectrum of post-sixties developments, including, but not limited to, perceived liberalism of the faculty, promotion of birth control and abortion, and any kind of "preferences" for minorities. "These were people who really didn't much like change, and who thought that the old Princeton had been just fine, and for many of them it was," recalls Bowen. "They didn't agree with the arguments in favor of moving Princeton to what it has now become."

For the students who were there to be the "educators," I can say that it wasn't always easy. I also went to Princeton, entering the campus in 1978, three years before Michelle, a white Southerner from southwestern Virginia, on the outskirts of Appalachia, and daughter of a housewife and a lawyer. I had never heard of the sport called crew, or any of the Northeastern prep schools that traditionally channeled alumni into the school. I'd never been exposed to kids who had grown up in New York City and attended schools where the playgrounds were on the roof, an image that seemed impossibly exotic. Or people whose families were so old and fabulously wealthy that their last names were chiseled into school dormitories. The school was full of wonderfully open-minded and remarkable students, and all in all, it was the presence of these students that dominated. But for a woman venturing onto a campus that had only recently gone coeducational, vestiges of the old sexist institutions were everywhere. There were organizations that had never had a woman or a student of color as president, and some professors were not welcoming. I remember wondering why, waiting tables at the university faculty club, I saw my own junior-paper adviser, a Shakespeare scholar, inviting a male advisee to lunch, when he had never asked me. My roommate, who was Jewish, was subjected to comments about whether she did, or did not, "look" Jewish, which she had never run into before. It was like being at a country club that had just loosened its admission policy and was still making uneasy adjustments. African American students recall newspapers slipped under their door with op-eds argu-ing that their presence on campus brought down university intellectual standards. In the fall of 1985, CAP sent around a letter to alumni warning that "alumni children comprise 14 percent of each entering class, compared with an 11 percent quota for blacks and Hispanics." Even some conservative students would see such missives as close to racist. "Is the issue the percentage of alumni children admitted or the percentage of minorities?" one CAP-affiliated undergraduate wrote in an internal memo. "I don't see the relevance in comparing the two, except in a racist context (i.e., why do we let in so many minorities and not alumni children?)."

They were a small group, these opponents, but a noisy one, and it wasn't just old alumni. A group of young conservatives were making their presence known, among them Dinesh D'Souza, a Dartmouth graduate who came to the campus in 1983 when he was hired to edit *Prospect*, a conservative monthly alumni magazine published by CAP. In his own writings, D'Souza would become a vocal critic of "black culture," which he portrayed as pathologically violent and inferior to white culture. The group disbanded in 1987; its heyday coincided with the period when Michelle was there. Not exactly a welcome banner for a black girl from the South Side of Chicago.

Even in her own dormitory—even in her own room— it must quickly have become clear to Michelle that she wasn't at cozy Whitney Young anymore. For the most part, her classmates' families had *not* sent their children to Princeton because they believed in diversity and inclusion. One of her new roommates, Catherine Donnelly, was a white woman from New Orleans whose mother, Alice Brown, had taken a job at a private school so her daughter could go there and increase her chances of getting into a good college. For Catherine, daughter of a single mom, Princeton was a much-worked-for achievement, as it was for Michelle. But when Alice Brown found that her daughter had been assigned to room with a black girl, she spent the night calling alumni friends and everybody she knew on campus, trying to get her daughter's rooming assignment changed.

"Mom just blew a gasket when I described Michelle," Catherine Donnelly, now a lawyer practicing in Palmetto, Georgia, would acknowledge later. "It was my secret shame." Both Donnelly and Brown would later give newspaper interviews, inspired by the candidacy of Barack Obama to engage in a public discussion of race. Brown would express her contrition and confirm that indeed, the joke had been on her: Here she was trying to protect her daughter from the influence of a young woman who would grow up to be a potential first lady. She said she regretted it.

In some of these interviews, Catherine Donnelly has said she doesn't think Michelle realized what her mother was up to. Certainly, if it was her private shame, she didn't share her mother's prejudice. She says she liked Michelle, who was friendly and told great stories about Chicago. But the dorm room was small and crowded, and when a bigger room became available a few months into the school year, Donnelly moved. She had little contact afterward with Michelle. "Michelle early on began to hang out with other black students," Donnelly told the *Boston Globe*. "I wish now that I had pushed harder to be friends, but by the same token she did not invite me to do things either."

Because that's just sort of how it happened: Tired of pinging like molecules, some people tended to withdraw into their own social systems. Michelle, at Princeton, seems to have been one of the ones who did. She has written that she felt, for the first time, self-conscious about her race. "My experiences at Princeton have made me far more aware of my Blackness than ever before," she wrote in her thesis. "I have found that at Princeton no matter how liberal and open-minded some of my White professors and classmates may try to be toward me, I sometimes feel like a visitor on campus; as if I really don't belong. Regardless of the circumstances under which I interact with Whites at Princeton, it often seems as if, to them, I will always be Black first and a student second."

In her thesis, Michelle also expressed her belief that the university was not doing enough to support black students' needs. "Due to the small number of Blacks in attendance, the University does not often meet the social and academic needs of its Black population because these universities focus their attention on accommodating the White students who comprise the majority of their enrollment," she wrote.

Noting that many clubs and campus institutions served to uphold the status quo, she wrote, "[I]t is often difficult for some Black students to adjust to Princeton's environment; and unfortunately there are very few adequate support groups which provide some form of guidance and counsel for Black students having difficulty making the transition from their home environments to Princeton's environment." She pointed out that there were "only five Black tenured professors on its faculty; and the program of Afro-American studies is one of the smallest and most understaffed departments in the University, only offering four courses during the spring semester of 1985; and there is only one major University-recognized organization on campus designed specifically for the intellectual and social interests of Blacks and Third World students." She also said that campus speakers were rarely selected based on the likelihood that they might appeal to communities of color, so black students formed groups such as the Organization of Black Unity and the Princeton University Black Thoughts table.

She was not the only one who felt that way. Because of the opposition they encountered, some black students also objected to race-sensitive admissions. Their dissatisfaction propelled them into the office of Eugene Lowe, who graduated from Princeton in 1971. Lowe, who is African American, in 1983 became dean of students. In that position, he caught much of the cross fire of the era. Students of color "basically would come in and say to many of us, 'You've brought us here to educate the white majority; we're sort of the guinea pigs,'" recalls Lowe, who is now assistant to the president of Northwestern University. "I've scratched my head about that. I have heard that a lot. I think part of the dynamic here is an intensification of the consciousness of oneself as being an educational ingredient in a process for the wider community." For some African American students, being seen as a pedagogical opportunity for white people "reinforced their sense of being differentiated." Lowe respected their view even as he did not agree with it. He believed, and still does, that all students were there to educate one another. They all were guinea pigs.

And the university did respond, or tried to. "We all learned painfully that not all of this was easy," says Bowen, who is now retired from the presidency and is a senior research associate at the Andrew W. Mellon Foundation, where he continues to write about college culture and defend affirmative action. "Many people thought that simply admitting minority students in and of itself was all one had to do, and everything would be fine," says Bowen. "The university learned slowly, because mistakes of course were made, that it was necessary to have support systems in place."

Among the institutions it did put in place was the Third World Center, a building that opened in 1971 and was designed to give students of color—black and Latino, mostly—an "address on campus," in the words of Lowe. The building was located at the corner of Olden Street and Prospect Avenue, positioned as an alternative to, and commentary on, the clubs. While it mostly was a venue for presentations and socializing, some students at the Third World Center also formed a food cooperative, taking turns shopping and cooking. The name was a political statement, an expression of solidarity with populations of color at a time when activists on many campuses were trying to persuade institutions to stop investing in South Africa's apartheid government. But even at the time the name seemed marginalizing to some students, since "Third World" also connoted poverty and underdevelopment. "I suppose it seemed a bit embarrassing to me, it had this feeling—it sounded so remedial," says Robin Givhan, an African American Princeton alumna who is now the Pulitzer Prize–winning fashion critic for the *Washington Post*. In 2002, the center's name would be changed to the Carl A. Fields Center for Equality and Cultural Understanding, a name that suggests more clearly that students of all races are welcome. "Essentially, the board believes that the new name will help encourage a more inclusive membership and, consequently, a more robust, diverse program," said Kathleen Deignan, Princeton's dean of undergraduate students, when the name was changed.

At the beginning of the year, the school held an introductory session for some black students. Michelle's classmate and friend Angela Acree would later note that the session puzzled both of them. "We weren't sure whether they thought we needed an extra start or they just said, 'Let's bring all the black kids together.'"

But the upshot was that Michelle did most of her socializing at the Third World Center, or around campus with students of color. In addition to Acree, one of her best friends was a young woman from the Washington suburb of Silver Spring, Maryland, Suzanne Alele. The three became "inseparable companions," noted a *Newsweek* profile. "The three of them talked often about the racial divide on campus—especially how white kids they knew from class would pass them on the green and pretend not to see them."

Michelle and her close friends were not alone: A number of classmates felt that at Princeton they were made aware of their race in a way they had never expected. "That was the first time that I was made very conscious that I was black, and it was very negative," recalls one molecular biology major who, like Michelle, came from an urban public high school, had come to college looking forward to the opportunity to meet people from all backgrounds, and continued to do so even when it felt like swimming upstream.

"I'd say hi to people and they would ignore me and I'm standing looking right in their face talking to them," he says. "People would make comments that were either overtly racist or extremely ignorant, very offensive and hurtful in all kinds of circumstances. People would make racist jokes and then turn to me or whoever was not of their particular background and say, 'No offense, I don't mean you.' Of course it was offensive, and how could it not include me? I had students come and rub my head for good luck."

Lisa Rawlings, a classmate of Michelle's who had gone to a public high school in Baltimore and who majored in engineering at Princeton, had a similar experience. "Definitely you got the feeling that you didn't belong. Like Michelle, it was my first experience with any kind of prejudice. I wasn't used to people asking me what my SAT scores were, with the implication that I didn't have the scores to get in, I didn't have the grades to get in." And, she says, "I knew that if I went down Prospect Avenue late at night, by myself, or with other black women, that there was a good chance that I would get called Brown Sugar."

Years later, Rawlings, though, has somewhat reassessed her own social choices as a black undergraduate at Princeton. She talks now about feeling she should "take more responsibility for my experience there. Would my experience have been different if I'd joined an eating club? If I had used that opportunity to reach out to nonethnic students and make those connections? I chose to be with who I was comfortable with, and you know, that's my responsibility."

For Michelle the Third World Center was a social magnet. According to her yearbook, she took some meals at Stevenson Hall, an inexpensive dining option known by its members as the "poor man's eating club." But she spent much of her free time at the center, where, among other events, she attended seminars that featured the last surviving Scottsboro boy—a member of a group of nine black Southerners who were falsely accused of raping two white women in the 1930s—and another featuring Rosa Parks. She did a number of work-study jobs, including running child care for children of university workers. At Princeton, there was a real town-gown divide; students had little contact with Princeton residents, many of whom were African American. The Third World Center made a point of bridging the two communities, and in this it was unusual.

The day-care position must have been a real pleasure for Michelle, who has always been very child-oriented. The center's director at the time, Czerny Brasuell, knew Michelle well, in part because Brasuell's son Jonathan was a preschooler and Craig and Michelle were like a big sister and big brother to him. Michelle, she says, was endlessly patient. "She was then, and remained thereafter, someone he felt close to, someone he felt listened to him," Brasuell says. "There was a bonding that took place there. When I read about what people describe her as today, in terms of her own mothering, that is very much the person that I saw then. Very empathetic," says Brasuell, who is now director of multicultural affairs at Bates College. "She was one of the most empathetic people I have ever met, in her ability to feel what people were saying, her ability to understand." She said she witnessed the same ability later, when she saw Michelle give a speech in Cincinnati and noted her ability to focus on every individual who came to talk to her afterward.

Brasuell also remembers how attached both Michelle and Craig were to their parents, and how important it was to make their mother and father proud. Fraser Robinson was a "tremendous example," Brasuell recalls. "He was more than a role model. He was a beacon, and the pride he felt in his kids, and what it meant to them to be able to make him proud, and to be able to make their mother proud—these were guiding signposts for them." She recalls Marian Robinson as "what people call the salt of the earth—one of those women. When she says, 'Stop,' you don't have another conversation or debate. That's always the impression I had, the kids had the utmost respect for her."

Craig's presence also made a difference for Michelle on campus; when she entered as a freshman, she enjoyed a certain stature and had an entrée into the social life as the sister of a basketball star. "She knew a lot of people just because of him," says Rawlings, who recalls Michelle as being "mature, hardworking, smart. She didn't get, you know, sucked into a whole lot of gossip and drama and that kind of thing." But Craig sometimes worried that his presence might have put a damper on Michelle's dating life, in the sense that guys were aware that he was nearby keeping a brotherly eye on her, and felt self-conscious. "My sister and I are really close, and have always been, and as a matter of fact, without even trying I think I was in the way," he told me in 2007. "Her first two years at Princeton were my junior and senior year, and I think people didn't ask her out—she could certainly take care of herself, but if you're going to take out . . . a guy's sister, you sort of know what you're doing. I was in the way in a certain indirect way." Later, Craig would remark on how, because of the example set by their father, Michelle's expectations for men were almost impossibly high. "Very few of my sister's boyfriends made it to the meet-the-family stage."

For her, racial awareness was sufficiently acute that in her senior year she wrote her thesis on the subject—a document that by now is probably one of the most debated and analyzed the school has produced. Some detractors have concluded that "Princeton-Educated Blacks and the Black Community" is an ill-disguised argument for racial separatism. In a piece for the online magazine *Slate,* Christopher Hitchens drew this conclusion based in part on the fact that she cites the black nationalist Stokely Carmichael. This seems strained and unfair. She invokes Carmichael not so much to endorse his viewpoint as to use his definition of *separationism,* and cites others in arriving at a definition of *assimilationism,* which is the other impulse she wants to explore. The goal was to survey black Princeton alumni to determine whether they felt more comfortable with blacks or whites at different times in their lives: before Princeton, at Princeton, and afterward. In many cases it's hard to know what she does conclude, because parts of the thesis are dense and turgid. It should also be remembered that senior theses are ragged snapshots, at best, of a student's abilities and thoughts and certainly don't reflect their intellectual profiles as full-fledged adults. For all undergraduates they are a bête noire, worried over, the focus of anxiety dreams, sometimes written at the last minute.

I read her thesis several times, empathizing with anybody whose twentysomething psyche is exhumed for public debate and analysis. That awkward summary that you wrote in desperation in your carrel the night before it was due, the tentatively baked idea inserted at the off-hand recommendation of your adviser, all of it now quoted by political opponents who want to defeat your husband! Who would have thought? Overall, it struck me that the thesis was the work of a young woman who was thinking a lot about her past and especially her future, and who even then was capable of reassessing her views.

In it she talks about how she felt transformed by Princeton, and not necessarily for the better. "Earlier in my college career, there was no doubt in my mind that as a member of the Black community I was somehow obligated to this community and would utilize all of my present and future resources to benefit this community first and foremost," she wrote. After her career on campus, she was not nearly so sure where her obligations lay. "It is conceivable that my four years of exposure to a predominately White, Ivy League University has instilled within me certain conservative values. For example, as I enter my final year at Princeton, I find myself striving for many of the same goals as my White classmates—acceptance to a prestigious graduate or professional school or a high-paying position in a successful corporation. Thus, my goals after Princeton are not as clear as before." She seems to be saying that attending Princeton introduced her to some of the privileges of upper-middle-class life, and made prestige and money more appealing.

It also seems fair to say that, after surveying black alumni, she anticipated that life would lead her further into a white-dominated culture, and did not look forward to it. "The path I have chosen to follow by attending Princeton will likely lead to my further integration and/or assimilation into a White cultural and social structure that will only allow me to remain on the periphery of society; never becoming a full participant," she concluded, in what has already turned out to be one of the most ironic sentences ever written.

"This realization has presently made my goals to actively utilize my resources to benefit the Black community more desirable." In this sentence, she seems to be steeling herself for a renewed commitment to the black community. And given the exclusion she had experienced at Princeton, she may well have had reason to dread more of the same in later life. But she also looked hard at the data and revised some of her old ideas. After evaluating the survey results, she concluded that blacks who felt comfortable around whites were not less committed to the welfare of the black community.

She also reveals just how much African American alumni had benefited by their admittance. Statistics she collected showed that 71 percent of respondents reported being in careers that made them upwardly mobile from their parents' socioeconomic class.

Mostly, she was struck by how, while at Princeton, black students were more likely to seek solace from one another than they were either before or after. Speculating on why this was, she concluded that African American students at Princeton often missed their families and the refuge they provided. Students who had attended integrated high schools, she conjectured, "could always escape from these frustrations when they left these environments to go home. Thus, respondents' families and home lives provide relief from any problems or tensions encountered in predominantly White environments." In the absence of parents and siblings, students turned to one another.

In that sense, her thesis sometimes seems, rather simply, the work of a young woman who badly missed her parents. In a later interview, Marian Robinson said she did not realize what Michelle was going through at college. Her daughter was in an environment with which Marian was unfamiliar, so there was probably no point in confiding. This was a common phenomenon at the time. In describing the impact of affirmative action, Byron Brazier points out that "during that time, you could not rely on your parents to help you through this, because they were locked out of that. It was a period when you had to live in multiple worlds at the same time. You had to begin to manage differently." Michelle may also have felt reluctant to disappoint parents who had worked so hard to get her into school.

But it is also worth noting that not all African American students felt alienated or chose to dwell mostly in an African American circle. Sharon Fairley, who was in the class of '82 and would later move to Chicago and become part of the Obamas' social circle, had a great experience at Princeton. She was an engineering major, performed musical theater with the Triangle Club, felt happy and at home. "It was awkward," she says, being an African American who didn't hang out only at the Third World Center. "It's almost like you had to make a choice."

Similarly, Robin Givhan says her rationale for attending Princeton was to meet people of different backgrounds, and for her, college lived up to her hopes. "I always felt like the Third World Center was, for a lot of black students, really, the center of their social world," says Givhan. "There were definitely black students who joined clubs, who were very much part of the wider social world, but there were some who really, I felt at the time, really sort of relied on the Third World Center as this kind of security blanket. And my feeling was always that I kind of needed or wanted to pop into the Third World Center as a way of saying, yeah, I'm black, I know that, I'm aware of that, but I never wanted or was interested in that being the center of things for me. If I'd wanted that experience, I would have gone to Howard or Spelman. I came to Princeton because I wanted to expand my horizons and wanted to meet people who were very much not like me." She remembers getting the impression from one Third World speaker that "if you didn't believe what I believe, or operate the way I operate, you're denying that you're black. I came back to my dorm room and was in tears, relating my experience to my roommate, who was Chinese American. She looks at me and goes, 'I get that all the time from the Chinese kids.' "

Givhan says she does have insight into the forces and obligations Michelle must have been contending with. She herself grew up in Detroit in a neighborhood transformed by white flight, and was aware of how the community that had nurtured her felt proud of her admission. When she would go home for a visit, she recalls, the minister in her family's church would say, "Robin is home from Princeton." She feels certain Michelle had the idea drilled into her that she was responsible not only for herself but for her community. "She probably heard the phrase 'to whom much is given, much is required'—the whole notion of giving back," says Givhan. Just as she says, Michelle Obama uses that exact phrase in her speeches.

The university was, for many, a time of thinking through how the place had changed you, whether you still belonged—or not—in the community you had come from, and what you owed that community. According to Marvin Bressler, a Princeton sociology professor, Michelle "was troubled by the questions that troubled every student in that situation. They all walk around saying, 'Who am I?'" Howard Taylor, a former chairman of the Center for African American Studies, said, "Michelle's central question was what good does a Princeton education do for the black community. What will it do for me? Will it separate me from the black community?"

"Princeton was a real crossroads of identity for Michelle," says Charles Ogletree, her adviser at Harvard Law School. "The question was whether I retain my identity given by my African American parents, or whether the education from an elite university has transformed me into something different than what they made me. By the time she got to Harvard she had answered the question. She could be both brilliant and black."

Czerny Brasuell also saw a sense of confidence and self-definition grow in Michelle over her four years as an undergraduate. "I would not say [Michelle] was shy. She was a person who I think kept her own counsel. [But] I saw her become more willing to speak out and express her opinions. I think that's what most students do, if they are basically quiet, if they're in an environment where they are encouraged to speak," she says. Crystal Nix Hines, a classmate of Michelle's who became the first black editor of the *Daily Princetonian*, the student-run daily newspaper, had a direct experience of this. She recalls that when the paper ran an article that characterized a black politician in a way Michelle felt was inappropriate, Michelle told her calmly, "You need to make sure that a story like that doesn't run again."

At no time, however, did Brasuell get a sense that Michelle was nursing a sense of racial grievance: "I would not characterize her as a person who was burdened by race," says Brasuell, "and I find that a very odd kind of comment [about her]. . . . In this society, those persons for whom race is a burden are persons for whom race has been *made* a burden."

Brasuell also remembers trying to help Michelle sort out what to do after graduation. At Princeton, for all students, there was considerable social pressure to interview with banks and corporations or to apply to law school, or choose some other conventional route. Michelle decided to apply to law school not, Brasuell sensed, because her parents were pressuring her. Rather, the impetus came from within, perhaps out of the view that the law could be an agent of change. "This is the generation that all read *To Kill a Mockingbird*," she says.

Brasuell tried to encourage Michelle to think twice about going into the law, unconvinced that it was the right path for her. "This had nothing to do with capability or anything like that. It had to do with understanding what the process of becoming a lawyer was like. There is a big gap between what you see on television or read about, when you see a lawyer, and what is the process that you go through. I was pretty certain that she probably would, once she got into law school, see what I was talking about. And she did—I did get the phone call where she talked about the things she did not like, and [said], 'If I could do this over, I'm not sure that I would.'" Michelle would later say she wished she had taken a year off before going to law school.

But she stuck with it. "I have to say that in addition to things I would place high in a list of things about Michelle—the empathy, the loyalty, the respect for people's humanity—she is not a quitter," says Brasuell. "She went in, she was going to see how this choice would allow her to make certain kinds of things happen in her life." And, of course, it did.

5

ARRIVING AT HARVARD LAW SCHOOL IN THE FALL of 1985, twenty-one-year-old Michelle would emerge as a hardworking young woman who was less outspoken and radicalized than some of her peers, but harbored a quiet commitment to social change. "She was never overtly political," says her classmate, Peggy Kuo, even during a period marked by continued rancor over any number of hot-button culture-war topics. On a campus that included outspoken activists as well as a silent majority of conformists, Kuo notes that "people who cared about social justice issues tended to find each other." Michelle was one of these; outside of torts and contracts classes, she spent her time working on behalf of poor people who had legal problems.

On that campus at that time, many of the same arguments Michelle had heard at Princeton about how to integrate the campus were being engaged. Harvard president Derek Bok was an ally of Princeton's Bowen in shaping a national policy on affirmative action, and the consequences for students were still playing out. At the law school, there "were always issues about affirmative action, there was still quite a bit of white resentment, you're taking a position that could be filled by a white person who deserved it more" says Kuo, who is Asian, describing the backlash she felt her black and Hispanic classmates faced. Meanwhile, the school's faculty was split over something called Critical Legal Studies (CLS), a movement in legal thought that originated at Harvard in the late 1970s. CLS held that the law, far from being an instrument of social change, was deployed to affirm the status quo, perpetuating the control of the rich and powerful over the poor and minorities. Some faculty members were so dismayed by CLS that they left the school. In May 1986, during Michelle's first year, Paul M. Bator, who had been with the school for twenty-six years, gave a public speech in New York criticizing the CLS movement and saying that Harvard's participation in the movement had undermined its reputation. He would decamp for the University of Chicago. "There was a lot of academic tension," recalls Neil Quinter, a classmate of Michelle's, "which frankly I think was a pretty healthy thing."

This was also a period marked by partisanship and rancor over Supreme Court nominees of President Ronald Reagan. In 1986, Chief Justice Warren Burger announced he would retire, and Reagan elevated William Rehnquist to the chief justice position. To fill that opening, Reagan appointed Antonin Scalia, also conservative, to the court. Then, in 1987, when the moderate Lewis Powell announced he would retire, Reagan's first choice was Robert Bork, whose nomination was such anathema to liberals that their vehement opposition led to a new verb, "borked." The Senate rejected his nomination and Reagan eventually appointed Anthony Kennedy. The yearbook for Michelle's class has a photo of a professor lecturing behind a classroom blackboard with "STOP BORK" written on it in huge capital letters.

Tenure of minority and women faculty members was also an issue. The faculty photo in the class of 1988 yearbook shows an assemblage of bespectacled white men, some wearing bow ties, some suits and vests, some horn-rims, many well advanced in years. The composition of the faculty did not reflect the composition of the student body, and there was long-running agitation over this. In the spring of 1988, a sit-in was held in the dean's office to win greater minority representation on the faculty. Michelle did participate in one protest, probably that one. But overall, she kept her head down, remembers Kuo, who ran for the class council with Michelle's friend Verna Williams on a platform of divestment from the apartheid government of South Africa. She got the impression that Michelle held liberal views, but was less likely to mount the barricades.

"I always felt she was supportive, but she was never out front," says Kuo. In class, she remembers, "My impression was that she had very strongly held beliefs that she mainly kept to herself unless it was necessary—she couldn't stand it any more." Similarly, Mark Blocker, who sat beside Michelle in a course on race, racism, and American law, does not remember any comments she made during class, just that she was "an extremely nice and affable person."

Part of Michelle's reticence may have been her nature. Part of it may have been the desire, shared by many students, to avoid attracting professorial attention and with it professorial interrogation. But part of what kept her quiet may have been forces of conformity embodied by some fellow students. Compared to Princeton, Harvard probably seemed a more active and engaged campus; there were always demonstrations for this or that progressive cause, and a small but hardy group of conservative students who belonged to the campus chapter of the Federalist Society. Overall, though, Kuo felt the most powerful ideology was the pressure to avoid having one. Students who had strong beliefs were mocked by those who didn't have any at all.

"Class discussions were often *Paper Chase* mean," she recalls. Outside the classroom, "people would be labeled 'fascists' or 'communists,' or 'feminists,' or whatever pejorative term, just because of what they said in class. It was not a very touchy-feely student body. It really was not a friendly, happy atmosphere." Conformists sat in the back during class and played "turkey bingo," a game designed to deride any student with convictions. Turkey bingo worked like this: Certain students became identified with certain viewpoints, and each time one of these students used a predictable buzzword—*woman,* say, if the person was regarded as a tiresome feminist—the turkey bingo player would get a point. It was a way of underlining how obnoxious they felt it was to have, you know, an opinion.

"There was that kind of social nastiness," says Kuo,

"and that may be one of the reasons people like Michelle didn't talk. I know it's one of the reasons I didn't." When Michelle did speak up in class, Kuo says, it was usually to challenge a professor who was looking at a situation in a way that did not take into account how the law in question might affect African Americans. An example might be something like stop-and-search, where, Michelle might explain, "if you are black, it's a completely different set of rules."

At Harvard, as at Princeton, Michelle joined several African American–oriented organizations. One was the *BlackLetter Journal,* founded in 1982 "by a group of law students who were disenchanted with the relatively small number of minority students represented on major law school journals, mainly the *Harvard Law Review,*" according to its yearbook entry. The goal of *BlackLetter Journal* was "the dissemination of legal literature, thought, and ideas which have direct impact on the minority community." She also belonged to the Black Law Students Association, which was primarily a social club.

But the place where she spent the bulk of her extra-curricular time was Gannett House, a white-porticoed Greek Revival structure that is the oldest building on campus. A few years later, Barack Obama would also spend untold hours in Gannett House, whose upper floors contain the offices of the *Harvard Law Review*. At the end of his first year, Obama was selected as an editor of the law review, itself a prestigious and much-competed-for position. In 1990, he survived an even more grueling competition and was elected the law review's first African American president, a signal achievement that would attract national media attention. For the students who worked on the review—and, even more so, for the president—editorial positions were a way to influence the direction of legal theory, a stepping-stone to any number of prestigious careers, including Supreme Court clerkships.

Michelle, unlike her future husband, toiled on a lower floor of the building, which housed the prestigious but less effete legal aid bureau. "There was a little bit of an *Upstairs, Downstairs* element to it," recalls Dave Jones, who was in Michelle's class and would go on to become a California state assemblyman. "There wasn't a whole lot of interaction when I was there between law review and legal aid bureau members, other than we would see them pass through the front door and go upstairs, while we were meeting with poor clients down in the basement." The legal aid bureau was essentially a student-run law firm. Students who worked there committed to spending at least twenty hours a week helping poor people with civil cases, a major time commitment on top of their studies. For many, it was a relief to get out of the classroom and do something that was useful and real along with other, public-minded students.

The bureau was entirely multiracial, and students enjoyed one another's company and commitment. They weren't staking out intellectual positions; they were helping people who needed a lawyer and could not afford one. "It was the most fun and the most memorable thing that I did my three years at Harvard; I loved going into the legal aid bureau," recalls Ronald Torbert, who was president of the bureau his third year. Students handled a variety of cases. "We provided legal services to the poor population in the Boston and Cambridge area, Suffolk and Middlesex County," says Torbert. "We handled landlord-tenant disputes, we handled public benefit disputes, we ran a pro se divorce clinic that empowered women to handle their own small, uncontested divorce matters." They did a lot of family law, handling child custody disputes. Housing also was a major part of the workload: people facing eviction who had not received adequate notice, or who had been mistreated by their landlord. This work must have felt familiar and vital to Michelle, coming from a city where housing had been such a major issue for the

African American community. "We would get a call from someone who had received a notice or summons from their landlord and was being evicted, sometimes from federally subsidized housing, sometimes private housing," recalls Torbert. The students could also appear in court, doing trial work under the supervision of a licensed attorney.

And when not in the courtroom, they were on their own, unsupervised, unbossed, exercising their own discretion. "We got to do the kind of work we thought we came to law school eventually to do, but we were also working with real people," says Torbert. People who were committed to the legal aid bureau spent a great deal of time there, and Torbert saw a lot of Michelle. "I remember being struck almost immediately by—although she smiled a lot and we had a lot of fun—[how she had] a serious side to her, the things she thought about. She was very mature, very very bright, she handled some of the more complex landlord-and-tenant issues. I just remember her being very serious about the work she did, and she really cared a lot about the people she worked with." Her colleague Dave Jones also remembers her as compassionate, someone who "came from a place in Chicago where she had very direct experiences with people living in dire and difficult circumstances, and I think she brought that to her work at the legal aid bureau."

The other thing Torbert noticed was that Michelle expected a lot from other people. "She's not easily impressed," says Torbert, now vice president and general counsel for Barton Malow, a construction management company based in Michigan. "If there's one thing that stood out about her—she is not easily impressed. You think you're working hard, and I think her attitude is: 'Well, that's what you're supposed to do.' "

Their third year, they had to decide what to do with the rest of their lives. Or at least the immediate future. Michelle had always been interested in life after the Ivy League. It was the subject of her Princeton thesis, and at Harvard she was active in organizing a Black Law Students Association event in which African American alumni were invited for what would become an annual symposium on careers, talking about what it was like to work in government, or public service, or private practice. "I think the hope was that we could sort of remind people that we had a responsibility, we were given the privilege of attending a school like Harvard, which opened a lot of doors for us, but it also meant that we had a responsibility after we left to do something with that education besides just go to a big firm and make a whole lot of money," says Torbert. Michelle, he says, "was a huge part of that."

Students in the legal aid bureau were perhaps the ones most likely to go into public service, or legal aid, or, if they went with a private firm, to find one with pro bono opportunities. "It was something that a lot of us talked about and thought about—you know, that going into a big firm you were going to get excellent training and experience," but that public service was also compelling, says Torbert. Even so, as her classmate Neil Quinter puts it, "the process channels you toward a corporate legal practice." Private firms interviewed incessantly and vigorously, "offering all this money." Michelle had student loans to pay off. In the end she went with a private firm, a conventional choice and one she would eventually urge other Americans not to make.

Before she graduated, Michelle's parents made a financial contribution to the class of 1988 yearbook, which entitled them to write a message to her in the back, in a space for parent patrons. Most parents wrote flowery tributes to their children, saying "We are very proud of you" and "Congratulations, son, and good luck [at] the most prestigious law firm." The one the Robinsons came up with demonstrates their trademark humor, and suggests that, while deeply supportive, they—like

Michelle—were not ones to engage in ego massaging. To mark her graduation from the most prestigious law school in the country, Fraser and Marian Robinson wrote: "We knew you would do this fifteen years ago when we could never make you shut up."

6

GIVEN MICHELLE'S WELL-CHRONICLED MISGIVINGS about aspects of Princeton, there is some irony in the fact that one person who went out of his way to help her get launched in a legal career was a white male Princeton alumnus named Stephen Carlson. Though he describes himself "as conservative as anybody comes," Carlson supports diversity, abhors racism, and believes that the fanatically loyal Princeton alumni network can—and should—be used to advance social progress by helping any graduate who calls upon that network for assistance.

And Michelle did call upon that network, as early as

her junior year at Princeton, as evidenced by a visit she paid to the Career Services office. In the 1980s, Career Services was a rather sleepy, underutilized campus office with bookshelves containing well-thumbed copies of *What Color Is Your Parachute?* and a space for corporations to interview. The office also maintained a binder containing contact information for alumni who had volunteered to help undergraduates who lived or wanted to work in their regions. Carlson had offered to talk to students in Chicago. He is a suburban-bred, Republican-leaning partner at the corporate law firm then called Sidley & Austin (now Sidley Austin LLP) who entered Princeton in 1969, the same year that a small group of women undergraduates were permitted to enroll. More women showed up in subsequent years, and he married one of the new coeds. Upon returning to campus, he would enjoy his wife's reunions more than his own because they were more diverse. No retrograde who pined for the old days of gin and tonics on the lawn with like-minded gentlemen, Carlson believed a central point of going to college was to mix with and meet people you might not otherwise encounter.

Once he graduated, Carlson realized that the great upside of Princeton's legendary clubbiness was that it could be used to help newcomers get a boost up the corporate ladder. "I figured that was part of the obligation of belonging to the old-boy network. I have talked over the years to anybody and everybody who has expressed any interest in talking to me. I remember what it was like when I was a college and high school kid. You can write off anybody's advice, but it doesn't hurt to hear lots of people talk about what they do."

More than talking, Carlson made a point of offering Michelle Robinson even more help than she asked for. In a letter she wrote him sometime around 1984, he recalls, she asked whether his firm might have a summer job for a college student with an interest in the law. "She obviously knew I was from a big firm, a big corporate law firm, and she was at least interested in finding out what we did." He wrote her back explaining that Sidley's summer positions were only offered to law students. But he also assembled the names of legal services organizations in Chicago, reasoning that a public service group might be more likely to hire college students, and sent the names to her. Though he never learned what she did that summer, he continued to keep her in mind. Two years later, estimating that she would have graduated from college and might be in her first year of law school, he found Michelle's Euclid Avenue address and sent a letter to her home, offering to talk to her about her prospects, if she had decided to pursue the law. "She eventually wrote back to me saying, yeah, she was at Harvard, and in fact, she would love to." So Carlson took her to lunch at a Greek restaurant called Yanni's, and they talked about the law and the things you could do with it.

Carlson does not remember whether they discussed the merits of going with a private firm versus, say, public interest or civil rights law, but if they did, Carlson, who has had this conversation any number of times with prospective hires, would have said what he always does: The public good can be served in any number of places. "One can do good even by just making choices as to where one lives and what one does." For example, though he had been raised in the suburbs, he had settled downtown in the south Loop, because it seemed to him a civic contribution, however small, to be "walking the city of Chicago at night," declaring his faith in urban America at a low time in the life cycle of American cities, when inner-city gentrification had not yet made this a relatively easy position to take. He could also tell Michelle he loved his practice—doing civil trial work involving issues such as privacy, breach of contract, and corporate governance—so much that every day felt, to him, like playing hooky. Though they did not stay in contact, the lunch must have had some impact. In her second year at Harvard, Michelle was hired by Sidley Austin as a summer associate. Around that time, Carlson recalls, "Somebody on our Harvard recruiting team came to me and said that this woman Michelle [Robinson] had said in part she was interested in talking to Sidley because Steve Carlson was so nice to her." Carlson was delighted she was there.

Like most of the firm's fifty-odd summer associates, Michelle spent the summer of 1987 going to baseball games and lunches and happy hours; like many, she was offered a full-time job at Sidley upon her graduation, which she accepted. The starting salary was around $65,000.

At Sidley, however, she did not follow the conventional course of doing, say, general litigation or antitrust work, but allowed herself to be recruited by the rather more fun-loving lawyers in the "marketing group," which nowadays would be called intellectual property or entertainment law. These attorneys represented entities who sold goods to the public: advertising agencies, car companies, beer manufacturers, anybody who had something to sell. One of the clients was the flamboyant boxing promoter Don King, whose appearances always created a stir in the otherwise sedate corridors. The marketing group "had the reputation in the firm of being a little more glitzy," says Brian Sullivan, an associate at the time who now practices in Vermont. "This would have been a group where people were a little less buttoned down." Sullivan remembers Michelle as being "pretty down-to-earth," and wondering "how long is she going to stick with this kind of glitzy" group?

Glitz, of course, is relative. They were still lawyers, they still wore suits, and they still worked long hours. But some of the associates in that group think Michelle came to them because they were congenial and relaxed, and had the most interesting work. "It was the most fun area of practice in the firm, bar none," says Mary Carragher, who as a midlevel associate was charged with supervising Michelle. "We were the coolest people and we had the best work. It was all popular culture stuff. You could do a lot of dull things in law, and this was, and still is, in my opinion, the best stuff." It was also a relatively small group where a new associate could get a fair amount of responsibility, and it had a sizable complement of women. One of the partners was Mary Hutchings Reed, a good-humored and gregarious attorney who had worked hard to win advancement for women in the top echelon of the legal profession. Reed, who also writes fiction, would later insert Michelle as a bit character in a novel, *Courting Kathleen Hannigan,* that explores the perils of being a woman trying to make partner in the 1980s and 1990s.

"I loved her," says Reed, who left Sidley in 1989 and is now of counsel at Winston and Strawn. She remembers Michelle as a stylish dresser with a ready sense of humor, not cowed by the senior partners, a young woman with poise and self-confidence who nevertheless was willing to admit what she did not know. Michelle knew she was an inexperienced lawyer, but, recalls Andrew Goldstein, another associate at the time, she would "push back" if she disagreed with an approach or had a different idea. "Michelle—you didn't want to underestimate her." They went out of their way to give her work well suited to her interests; when an opportunity came in to handle the budding television career of Barney, the purple dinosaur, who at the time was poised for his breakthrough moment in the hearts and minds of American children, they felt the client had Michelle's name written all over it. "Michelle had some smattering of public interest background," says Goldstein, who is now at the firm of Freeborn & Peters, "and so we said that's it, public television, you're in on it." The firm's task was to manage the trademark protection and distribution of Barney plush toys and other merchandise, and to negotiate with public television stations who wanted to broadcast the show. "She had very little experience in that area," recalls Goldstein, "but she latched onto it and did a very good job with it."

At least one person, however, found Michelle a challenge to manage. The head of the marketing group was a partner named Quincy White, whom people in the group referred to, fondly, as "Q." White, now retired, recalls that he recruited Michelle to the group and endeavored to give her the most interesting work he could find, in part because he wanted to do right by her and see her advance, but also because she seemed perennially dissatisfied. She was, White recalls, "quite possibly the most ambitious associate that I've ever seen." By this he means that she wanted significant responsibility right away, and was not afraid to object if she wasn't getting what she felt she deserved. At big firms, much of the work that falls to young associates involves detail and tedium. There were all sorts of arcane but important rules about what could and could not be said or done in product advertisements, and in the marketing group it fell to all associates, not just the new ones, to review scripts for TV commercials to make sure they conformed. As far as associate work goes, it could have been worse—"advertising is a little sexier than spending a full year reading depositions in an antitrust law suit or reviewing documents for a big merger," says White—but it was tedious and relatively low-level.

Too tedious for Michelle, who, White says, complained that the work he gave her was unsatisfactory. He gave her the Coors beer account, which he considered one of the sexier clients they had. Even then, he says, "She at one point went over my head and complained that I wasn't giving her enough interesting stuff, and the person came down to my office and said, 'Basically she's complaining that she's being treated like a second-year associate,' and we agreed that she *was* a second-year associate. I had eight or nine other associates, and I couldn't start treating one of them a lot better." Even if he did give her privileged treatment, White is not sure any work he had would have satisfied her. "I couldn't give her something that would meet her sense of ambition to change the world."

"Not many people went over my head," says White, who is now living in Michigan. It was an unusual move for a young associate to make, and he believes it was consistent with her personality. "She was extremely ambitious," he says, and wanted "something that pushed her harder, something that was a more general challenge." He reflects, "Waiting five to seven years to make partner was a good career move for me but not for [her]. There are too many other opportunities out there . . . that mature faster than that."

His description is in line with the image of the Michelle Robinson who as a high school student gave her typing teacher a hard time when she didn't get the A she believed she had earned or complained that the Princeton professors were teaching French incorrectly; it is also consistent with someone who wasn't impressed with how hard her Harvard legal aid colleagues worked. Abner Mikva, who met Michelle in the late 1990s, when he returned to Chicago from Washington, is amused when he hears this description. "That doesn't surprise me at all," he says. "She's clearly somebody who likes to make decisions and likes to be involved in exciting and important stuff. I can imagine, writing memos for other lawyers—I don't think that would have been her favorite dish of tea."

In that sense she seems to have had much in common with Barack Obama, whose political ambition was already very apparent to those who knew him at Harvard Law School, where he graduated in 1991 and began his history of jumping ahead of the line to run for a higher office. Michelle had some of the same qualities—she was impatient, driven, and eager to make an impact on the world.

Though the marketing group was extremely social and went out often to restaurants, her colleagues knew relatively little about Michelle's personal life. Sidley Austin is located in the Loop near the Chicago River, but Michelle was still living in the bungalow on Euclid Avenue, according to her voting registration. One of her Euclid neighbors, who worked at a bank in South Shore after retiring from a career in the federal government, recalls Michelle coming into the local branch to do her banking. Like many African Americans of her generation, her life was compartmentalized—work in one part of the city, home in another.

Her Sidley colleagues were unaware, for example, when her father, Fraser Robinson, died in 1991. This was an event of enormous emotional and psychological magnitude. Michelle loved her father so much that even as an adult, she would curl up in his lap. She has said that the death of her father made her aware of how short life can be, and prompted her to reflect, "If what you're doing doesn't bring you joy every single day, what's the point?" But all in all, say her former colleagues, she talked little about her family.

There was, however, one aspect of her personal life they couldn't miss: a nascent romance.

In 1989, Barack Obama was brought into Sidley Austin as a summer associate. He had just finished his first year at Harvard Law, which was noteworthy; the firm did not often hire first-year students as summer associates, so that in and of itself conferred distinction. Martha Minow, a professor of law at Harvard, told her father, Newton Minow, a senior partner at Sidley Austin, that Barack was possibly the most gifted student she had ever had. Michelle heard the buzz and felt annoyed by it; she figured people were surprised that a black man might be articulate and capable. Hearing his name and the fact that he had been raised in Hawaii, she later said that she assumed he would be "nerdy, strange, off-putting," and resolved to dislike him.

"He sounded too good to be true," she told *Chicago Tribune* reporter David Mendell, in an interview for his biography of Barack Obama, *Obama: From Promise to Power*. "I had dated a lot of brothers who had this kind of reputation coming in, so I figured he was one of those smooth brothers who could talk straight and impress people. So we had lunch, and he had this bad sport jacket and a cigarette dangling from his mouth and I thought, 'Oh, here you go. Here's this good-looking, smooth-talking guy. I've been down this road before.'" Craig has talked, many times, about Michelle's high standards and the obstacles they created for would-be suitors: "She would meet guys and go out on a couple dates and that would be it."

The firm appointed her to be an adviser and mentor to Obama, something that apparently made her feel self-conscious; she often has said that when he asked her out she resisted, feeling it would be "tacky" if they started to date, "the only two black people here" at the firm. In fact, as Newton Minow and others are quick to point out, Michelle and Barack were not the only black lawyers at the firm. Sidley Austin made an effort to be socially progressive: The firm had a black partner, Charles Lomax, and more African American attorneys were brought on every year, some of them following Michelle into the intellectual property group. "I remember one of the members of the management committee talking about the decision to hire Charles Lomax, and how important it was to have some examples to show that people can succeed and be prominent at establishment law firms who come from a variety of different backgrounds," recalls Carlson. Even so, there certainly weren't many, and it must have felt to Michelle as though they were under a microscope.

She has also said that she resisted his advances for a while, even introducing him to other women, before agreeing to go out with him. She later said, "I had made this proclamation to my mother the summer I met Barack, 'I'm not worrying about dating . . . I'm going to focus on me.' " But if she was reluctant, it could not have lasted long. During the period when they still weren't officially dating, Newton Minow and his wife, Jo, ran into them at the popcorn stand at a movie. "I think they were a little embarrassed," Minow says with a laugh. Others say it's no wonder she succumbed: Given the impact Obama makes on political supporters, "You can only imagine . . . how charismatic he must be when he was trying to court somebody," says Carragher. Goldstein got the impression she was pursuing Barack as much as he was pursuing her, and with plenty of resources. "She is just as charismatic as he is," he says.

Her colleagues got the sense of a woman smitten. During that summer, Carragher remembers that sometimes, in the slow hours around five-thirty, she would go to Michelle's office to talk about a case or bring her a piece of work, and through the doorway she would see Barack in Michelle's office, sitting on one corner of her desk. Michelle would be seated, the two of them rapt, oblivious, chatting. "I could tell by the body language, he's just courting her," says Carragher, who would quietly depart without bothering them, thinking, "You know what, I'm going back to my office."

But between Barack's visits, Michelle would confide in Carragher, sharing the tidbits she was learning about him. It was clear that she was intrigued by his unlikely origins and upbringing, which she would relay piece by piece as she learned about them. "I can't believe he's got a *white grandmother from Kansas!*" Carragher recalls Michelle telling her.

"She had all these little facts about him," says Carragher now. "She was just learning about him and getting to know him, and she seemed to be quite taken with him." His biracial heritage was part of the appeal. "That he had this white grandmother, he had this very unusual upbringing—knowing what I've read about her life, which was pretty ordinary, pretty straightforward, she was just sort of amazed by him." Far from put off, Carragher says, "She was falling hard. But always cool. I mean never, even when you'd see their interactions, she was not falling all over him. She was very cool."

Michelle and Barack were both attracted to what was different about the other. Barack has written about how Michelle impressed him immediately, being tall, immaculately outfitted, well groomed, poised, and strong-minded. He was touched by what he saw as the occasional hint of vulnerability, the sense that her good fortune could vanish with one misstep, "as if, deep inside, she knew how fragile things really were, and that if she ever let go, even for a moment, all her plans might quickly unravel." He has also written about how appealing he found her rootedness, her close-knit extended family, all those uncles and aunts and cousins. Obama himself had endured a rootless childhood: After his father left, he saw him only one more time, when he was about ten, and the meeting was awkward. His peripatetic and intellectual American mother was also absent much of the time doing anthropological fieldwork, with the result that, apart from a stint in Indonesia, Obama was raised for much of his youth in a high-rise apartment in Honolulu by his two white grandparents. To him, it must have seemed an unimaginably rich emotional bounty that Michelle had enjoyed in her own childhood, growing up in a functional and loving two-parent family with an attentive big brother, a piano-playing aunt, and cousins sprinkled around the city, in one of the country's largest contiguous black communities.

Gerald Kellman, who initially hired Barack and brought him to Chicago to work as a community organizer in the South Side, witnessed Obama's attraction to and fascination with the black community, which, in a sense, he made a deliberate choice to be part of. Kellman speculates that this may have played into his attraction to Michelle. Kellman points out that Obama in his first book chose to meditate on his father, a black man, rather than his white mother. "It makes the case that this is what he chose for his future—the fact he chose to marry Michelle, the ideal person who could help him develop those kinds of roots, and the person to share this career with."

His attraction to Michelle would also be a source of pride among many black women; on theroot.com, a Web site run by the Washington Post Company and devoted to African American issues, Kim McLarin has written about the validation many black women feel, knowing that Obama, who had dated a white woman, chose an African American woman—"one of us"—to spend his life with. "I am thrilled," she wrote, explaining that "beautiful Michelle has the potential to counter in a real and powerful way the still all-too-real internalized belief by many dark-skinned black American women that we are still not pretty enough, not desirable enough, not worthy to be loved." The African American political commentator Debra Dickerson has pointed out that marrying Michelle helped Obama establish his credibility with the city's African American political leaders; having her at his side would help him surmount the objection, later raised by his detractors and competitors, that somebody with such an exotic pedigree, not to mention a white mother, was not "black enough."

What's interesting is that, even as Barack appears to have been drawn at least in part to her sense of place and stability—not to mention her looks and strong personality and, one assumes, the advice that she began giving him to improve his wardrobe—Michelle seems to have been attracted to his exoticism, the fact that he was different from those smooth-talking brothers she'd come to feel wary of. One senses in her a branching out, an attraction to a man who was not like anybody she had ever met before, but who did display the moral character and sense of social justice she valued and had loved in her own father. She frequently talks about how, on an early date, he took her to a church basement to watch him meet with a group he'd worked with as a community organizer and how his passion and desire to help poor African Americans swept her off her feet. His message then was much the same as his message now. In speeches, she would later describe how he took off his suit jacket and tie and talked, to an audience mostly of grandparents raising grandchildren, about how all people are connected, regardless of their economic status or their race. She also laughs about the fact that the first movie he took her to was Spike Lee's *Do the Right Thing*, which she saw as an attempt to establish his own street credibility with her.

Much later, Michelle would confirm Carragher's impression that Barack seemed foreign to her, and that his difference was part of what made him appealing. As she put it in 2007 to the *Hyde Park Herald*: "This is the thing I marveled at when I met him. On paper we couldn't be more different. He is half black, half white, grew up in Hawaii, lived in Indonesia. I heard about him and I thought he was going to be weird." It's interesting that, in this interview, she did not call him black—she used the expression *half black, half white*, describing him as biracial. She went on to use this distinction to make a point about the need for integration of different communities, as though that's what she and Barack represent. "When there are people who are different from us, we automatically think well, that's nothing like me and we have nothing in common. But as he points out in his books, we have more in common than not. His grandparents are very much Midwestern and in that respect, the Midwestern value is [to] work hard, treat people with decency and respect, and do what you say you are going to do, your word is your bond. We're both worried about doing our best and doing the right thing."

Her mother also saw him as somewhat unusual. Speaking later to an interviewer for Chicago public television, Marian Robinson allowed that at first she had some qualms about the relationship. Asked about his biracial status, she said that it concerned her a "little bit," but not as much as it would have if he had been white. "I guess that I worry about race mixing because of the difficulties, not so much for prejudice or anything. It's very hard." According to Craig, Barack came over for dinner and the whole family liked him and felt sorry for him, assuming he wouldn't be around for long. "He was very, very low key," recalls Craig. "I loved the way he talked about his family because it was the way we talked about our family. I was thinking, 'Nice guy. Too bad he won't last.' " Craig likes to tell about how Michelle asked him to take Barack out on the court to test his character. He obliged her and emerged from that game able to give a positive report: Obama was self-confident and a decent player, but not a ball hog or a hotshot. Later that year, Michelle met Barack's family when they went to Honolulu for Christmas. His sister, Maya Soetoro-Ng, remembers, "From the start, Michelle was a ready convert to our lazy and fun Christmas rituals," which were hard-fought Scrabble tournaments and big egg-and-pancake breakfasts.

At this time, it was also clear to Michelle's colleagues that the couple were sharing their hopes and ambitions. "I am sure that from the moment they started talking, and their ice cream that they shared on that early date, he told about his dreams," says Martha Minow. "I don't know about president, but public service, politics, that's what he talked about as a student. He never had any other plans."

Michelle confided to Carragher that Barack was planning to write a book, a project that he would not embark on for several years. And they were also discussing, as twentysomethings will do, how exactly to change the world. "We had many debates about how to best effect change," Michelle would tell the *Daily Princetonian*, suggesting that they bonded over their commitment to lifting up the community, and believed they could do more if they worked at it together. "We both wanted to affect the community on a larger scale than either of us could individually, and we wanted to do it outside of big corporations." It's not quite the two-for-the-price-of-one offer that Bill Clinton initially promised to deliver with his wife, Hillary, as first lady, but it suggests that their personal and professional goals are melded. She may not have had much use for politics, but she shared her future husband's desire for civic action and social change.

But even as Michelle was discovering and relating Obama's marvelous qualities, Carragher recalls that she also spotted a drawback. One day, when she was reciting her new boyfriend's many wonderfulnesses, she added, unhappily, "But he smokes."

"I'm like, 'Oh man, that's too bad,'" says Carragher. "And she's like, 'Yeah, I try to tell him he shouldn't, I'm trying to talk to him about that.'"

She wouldn't succeed with this one until she made it a bargaining chip in his presidential run.

Even then it was clear to people at Sidley that Barack was presidential timber. Goldstein remembers conversations around the water cooler in which people would tick off his accomplishments, predicting that a set of résumé items like his could only be leading toward one place. "This guy's going to be the first African American president," commented a Sidley colleague. Mary Hutchings Reed got a clear sense of Obama's interest in public life: "I think it could be said without a doubt that the man had political ambitions." She had the impression that Michelle heard the chatter, shared a sense of his potential, and was aware of his goals. Certainly, his speech in the church basement had told her he was a man who could move crowds, and probably mountains. But Michelle herself holds that she was unaware, early on, of political intentions on Barack's part. "As we were dating, we didn't talk about politics specifically; we talked about issues of the country," she told me when I interviewed her in the summer of 2007, describing their early courtship. This is surprising, since Obama wasn't keeping his intentions secret to anyone else: Harvard sociologist Robert Putnam, who got to know him after law school, describes him as being "transparently and lovably ambitious." Newton Minow, who met him the same time Michelle did, says, "I think he saw himself with a political career even before I knew him." Craig also likes to talk about one of the first times Michelle brought Barack to a family function, during which Craig drew Obama aside to quiz him on his prospects and clue him into family members' personalities and eccentricities. When Craig asked Obama about his job plans, Obama replied, "I think I'd like to teach at some point in time, maybe even run for public office." Craig assumed Obama wanted someday to run for a post like alderman, but Obama let him know that his aspirations were higher. "He said no—at some point he'd like to run for the U.S. Senate. And then he said, 'Possibly even run for president at some point.' And I was like, 'Okay, that's great, but don't say that to my aunt Gracie.' I was protecting him from saying something that might embarrass him," continued Craig, alluding to the family's suspicion of politicians.

When I related this anecdote to Michelle, she laughed as though she had not heard it before. "He probably should have said: Don't tell Michelle!" she cracked, meaning that she shared her family's antipathy toward politics and implying that she didn't realize Barack had such aspirations. "She knew what she was getting into," Craig would say later, pointing out that Barack never made a secret of his inclinations. And the memory of some colleagues suggests that she set her sights for him high. "Michelle would be full speed ahead," says one Sidley lawyer, who believes that from the start she recognized in this man the ability to go far. It could be that she admired and responded to the qualities that would make him such a successful politician, even as she had reservations about politics itself. "History is littered with people who were attracted to individuals who were in politics, but who didn't like politicians," points out Al Kindle.

After Barack went back to Harvard, the couple had a long-distance romance and married three years after they started dating. Michelle tells a funny story on herself, about how, during this period, she began to pressure Barack in the direction of marriage, and how Barack put her off, rationalizing any foot-dragging by arguing that marriage was a meaningless institution and that the only thing that mattered was how they felt about each other. Then one night he took her to Gordon, a swanky Chicago restaurant, and she started to press him again. He went into his usual tirade against marriage, a dissertation that went on until they ordered dessert. When it came, the plate had a box on it, and in the box was an engagement ring. "That kind of shuts you up, doesn't it?" Michelle remembers Barack telling her. She admitted to a reporter for the *Chicago Sun-Times* that she doesn't remember what the dessert was, or whether she ate it: "I was so shocked and sort of a little embarrassed because he did sort of shut me up."

They married in 1992, at Trinity United Church of Christ, in a ceremony officiated by Reverend Jeremiah Wright, whom Barack had gotten to know during his work as a community organizer. Michelle wore an off-the-shoulder gown. They had the reception at the South Shore Cultural Center, the former country club that had once excluded both blacks and Jews. They honeymooned on the West Coast, and lived with Michelle's mother on Euclid for a few months before taking a walk-up condo in Hyde Park. The neighborhood is one of the city's most integrated communities and the geo-

graphic and spiritual headquarters for the liberal progressive coalition that had opposed Mayor Richard J.
Daley.

The year before they married, Michelle left Sidley
Austin, and with it the practice of corporate law. Newton Minow recounts an anecdote about how Sidley offered Barack Obama a full-time job upon his graduation
from Harvard and how Obama broke the news that he
wanted to go into politics and would not be taking a job
with the firm. Minow, who had spent a good deal of
time in politics, including serving as chairman of the
Federal Communications Commission under President
John F. Kennedy, affably replied that public service was
an admirable career and that the firm would do all it
could to help advance his political prospects.

"Well, I don't think you're going to want to help me,"
Barack replied, telling him to sit down because he had
even more bad news. "I thought, 'What the hell is
this?'" says Minow, who sat down, whereupon Barack
said, "I'm taking Michelle with me." Minow remembers
that he began to sputter at Obama, "You no-good
worthless rotten . . ." until Obama said, "Hold it, we're
going to get married."

In truth, of course, there was no need for Michelle to
leave Sidley Austin just because she was marrying Ba-

rack. He was coming back to Chicago after Harvard, and she easily could have stayed with the firm. "As far as the firm was concerned, we considered it a real loss," says Minow. "We thought she was going to eventually become partner and have a big role there." Far from being discouraged or held back—the experiences she dwells upon—Michelle in this case had, after just a few years, been marked down as a future partner.

In a number of interviews, Michelle has discussed her reasons for leaving: the soul-searching prompted by the death of her father, and by the tragic death, in 1990, of her beloved Princeton classmate Suzanne Alele. Alele died from cancer when she was only in her twenties, and Michelle recalls that Alele had always followed her heart and her natural inclinations, doing what felt right rather than what was expected of her. She has said that she resolved to live her own life the same way. It is something of the same epiphany that happened to Craig, when he was working on Wall Street and got a call about coaching. It also seems possible that Barack gave her a sense of the life that might lie beyond a fat paycheck. He, too, had agonized over working at a corporate firm, even for a summer, worrying that it "represented the abandonment of my youthful ideals, a concession to the hard realities of money and power." When her father died,

Michelle told the *New York Times,* "I looked out at my neighborhood and sort of had an epiphany that I had to bring my skills to bear in the place that made me. I wanted to have a career motivated by passion and not just money."

Explaining this to a *Chicago Sun-Times* reporter in 2004, she also expressed a lingering sense of guilt about enjoying material success while others who shared her origins and upbringing were not faring as well. She remembers asking herself, "Can I go to the family reunion in my Benz and be comfortable, while my cousins are struggling to keep a roof over their heads?" Moreover, she wasn't enthralled with the work, and apparently didn't think many of her colleagues were either. Explaining to *Newsweek* in 2008 why she left the firm, she said, "I didn't see a whole lot of people who were just thrilled to be there. I met people who thought this was a good life. But were people waking up just bounding out of bed to get to work? No."

It's a bit of a judgmental statement, implying that those colleagues who liked her so much were just marking time, doing work that didn't enthrall them. For the most part, they are forgiving of her dismissal. "I do understand," says Reed, who, contrary to Michelle's description, seems to have relished getting up every morning and winning a place for women in the corridors of legal power, and who has done it with humor and zest. Even so, Reed allows: "We're sitting here doing advertising." You can tell yourself that you're working for the protection of the American consumer, she continues, but "working at a large law firm like this, sometimes—looking for meaning, you can't look for meaning in your work."

"At the beginning it's so fun and interesting and new, and then after a few years you realize that it's pretty much all the same stuff," allows Carragher, who left in 1992 and now has her own practice. She points out that many young lawyers try big-firm work and decide that it's not for them. "It's not surprising that she would go the big-firm route for a while. When you're at a top school and you're a top candidate like that, you're getting recruited by every top law firm in the city. It takes a little while to say, 'Does this really fit for me?'"

After Michelle left, her colleagues mostly lost touch with her. Carragher ran into her on Michigan Avenue a couple of years later, when Michelle was executive director of the nonprofit organization Public Allies, which prepares young people for jobs in public service, and Michelle gave her her card and seemed very happy. In the late fall of 2006 Carragher ran into her again at a fund-raising lunch for St. Jude Children's Research Hospital; by then Michelle was the wife of a U.S. Senator widely regarded as a presidential prospect, and Mary had her own daughter with her, who was eleven. "I feel like I was eleven years old when I met you!" Michelle joked, marveling at how inexperienced she was. When Carragher introduced Michelle to her mother, Michelle politely said, "Mary was my mentor and taught me so many things," whereupon Carragher's mother, who, she says, does not hear well, thought Michelle simply said they worked together, and replied, "Oh yes, that's what Mary told me!" Carragher was mortified, and Michelle, she says, laughed.

"What a life you're having," Carragher said to her, and Michelle said, "I know."

But Michelle didn't just leave the world of corporate law; she would go on to repudiate it. She and Barack both make a point of talking about how they left corporate America and devoted themselves to public service. "We left corporate America, which is a lot of what we're asking young people to do. Don't go into corporate America," she said at a speech to women in Ohio, continuing: "You know, become teachers. Work for the community. Be social workers. Be a nurse. Those are the careers that we need, and we're encouraging our young people to do that. But if you make that choice, as we did, to move out of the moneymaking industry into the helping industry, then your salaries respond." At a Baptist church in Cheraw, South Carolina, in January 2008, she said, "We don't need a world full of corporate attorneys and hedge-fund managers." In Rhode Island in 2008, talking about how Barack chose work as a civil rights lawyer rather than on Wall Street, she shouted, "When you're given the gift of advocacy, you don't sell it to the highest bidder!" She talks often about how Barack could be making much more money in private practice, a fact that is true of many government attorneys laboring in Washington to enforce this or that federal regulation. Virtually any attorney at the Federal Communications Commission or the Securities and Exchange Commission or the U.S. Justice Department could leave public service to make more money. The implication is that the Obamas are worthy of special praise, when the decision to eschew a private-sector salary is a decision many public servants make.

This has not been lost on Carlson, the corporate lawyer who took the time and made the effort to copy down names of potential summer employers, back when Michelle Robinson was a junior at Princeton. Without that effort, it seems quite possible that she never would have been drawn to Sidley Austin and might never have met Barack Obama. Her *Newsweek* comment about her Sidley colleagues not enjoying their work, he says now, is "the thing that has disappointed me the most about Michelle."

That's because, for him, it's not true.

"I'm perfectly happy doing what I'm doing," says Carlson. "I would think that most of us who stayed here are perfectly happy doing what we do, and most of us see the possibility of improving people's lives." If she had stayed in private practice, he thinks, Michelle would be accomplishing a public good through the power of example, showing what an African American woman can achieve. "Someone like Michelle . . . would perform an enormous public service of being an example of someone succeeding and thriving in private practice."

And he disagrees with her dismissal of corporate America. "People who don't want to go into corporate America, whatever the heck corporate America is, don't have to go into corporate America and can choose other paths, but one should not underestimate the good that has been done by corporate America. Michelle Obama herself has benefited enormously from the fact that there is a corporate America. Barack Obama has benefited tremendously from the fact that there is a corpo-

Michelle Robinson Obama in grade school and upon college graduation from Princeton University (Polaris)

CLOCKWISE FROM TOP LEFT: Michelle, center, with other students from Whitney M. Young High School after being inducted into the National Honor Society; Michelle with her fellow high school class officers their junior year; Michelle performs ballet for a high school recital (Courtesy of Whitney M. Young High School)

LEFT: Michelle Robinson and Barack Obama on their wedding day in 1992 (Obama for America/Handout/Polaris)

BOTTOM: Barack and Michelle arriving at the Legends Ball, an award ceremony hosted by Oprah Winfrey honoring women who paved the way in arts, entertainment, and civil rights, in May 2005 in Santa Barbara, California (Michael A. Mariant/AP Photo)

Michelle and Barack Obama with their daughters, Malia and Sasha, on the front porch of their home in Hyde Park (Callie Shell/Aurora Photographs for *Time* magazine)

Michelle reads to schoolchildren while campaigning in Monticello, Iowa, in November 2007 (Scout Tufankjian/Polaris)

CLOCKWISE FROM TOP LEFT: Michelle campaigning with Oprah Winfrey in Manchester, New Hampshire, in December 2007 (Polaris); with Hillary Clinton at the annual Jefferson Jackson Dinner in November 2007 (Scout Tufankjian/Polaris); the family is shown as Barack, the only African American member of the U.S. Senate, is sworn in by Vice President Dick Cheney in January 2005 (Jason Reed/Reuters/Corbis)

LEFT: Michelle, in January 2008 in Wilmington, Delaware, stumping for her husband and talking about his upbringing (Phil Mcauliffe/Polaris) RIGHT: Watching as Barack makes remarks at a Super Tuesday primary night rally in Chicago (Jason Reed/Reuters/Corbis)

Michelle, in a green dress, having lunch with Pittsburgh Steelers owner Dan Rooney (right foreground), on the day of the Pennsylvania primary, with Barack in the background (Scout Tufankjian/Polaris)

Barack and Michelle embracing after she introduces him at a campaign event at the fairgrounds in Atlantic, Iowa, in August 2007 (M. Spencer Green/AP Photo, file)

RIGHT: Michelle hugs Barack after he delivers his keynote address during the Democratic National Convention in Boston on July 27, 2004 (Ed Reinke/AP Photos)

BOTTOM: Michelle checks on Barack as he puts the finishing touches on his Super Tuesday speech at the Hyatt Hotel in Chicago (Callie Shell/Aurora Photographs for *Time* magazine)

rate America. That's why people vote with their feet and come to this country from all over the world. They know that there are certain benefits to this country. We all count on corporate America."

Not least, corporate America has helped bankroll the Obama campaign, including many African American businessmen and financiers whose success attests to what that sector can provide someone, anyone, who is driven and smart. "I think Michelle has underestimated how important it is to show that there are examples," says Carlson. It's his view that an African American woman in a prominent position sends a message to all.

But then he laughs. She'll also demonstrate the power of a living example, he reasons, "when she's sitting in the White House."

7

WHILE MICHELLE WAS AT PRINCETON, A WATER-
shed event had occurred in Chicago: Harold Washington was elected mayor in 1983, the city's first black
mayor. It was a tremendous victory for the African
American community, practically and psychologically, as
the newcomer Barack Obama would later hear from his
barber. Which is not to say that racial peace broke out in
the city. During his first term, Washington became engaged in a long-running battle with the white-majority
council that got so nasty that once, the mayor threat-
ened to punch out his chief antagonist, council leader
Ed Vrdolyak, telling him he would get a mouthful of

something he didn't want. On another occasion Vrdo-lyak taunted a Washington supporter, Walter "Slim" Coleman, so badly from the council floor that Coleman leaped over the rails and was about to attack Vrdolyak but was restrained by several bailiffs.

But Washington's tenure, according to Judson Miner, a white attorney who worked for Washington as corporation counsel, carried a basic lesson: It became clear to people that "an African American could run Chicago and it wouldn't fall apart." Running for his second term, Washington did better among whites; while he did not get a great many more white votes, fewer whites voted against him. Washington's death from a heart attack at his desk in 1987 was a tremendous blow, but his tenure changed racial dynamics in the city.

This wasn't clear at first. Barack told me that after Washington's death, he felt disillusioned by the splintering of the progressive biracial coalition that had supported the mayor, who was replaced by an undistinguished councilman picked by the old Machine. "I was, like many people, impressed by the degree to which he could mobilize the community and push for change. I was frustrated by the inability to build an organization that could sustain all that excitement and deliver [results]." At that point, Obama says, "I was somewhat disdainful of politics. I was much more interested in mobilizing people to hold politicians accountable."

That attitude helps explain what Barack decided to do after he graduated from Harvard Law School in 1991. He was offered many jobs and could have gone to work anywhere. Abner Mikva, a former U.S. congressman who was a judge on the U.S. Court of Appeals for the D.C. Circuit, called to offer him a clerkship, and when Obama turned him down, Mikva jokingly says he assumed Barack was an "uppity black" who would only clerk for a black judge. Michelle was also surprised that he was uninterested in clerking, even for a U.S. Supreme Court justice. She said Barack had gone to law school because he realized, working as a community organizer, that to bring about change he needed to better understand how laws are created.

"You've got to have a grasp of the law, so he goes to law school, he goes to law school for more than just being a lawyer," Michelle told me. "Even though he was head of the law review he didn't become a Supreme Court clerk, which is the natural progression. Never did it cross his mind. Here I am, knowing the power of his position: 'You're not going to clerk for them? You're kidding me!' He's like, 'No, that's not why I went to law school. If you're going to make change, you're not going to do it as a Supreme Court clerk.' It was change, it was always change. It was always this notion, how do you help move this country."

Instead, Obama took a job at Judson Miner's civil rights law firm, though he first spent six months on a voter registration drive, Project Vote, targeting low-income African Americans. It was an effort strikingly reminiscent of what Michelle's father, Fraser Robinson, the genial precinct captain, had done, walking the streets of South Side exhorting folks to go out on election day and vote Democratic. The drive was so successful that it helped Bill Clinton win in Illinois and assisted Carol Moseley Braun in becoming the first black woman elected to the U.S. Senate. He also embarked on his book project, writing his first memoir, *Dreams from My Father: A Story of Race and Inheritance*. Obama got the book contract after his election to law review president attracted admiring profiles in newspapers around the country. Miner laughs, though, at the fact that publishers—making a clichéd assumption about his background—assumed it would be the tale of how a young black man heroically rose from the ghetto. Instead, Obama would write a complex memoir about growing up biracial and fatherless in Hawaii and Indonesia, then leaving for the mainland to find his identity as a black man in a variety of American landscapes. Miner says that during a series of lunches, Obama quizzed him on race relations under Harold Washington, asking what it had been like for him, working in a government run by an African American. Miner's firm did mostly civil rights litigation, including voting rights and discrimination cases, often suing the city. The firm, Davis, Miner, Barnhill & Galland, was small and the work didn't pay particularly well, Miner says, but it was prestigious and had a reputation for hiring up-and-comers. Moreover, Miner—along with Newton Minow and Abner Mikva—would introduce Obama to a range of supporters and political contacts, including African Americans, Jewish leaders, progressives, so-called lake-front liberals, politically involved socialites. During those lunches, Miner says, "It was really clear that he was interested in government."

But while Barack was reaching out to Chicago's progressive coalition, Michelle was embedding herself in a mayoral administration that many of the same people regarded with suspicion. During her last, dissatisfied year at the law firm Sidley Austin, Michelle began sending letters to general counsels for universities, trying to find an area of the law that might be more satisfying. In

1991, she wrote to Valerie Jarrett, a high-level operative in the second Daley administration who came from a distinguished Chicago family. Jarrett had grown up in Hyde Park and she had attended one of the top private schools in the country, the Laboratory Schools affiliated with the University of Chicago. Her mother was a child psychologist and her father, a pathologist, was the first African American to receive tenure at the University of Chicago's department of biological sciences. Jarrett, who had a law degree from the University of Michigan, was working as deputy chief of staff for Richard M. Daley, the first Mayor Daley's son, who was now himself mayor. She was instantly impressed with Michelle. "I offered her a job at the end of the interview . . . She was so confident and committed and extremely open," Jarrett would say later. But before Michelle would accept, she asked that Jarrett have dinner with her and Barack.

According to one account, Barack was concerned, even then, about how it might affect his nascent political career if his wife were to work for Daley, who, while not the Machine politician his father had been, was regarded by many as representing the establishment that independents had long been fighting against. "Certainly, it would be something that they would look upon [unfavorably] in Hyde Park—anyone who worked for Daley would be highly suspect," says the political consultant Don Rose, which may be one reason why Michelle did not stay long in the job. Obama was also worried, according to biographer David Mendell, that Michelle might be too straightforward and outspoken to survive in a political setting. He fretted, too, that if she was going to enter this realm, she needed someone to look out for her. Patronage was waning as a style of doing business, but in Chicago it still helped to have a mentor. Jarrett agreed to have dinner with Michelle and Barack. "My fiancé wants to know who is going to be looking out for me and making sure that I thrive," Jarrett recalled Michelle saying. At the end of the evening, Jarrett asked, "Well, did I pass the test?" and Barack smiled and said she did.

That dinner would set a pattern. While many professional husbands and wives operate in spheres that don't overlap, Michelle and Barack have been more of a tag team, making speeches at each other's behest, inviting each other to sit on panels, in large part because they share the same academic and professional training—Ivy League, Harvard Law—as well as the same mission. Michelle would later assert, "Barack hasn't relied deeply on me for his career path, and I haven't relied on him at all for mine." This is true in the sense that she is a highly qualified person perfectly capable of securing jobs on her own merits. Still, it's also fair to say that the two of them are more closely melded, personally and politically, than many couples, and have helped each other along. "Fundamentally we work well together because we share the same values," Michelle would later say to the *Hyde Park Herald*.

Michelle was valuable to Barack, politically, in a number of ways. Through his work as an organizer, he already made contacts and earned stature with leaders and politicians on the South Side, but she helped him deepen and broaden that stature, having grown up there herself. "There are a lot of successful people who have a hard time working in the community because they're not from there," their friend John Rogers told *Newsweek*. "Craig and Michelle can do it because it's where they come from." She knew some of South Side's political leaders; her friendship with Santita Jackson would be an entrée into the Jackson household and an introduction to Santita's father and brother, Jesse Jackson Sr. and Jr.

And at the same time, thanks to her own ambition and achievements, Michelle would provide him with contacts in the new professional class, introducing Barack to some of the people who would be his well-connected friends and most important financial supporters. Through her job with the city, she had made contacts in Daley's inner circle. Jarrett was chief among them; she became a friend and confidante, and an extraordinarily useful person for Barack to have in his corner. One of the most powerful women in Chicago, Jarrett would go on to serve as chair of both the Chicago Transit Authority and the Chicago Stock Exchange, on the board of the University of Chicago Medical Center, and as president and CEO of Habitat Company, a major real estate development and management company. And she would chair Obama's finance committee during his 2004 campaign for the U.S. Senate.

Michelle also was the conduit to John W. Rogers, Jr., a Chicago native who founded the first African American–owned money management firm and proved a tremendous fund-raising asset. Rogers had played basketball with Craig Robinson at Princeton. Craig also introduced the Obamas to Martin Nesbitt, chair of the Chicago Housing Authority and another basketball-playing buddy of his who would become one of Barack's closest friends. Both Rogers and Nesbitt would provide Obama with a way in to Chicago's growing black business class. The city had always had a group of affluent black families, some of them magnates who made their money early on from businesses and media serving the South Side. But that group had matured and expanded to include a lot of younger, dynamic black Chicagoans. By this point, says Don Rose, Chicago had a black upper-middle class "that would include a fairly wide range of people, some of them of economic substance, some of them of political substance. It might include judges, lawyers—by the eighties you've got the Chicago Bar Association beginning to absorb a lot more African American lawyers, and things have taken hold. You've got brokers and underwriters and professionals in the knowledge field. [Michelle] moved rather naturally into [this sphere] as a Princetonian and a Harvard graduate."

All in all, they constructed an enviable life of friendships both genuine and useful, with people of all ethnicities and religions. Michelle has always valued friendship. Her Princeton thesis was dedicated to her family and to "all of my special friends"; and her yearbook entry expressed her philosophy that "there is nothing in this world more valuable than friendships. Without them you have nothing." She and Barack went on golfing weekends with Miner and his wife, attended music festivals with the Minows, enjoyed a range of relations with people who shared their lifestyle as well as their progressive values and political involvement. "These are folks," says Marilyn Katz, a member of their social circle, "who talk to their friends a number of times a day."

Katz is struck by how Chicago, in so many ways, turned out to be the ideal incubator for Obama's career. The city never quite saw the physical decline and out-migration of other industrial cities, in part, ironically, because the first Mayor Daley kept white residents there by preserving segregation as long as he did, but also because of some of the city's own innate strengths. It has a diverse employment base, and even as the manufacturing sector declined, there were other industries—the financial sector—to keep the city afloat and keep people living there. As a result, the city had a vibrant professional class, and a politically engaged one, since Chicago has always been an intensely political city. It has a nexus of people who work, relax, and raise their kids together. "There is a core of urban folks who play together, hang together, and who see each other on a regular basis," says Katz, who participated in the 1968 Democratic National Convention protests, worked for Harold Washington's campaign, and, like many '60s activists, has settled down a bit. She now runs a public relations firm.

When Michelle was hired by the Daley administration, she was an assistant to the mayor, making about $60,000 a year, but Jarrett was soon promoted to head the department of planning and development, and took Michelle with her. Michelle's new job was "economic development coordinator," which according to city records involved "developing strategies and negotiating business agreements to promote and stimulate economic growth within the City of Chicago." There is a lovely kind of closure here. After all those decades in which African Americans had had their lives hemmed in and circumscribed by city planners, Michelle Obama and Valerie Jarrett now *were* the city planners.

Colleagues in city government describe Michelle as a good problem solver and a manager who was unafraid to tell people their shortcomings, a trait that probably would not surprise her high school typing teacher. One colleague, Beth White, recalled that a junior staffer wanted a promotion and approached Michelle, who readily explained why she was not qualified, enumerating the ways in which the staffer fell short. "A lot of people are uncomfortable doing that," says White, but Michelle wasn't. She was kind, White said, but firm.

She and Barack had also, inadvertently, settled in a good place for working women. Unlike, say, Washington, D.C., a commuter city where most downtown workers go home to Arlington or Bethesda and end up living a long drive from their friends, Chicago is a place where many working women live in proximity. "From the time Michelle came [back] to Chicago she was immediately recognized as a young leader. She was recognized as brilliant and beautiful, and immediately accepted into a very sophisticated social circle," says Katz, describing how, in Chicago, a girlfriendy confederation of black and white women shops together, works out together, calls one another in the middle of the night to see who is up and making peanut-butter-and-jelly sandwiches to go into lunchboxes. Katz organizes an annual excursion to visit salons and go consignment shopping attended by city employees, journalists, politicians. At the May 2008 fund-raising luncheon for Jan Schakowsky where Michelle spoke, Katz says, "I could have gone to a hundred tables and known somebody at the table." The same, certainly, is true of Michelle. The circle, for one thing, is the most integrated in the city. In this context, "class is much more of a dividing line in the city than race," says Katz.

If Michelle was helpful to Barack, the converse was also true. In the early 1990s, Barack was on the founding board of Public Allies, a new nonprofit whose mission was to train young people to work in the nonprofit sector, with the hope of producing a fresh generation of public service leaders. The Chicago branch needed an executive director, and Obama suggested Michelle. In 1993, she was hired. Barack resigned from the board before she took over. Two years later she would be profiled in a *Chicago Tribune* article on so-called Generation Xers, young people born after 1964 who were being characterized as a "nomadic" work force with less employer loyalty than their boomer forebears. "I wear jeans and I'm the director," said Michelle, who was described as "having changed careers three times, with accompanying lower salaries—another characteristic of the age group that wants to do meaningful work."

According to Julian Posada, her deputy director at Public Allies, Michelle was as hardworking as her husband. Public Allies would soon become part of the Clinton administration's AmeriCorps program, and she was determined that the Chicago branch would succeed and excel, which it did. Among other things, she was a zealous money raiser, and left the organization, three years after starting, with cash in the bank. "There was an intensity to her that—you know, this has got to work, this is a big vision, this isn't easy," recalls Posada. "Michelle's intensity was like: We have to deliver." He was impressed with her sleeves-up attitude. "I'm sure she came from a lot more infrastructure. There was no sense that this was a plush law firm, that's all gone. It's like, 'Who's going to lick envelopes today?' Nothing was beneath her."

One of the first orders of business was recruiting "allies," young people who would spend ten months working in homeless shelters, city offices, public policy institutes, and other venues for public service. Allies were recruited from campuses and projects alike. Michelle knocked on doors in Cabrini Green, a notoriously rough public housing project, but also phoned friends to ask if they knew any public-spirited undergrads at Northwestern. "We would get kids from a very very lily-white campus to come sit down with inner-city kids, black, Hispanic, Asian," says Posada. In addition to recruiting and managing allies, she had to raise funds from Chicago's well-established foundations, competing with more established charities. As such, she had to be in touch with the old-money world of private philanthropy and the no-money world of housing projects, moving easily between almost every world that existed in Chicago.

Being a boss suited her. "Michelle was tough, tough in a good sense," says Posada. She was kind, he says, telling him when she thought it was time for him to move on and go to business school to develop more skills. She was attentive to every aspect of the program: raising money, inviting speakers, managing staff. "Even things she didn't know about—she was like, let's pick it up, let's go. She was very good about being meticulous about the details: Are you on message? Are we meeting people's expectations?" The person who hired her, Vanessa Kirsch, would later say that Michelle "had incredibly high expectations and was constantly asking questions, making sure we were using her time well." In this, she seems to be describing the same person Quincy White worked with: someone who wanted to be in charge and who grew impatient if she felt her time was being wasted. "There were days when, even though she worked for me, I definitely felt like I worked for her," Kirsch said.

There was also an ideological dimension to the program. Part of its goal was teaching people to work with peers of radically different backgrounds. Four days a week the "allies" would intern with a variety of nonprofits, but on Fridays they would be brought into the office for diversity training. "You'd take people through, what are your biases, people would learn how other people were feeling about stuff," says Posada, who describes the sessions as containing both a "lot of squishy stuff" and "incredibly powerful growth opportunities for individuals." Sometimes the workshops were led by outside experts, sometimes by Michelle. According to one ally,

Beth Hester, who is white, Michelle could be a forceful coach. "The most powerful thing she ever taught me was to be constantly aware of my privilege," Hester said, continuing, "Michelle reminded me that it's too easy to go and sit with your own. She can invite you, in kind of an aggressive way, to be all you can be."

The exercises were not for everyone at first. One ally at the branch of the program in Los Angeles later said she didn't feel comfortable in initial sessions. "It was too touchy-feely," said Nelly Nieblas, a member of the 2005 Public Allies class in Los Angeles. "It's a lot of talk about race, a lot of talk about sexism, a lot of talk about homophobia, talk about isms and phobias." But Nieblas, who has cerebral palsy, came to value the experience after doing an exercise where people had to take one step back for each disadvantage they had confronted, and she ended up with her back against the wall. After that, she realized that her liabilities were not any harder to overcome than those of others. In Chicago, the allies were matched in unlikely groupings and sent on scavenger hunts, assigned, say, to spend a day tracking down and interviewing five nonprofit leaders. It was a way of getting disparate people to work toward a goal. "That was part of what Public Allies was—you had to get over any phobias, or stuff you have," says Posada.

Many allies found Michelle inspiring. "You kind of know when you're in the presence of somebody who is really terrific," says Jobi Petersen, who was in the first class of Chicago allies. "I owed a lot to her. She's really fair, she's calm, she's smart, and she's balanced and she's funny, she doesn't take any crap. I get a little bit angry when I hear the thing about her being negative. She is the least negative person I've ever met. She is a can-do person." Petersen remembers a time when "one of the allies was despairing about how difficult things were, or the world wasn't bending their way, and [Michelle] would come back and say, 'You know what, today you have to get up and do something you don't love doing. If it's helping people, it's worth it.' She had a way of making you feel you could do anything. Humor, personal style, warmth, she can be strong and tough and not come across as negative. She's got timing. She can pass you one look and you'd laugh."

Part of Michelle's adult mission, clearly, was breaking down self-segregation and moving people outside their clans, a goal she talks about often in campaign speeches. These exhortations are one of the more controversial aspects of her public persona. Not everybody wants to be invited in a "kind of aggressive way" to be all they can be; not everybody wants to be forcefully reminded of their privilege. In January 2008, speaking at the University of South Carolina, Michelle embroidered on this theme, telling the students who came to hear her that "we don't like being pushed outside our comfort zones. You know it right here on this campus. You know, folks sitting at different tables—y'all living in different dorms. I was there. Y'all not talking to each other, taking advantage of the fact that you're in this diverse community. Because sometimes it's easier to hold on to your stereotypes and misconceptions. It makes you feel justified in your own ignorance. That's America. So the challenge for us is, are we ready for change? Real change?"

She took some heat for this speech, which is posted on YouTube with notations like "Michelle Obama—That's America!" Critics complained she was chastising whites, but in fact she was chastising everybody. It's easy to see from the video that the students in the front row, the only ones visible, are black. Critics also point out that her vision of America can seem strikingly negative; hers is a country in which people are disconnected and still segregated, a theme she returns to over and over. "We are still a nation that is too divided," she told the USC students. "We live in isolation from one another . . . Throughout this country, people live in isolation, and they tend to believe that their pain is unique to them, and their struggles are unique to them, and we become more isolated." In her view, it's social and racial isolation that leads to inequality and a lack of empathy—leads, for example, to a situation where American soldiers are bearing the brunt of the Iraq war and the rest of America is out shopping, unaware, in many cases, that a war is even going on. Her message is the same as Obama's—we are one another's keepers; our fates as citizens are inextricably tied—but he tends to deliver it in loftier, more majestic terms, and she tends to sound bleaker and, possibly, more realistic. In another speech, she told an audience that Obama would require people to conquer their inner isolationist: An Obama administration, she declared, would "demand that you shed your cynicism. That you put down your divisions. That you come out of your isolation, that you move out of your comfort zone. That you push yourselves to be better. And that you engage." Obama, she said, "will never allow you to go back to your lives as usual, uninvolved, uninformed."

This comment agitated conservatives, who rushed to defend Americans' constitutional right to remain in whatever comfort zone feels most comfortable. In the *National Review,* Mark Steyn argued that Michelle's urgings sound totalitarian, as though under an Obama administration there might be a national community reeducation day in which we all would be required to walk around our suburban cul-de-sacs reciting our biases. And it's true, she does sound a little schoolmarmish in that snippet. But these speeches, above all, prove that Michelle is hardly the militant racial separatist some of the same detractors portray her as. Just the opposite; she could be described as a passionate and even radical integrationist. During that same speech, she lectured the USC students about how, "when you are on a college campus, it is a rare opportunity that you have to live with people who are not like you, where you are forced to engage and have conversations . . . where you are potentially going to talk to somebody who doesn't agree with you, who lives in a different way." It almost seemed as if she were talking to the young Michelle Robinson at Princeton, as if she were looking back, wishing she had reached out even in an atmosphere that did not encourage it.

In a way, Michelle Obama can't win, not against the people who are determined to dislike her. Critics read her Princeton thesis and argue that she's Angela Davis in designer sundresses, an upper-income black nationalist, harboring all sorts of resentment despite her unity-modeling black-and-white outfits. When she urges integration and commingling and leaving one's own personal Green Zone, she's dismissed as a Stalinist. But her work at Public Allies and her campaign speeches show how passionately she feels about the value of different Americans surmounting their instinctive boundaries. "We have so much more in common as people," she told *People* magazine in 2007. "It's just that we don't cross paths enough as communities."

At Public Allies in the early 1990s, she recruited Barack to the cause. Posada remembers Barack came to do one of the Friday workshops, delivering a riveting lecture on community transformation, what might be called Changing the World 101. At the time, Posada says, Barack was "really intense—I think a lot more intense than I've seen him now." He says, "I remember him giving a speech about how you have to really understand who has power and what their self-interest is, if you want to move an agenda. That message still has stuck with me today."

Posada got the sense that the Obama marriage consisted of two highly driven, highly intense, highly functional, highly intelligent people who believed in the same things, shared the same goals, wanted to accomplish the same social program, and who both were able to throw themselves into their work. Michelle, he says, was in the office all the time. The marriage was new enough that sometimes she would sign a check "Michelle Robinson" and he would have to bring it back to sign with her married name. Barack still had his crummy car, a ridiculous old copper-colored jalopy; sometimes it would break down and Michelle would ask Posada to pick him up from a basketball game. Posada was invited to their Hyde Park condo and recalls that she was proud of it, and tidy, directing him to take off his shoes before he entered. "I can tell you that Michelle was very, very disciplined as far as her household. She ran a tight ship. It was always clean."

They would continue to have a collaborative marriage. Michelle would invite Barack to speak at events and panels, and she would consult him on her career choices. Newton Minow stayed in touch with both of them, and later his wife, Jo Minow, recalls wooing Michelle to the board of what is now called the Chicago Council on Global Affairs, an organization for movers and shakers with an interest in international politics and law. She took Michelle to lunch with the head of the group, they worked on her for a while, and Michelle told them she was flattered but had a lot of things on her plate. A few months went by and Jo called and asked if she had given any thought to it. "I really want to talk to Barack about it," Jo remembers Michelle saying, "which,

I thought, was very indicative of the relationship they have—they do things as a team." She did join that board, one of six she belongs to. Among the other groups whose boards she sits on is Muntu Dance Theater, a South Side dance company that performs traditional African and contemporary dance, and Facing History and Ourselves, whose mission is educating young people about prejudice, by fashioning curricula to help students learn about the Holocaust, the Rwandan genocide, and segregation in America.

Work aside, others who know the Obamas say that the personal dynamic of their marriage is one in which Obama simply adores his wife and makes a point of saying so. Michelle has described him as a romantic husband, in a kind of limited way. "He is not Mr. Door Opener," she told the *Hyde Park Herald*. But he does bring her flowers and is good about remembering anniversaries.

"He worships her," says Martha Minow. "Barack says, 'If I'm a ten, Michelle's an eleven.' "

He also defers to her authority. "He's always saying, 'She's the boss. Gotta check with the boss,' " Minow continues. "This is a partnership. This is real partners."

Michelle—the boss—has said that there's a rule in their marriage: She gets to tease, and Barack does not.

She is the one who gets to rag him publicly about leaving his socks around and not putting away the butter, and he is the one who does not get to rag her publicly about . . . anything. (He does allow himself the indulgence of mentioning, in *The Audacity of Hope*, that early in their marriage Michelle had a talent for acquiring parking tickets.) A mutual friend says it's sometimes hard when he and his wife have dinner with Michelle and Barack, because Barack will so elaborately praise Michelle that at the end of the dinner, his wife always wants to know why her husband doesn't talk about her that way. "He is so wonderful about Michelle, both about what he writes and says . . . it's not praise for praise's sake, it's honest and believable."

It must also have become clear to her, early on, that money was not something that motivated the man she had married. It might be an overstatement to say this gave her pause, but Barack's absence of financial ambition is something she gave thought to. When she first met him, "He had no money; he was really broke," she told the *Hyde Park Herald*. "He wasn't ever going to try to impress me with things. His wardrobe was kind of cruddy . . . He had five shirts and seven blue suits and a bunch of ties. He looks good in his clothes because he is tall and thin, but he has never been into clothes. I had to really tell him to get rid of the white jacket. He had good taste, but he just doesn't care about those things. His first car had so much rust that there was a rusted hole in the passenger door. You could see the ground when you were driving by. He loved that car. It would shake ferociously when it would start up. I thought, 'This brother is not interested in ever making a dime.' I would just have to love him for his values."

8

IF MICHELLE WAS INTENSE AND DRIVEN, BARACK soon emerged as more intense and more driven, at least when it came to making a mark in politics. In 1995, Obama, now thirty-three, decided to run for the Illinois state senate. It was the first in a striking number of occasions in which his political advancement would be facilitated by somebody else's catastrophic personal life. That year, Mel Reynolds, who represented Illinois's Second Congressional District, was facing charges related to sexual misconduct with a sixteen-year-old campaign volunteer and would eventually resign his seat. There were several contenders in the special election to replace him, including Alice Palmer, the progressive state senator who represented Hyde Park. Obama came to his alderman, Toni Preckwinkle, and told her he wanted to run for Palmer's seat.

Michelle told me in a 2007 interview that this was the first time she and Barack seriously discussed his having a political career. "We would always have discussions about how do you create change," she said. "Politics didn't come into the discussion until the seat opened up, and . . . that's when we started, and I was like, 'What are you talking about, politics, why on earth?' And of course I'm like, 'No, don't do it, we're just married, why would you want to do this?' "

But according to Dan Shomon, a political consultant who would become one of Obama's closest advisers during his career in Illinois politics, the problem wasn't so much that Michelle disliked politics; it was that Michelle was disdainful of this particular political post, viewing the state senate as beneath Barack and his talents. "She thought he was *so* outstanding that if he became mired in local or state politics, he'd never achieve greatness," Shomon told Melinda Henneberger of *Slate* magazine. "I remember him saying his wife thought he could do more," a state senator and Obama friend, Denny Jacobs, also told *Slate*.

Whatever her exact reservations were about the senate seat, Barack convinced her to abandon them, effectively arguing that you have to start changing the world somewhere—might as well start in Springfield. "You know, Barack is very convincing and very passionate," Michelle told me. "You have this conversation—we could build a very comfortable life for ourselves, we've gone to the right schools, and have all these advantages, [but] look around, I grew up in the city, most of my family are not in the position I [am], so you can't deny the fact that it isn't enough for the Obamas to be okay, and for our kids to be okay. And you know, that was a struggle that I had—going to top schools, leaving a very working-class [background], seeing the really grand distinctions, the opportunity for kids to get into Princeton and kids who can't get into college at all. Knowing that the chasms are so vast. I understand it, and eventually my conscience said okay, you're right, we do have an obligation. This is what we got this education for. We're in a position to make sacrifices . . . forgoing income."

As she often does, Michelle seems to be articulating some survivor's guilt—the awareness that, while she has prospered in her life, she can't fully enjoy that prosperity and seek more of it when other people have none at all. It's important to remember that while Michelle was away at Princeton, Harold Washington may have been elected, but as a counterweight to that advance, the poverty and problems in many South Side neighborhoods became worse. The disappearance of the working-class jobs that created and sustained the South Side was a tremendous blow to many of its various parts, as was the decline in federal support for cities.

Many sociologists have studied the neighborhoods that make up the South Side. Among them is the Harvard sociologist William Julius Wilson, who based his book *When Work Disappears: The World of the New Urban Poor* on areas with which Michelle was familiar, including Woodlawn, right next to South Shore. That neighborhood has declined to the point where it is a textbook example of what Wilson refers to as the new urban poverty, an especially bleak version that is brought on by "concentrated and persistent joblessness," resulting in "poor, segregated neighborhoods in which a substantial majority of individual adults are either unemployed or have dropped out of the labor force altogether." In the 1950s, Woodlawn had over eight hundred commercial and industrial establishments; it now has one hundred, many of them tiny enterprises such as barbershops and thrift stores. In neighborhoods near Michelle's childhood home, the consequences of job disappearance are impossible to ignore. And, Wilson points out, while joblessness affects working-class people of all races, it has a particularly devastating effect on African Americans living in communities into which for years and years they were corralled.

The effects of segregation have by no means gone away. Blacks living in projects that were deliberately built in poor neighborhoods by city planners are at a particular disadvantage, because it's harder for them to move when jobs go to the suburbs. "There is no doubt that the disproportionate concentration of poverty among African-Americans is one of the legacies of historic racial segregation," Wilson writes. "It is also true that segregation often compounds black vulnerability in the face of other changes in the society." Even the more stable South Shore has not been immune: the block Michelle's mother lives on is still middle-class and relatively prosperous, and has many of the residents who were there when she was growing up. But neighbors voice concerns about more crime and less of a sense of community. Reporting one day in her neighborhood, I went for lunch not too far away, at Harold's Chicken—Harold's is an institution in Chicago—and while I was waiting for my order, I listened to a couple of men discussing a recent street shooting.

And this is where Michelle's life experience is so unlike Barack's. For all that he has resolved to work on behalf of the American black community, he was not incubated and nurtured in the heart of it, as she was; he did not leave the community to go to an Ivy League school and then return home on visits, as she did, to witness the devastating changes.

In fact, it seems fair to wonder whether this may have always been Obama's trump card in marital arguments. He could always—always—convince Michelle of the rightness of his run, pleading the cause of the community she came from. As Michelle would later put it in an interview with the *Hyde Park Herald,* "I have a ton of bright friends from my neighborhood who could be doing what I am doing, but they didn't get the breaks. They did not have the right inspiration. It is such a flimsy difference between success and failure."

This quote defines and articulates a significant aspect of her psyche. As Barack observed when he met her, Michelle does seem to harbor a sense that things could have so easily gone wrong for her, just as they went wrong for some of the people she grew up with—a sense that if she doesn't work hard to hold it together, everything could still fall apart. She is also aware that things might have gone badly for Barack if he had done his youthful experimenting in a place other than Hawaii. When a Chicago television interviewer spoke with her for a 2007 special, the topic of Barack's teenage drug use came up. The interviewer mentioned the fact that Barack, as he has acknowledged in *Dreams from My Father,* dabbled in marijuana and cocaine while in high school, and Michelle responded by saying he was lucky he lived where he did.

"If he had been the same kid growing up on the South Side of Chicago, I think his outcomes might be a bit different," Michelle pointed out. "But there wasn't a lot of trouble to get into in Hawaii. You could screw up in Hawaii and still be okay."

When Barack convinced her that running for the state senate was a good move, Michelle says she had no real understanding at the time of how a political career would affect their marriage or their home life. Who could? As intense as Barack seemed, who could foresee that, barely a decade later, he would be talking her into a run for the presidency? "I didn't know at the time how much" his going into politics would take away from their family, she told me in 2007. "There was my naïveté. So I eventually said sure, let's do it, okay, you win.

"And then," she said, "you're in it. You're feeling the passion, the desire to try and be part of moving things to a better place for people."

Not surprisingly, she was a valuable political partner in the sense that she was wonderful at fund-raisers, elegant and funny and spontaneous and at ease. When Barack called Newton Minow and said he planned to run for public office, he acknowledged that Michelle had reservations about the undertaking. "She did not like politics, period," says Minow. "She did not want him to run for office. I know this because he told me so himself." But Minow says she was charming at an early fund-raiser held in Minow's apartment overlooking Lake Michigan, which is decorated with photos of the Kennedy administration, sunlit images of Camelot. Those people who know Barack well have enjoyed listening to him become a more effective public speaker, and he was at the beginning of the learning curve that night. "She came—she sat right next to the fireplace; he was just learning how to speak to a group," Minow remembers. "He was okay. For questions, he would give too long an answer. Martha says that's because he's very intellectual."

And he was very determined. When Alice Palmer gave him her blessing to run to replace her, Barack asked her whether, if she lost in the Democratic congressional primary, she might want her old state senate seat back. He would say later that he warned Palmer that once he committed to the race, he would not step aside. Palmer did lose the primary—to Jesse Jackson Jr., who would go on to win Mel Reynolds's congressional seat in the general election—and she did come back and seek her old seat. But Obama did not step aside. Far from it. When his staffers looked at the petitions Palmer had hastily garnered, they saw irregularities and challenged them. Then, noting irregularities in the petitions of his other primary opponents, he knocked them all out of the race. He went on to win and was sworn into the state senate in January 1997.

Abner Mikva, who returned to Chicago in the late 1990s and met Michelle then, got the sense that her reaction was similar to that of many political wives: She was glad her man had prevailed. "At first she was kind of proud of his becoming state senator," Mikva said. "That's the usual arc. The wives are kind of pleased that their husbands have performed so well. But then the burdens begin to get more and more, taking care of the household and raising the family. I'm sure they had many conversations. Clearly, her point of view was important; there was the constant struggle of her trying to maintain a family life and some relationship, not only between them, but especially when the kids came along, trying to make sure he was performing some of the roles as father. The higher up he went, the harder it became."

Mikva liked Michelle immediately. He and his wife were invited to their Hyde Park condo; there were just six or eight people, he says, and "I was impressed then, first of all with how she fills a room when she comes in. She has such a great bearing. You know she's there. She was not the shy retiring political wife, taking the back-seat—she very much enjoyed the conversation, there was lots of give-and-take on Chicago politics." And, mindful of nonlawyers in the room, she was careful not to let the conversation get mired in legal minutiae. But from his own experience as a politician, Mikva had perhaps a better sense of what she was in for than she did. "Being a political wife is not the greatest job in the world. Your ego is stomped on, and you're pushed aside, and you're always the senator's wife, the congressman's wife, the state legislator's wife—you're never a person in your own being. It's very, very hard on the family. The hours are crazy. Elected officials are gone on weekends and at night. My wife always used to be furious that our social engagements had to be made through our campaign staff. There's good cause for resentment."

This would quickly become clear to Michelle. Formerly, their marriage had consisted of Obama's doing two or even three things at once; before the race he had been writing a book and practicing law, and he had taken a job lecturing on constitutional law at the University of Chicago, which was so avid to hire him as a permanent faculty member that later the law school would offer to hire Michelle, as well, if only he would sign on. He didn't. His work habits were hard on them even as newlyweds. Barack had a little writing cubby in the apartment, which they referred to as the Hole. He would later write, in his second book, *The Audacity of Hope:* "I would often spend the evening holed up in my office in the back of our railroad apartment; what I considered normal often left Michelle feeling lonely." Now that the election was over, he was working as a legislator, working as a lawyer (though he did take leave from the firm when the legislature was in session, because he didn't want to be paid for not working, according to Miner), and teaching law, a job that paid well and could be worked into his political schedule.

And they were starting a family. During this period, Michelle was trying to get pregnant; when it didn't happen right away, she has said, she started to worry. Then on July 4, 1998, Malia Ann was born. According to the *New York Times,* early in their marriage the Obamas had agreed that their children would have "the kind of dinner-together-every-night childhood" Michelle had known growing up. It was a resolution that would prove laughably difficult; they would never have that kind of household, not even briefly. She had married a man who was operating on an almost inhumanly accelerated timetable, driving on his own personal autobahn faster than all the other traffic. As Barack would later tell David Mendell of the *Chicago Tribune,* one of his greatest strengths and weaknesses is the desire to, in effect, have it all—to be a politician, husband, father, writer.

"There are times when I want to do everything and be everything," he said to Mendell. "I want to have time to read and swim with the kids and not disappoint my voters and do a really careful job on each and every thing that I do. And that can sometimes get me into trouble. That's historically been one of my bigger faults." Barack has never sought to correct this aspect of his personality, and as a result, it would be Michelle who found it impossible to have it all. Early on, Gerald Kellman was struck by Barack's terror of living a repetitive and ordinary and unremarkable life—the kind of life, presumably, where a man might come home from work to gather round the dinner table with his family.

"He didn't want to be on one of those [commuter] trains every day," says Kellman. "The image of a life, not a dynamic life, of going through the motions . . . that was scary to him."

Barack was an adoring parent and, like many first-time fathers, gleeful and grateful and willing, and charmingly clueless. Right after Malia was born, he ran to a Hallmark store in Hyde Park and tried to find something commensurate to the occasion. "He had no idea what to get his newborn baby and his amazing wife who was still in the hospital with her," remembers the store's owner, Joyce Feuer. "He was a very typical first-time dad but incredibly nervous. We put together this really adorable gift bag with a teddy bear, balloons, a card and some other things. He was acting like there was no other new father on earth. He was just in his glory like a kid in a candy shop—ecstatic beyond belief." That Malia was born in the summer made things easier: The legislature wasn't in session, and he didn't have to teach. Michelle had left Public Allies and was now working part-time at the University of Chicago, where she had been hired to put together an Allies-like public service program for undergraduates. She was on maternity leave and not due to start work again until the fall. So, Barack would write in *The Audacity of Hope*, "for three magical months the two of us fussed and fretted over our new baby." The fact that she was a morning person and he was a night person worked well. "While Michelle got some well-earned sleep, I would stay up until one or two in the morning, changing diapers, heating breast milk, feeling my daughter's soft breath against my chest as I rocked her to sleep."

But when fall came, domestic life became more complicated. Michelle went back to work, and he was gone for three days at a time, then back in Chicago with papers to grade and briefs to write. When the legislature was in session, he would leave on Tuesday and be back from Springfield on Thursday. Far from eating dinner together every night, the family got used to a schedule where Michelle was the resident parent during the week. "Our kids are used to the fact that Dad's a weekend dad," Michelle would tell the *Herald* in 2007. "They see him on Sundays and Saturdays. That's been what they know." During the week, it was Michelle's duty to get Malia up and cared for and bathed and fed and read to and in bed and taken to the doctor, and to perform the other ceaseless, often invisible tasks that fall to a young parent, while trying to maintain her own career.

Meanwhile, Barack took on even more obligations and opportunities. While he was in the state senate, he was invited by Harvard sociologist Robert Putnam, author of *Bowling Alone: The Collapse and Revival of American Community*, to join the Saguaro Seminar, a group of leaders interested in enhancing "civic engagement in

America." It was an ideologically diverse group that included liberals and conservatives, ministers, academics, community organizers, big thinkers, people like the Christian conservative leader Ralph Reed and the liberal columnist E. J. Dionne. The group held its meetings on weekends. Later, Putnam would remember that Obama's political ambition was so apparent that members began teasingly calling him "Governor." Martha Minow, who was also part of Saguaro, recalls that Barack was gifted at reconciling opposing viewpoints, and how, after one session, "we'd had some intense discussion about some complicated issue, and Barack was summarizing, 'This is what everybody said,' and he was so terrific" that they gathered around and asked him when he was running for president.

"I try to remember: Why did we think this?" Martha Minow says now. "It was his way of listening astutely to the conversations, offering an embracing, objective view: Here's how what everybody says fits together." He made some polite demurral to the question, says Martha, who also remembers that Barack would often show pictures of his family, sometimes mentioning "that Michelle wasn't happy that he wasn't home for the weekend." Sometimes he would explain that was why he wasn't staying for the concluding dinner. Her displeasure—or, simply, loneliness—was not something he took lightly, but it didn't keep him from doing what he wanted to do.

Barack's first term in the senate was not an easy one. The politicians there resented his résumé and his new-comer status. As Mendell puts it, in Springfield, people often viewed him as "an aloof Ivy League good-government type who too often mentions his years of sacrifice as a community organizer and his Harvard Law pedigree."

And the resentment intensified when, in 2000, Obama had the hubris to challenge Representative Bobby Rush (D-Ill.), a member of Congress and former Black Panther, in the Democratic primary. It was a pre-mature move, though it's possible to understand why he did it. He was an exceedingly ambitious politician, now in his mid-thirties, restless in the state legislature, with a wife who expected great things of him. "I wasn't pre-pared to be a lifer in the state legislature," he told me in 2007. And for an African American politician anxious to move out of the minor leagues of political service, it was a sorry truth that in Illinois, as around the country, there were limited options. Then, as now, it was gener-ally thought that if you were a black lawmaker, you needed a district with a black base in order to win. Jesse Jackson Jr. represented one of these districts, and Rush another. There weren't a lot of other avenues to higher office. In 1999, Rush had challenged Richard M. Daley for mayor and lost, an event that suggested he might be vulnerable. Even so, some people tried to talk Barack out of running. "I was a little bit questioning about whether Rush was vulnerable at all, but Barack was sure that he was," says Mikva.

Both Michelle and Barack have said what a difficult period this was for them. They had a baby and Barack was gone all the time, legislating or campaigning. According to Dan Shomon, his political consultant and confidant at the time, Michelle was not yet willing to throw her life into disarray to help her husband. During the campaign, Barack would sometimes get stuck in Springfield during extended sessions, and when his staff would call Michelle to ask her to fill in for him at an event, she would do it if it worked into her schedule, but felt free to decline if it didn't. "It was no secret among us who were helping to run his campaign that Michelle was not wild about it," says the political consultant Al Kindle, who worked for Obama on that campaign.

Barack Obama got the same idea—only a lot more directly. "When I launched my ill-fated congressional run, Michelle put up no pretense of being happy with the decision," he wrote in *Audacity*. "My failure to clean up the kitchen suddenly became less endearing. Leaning down to kiss Michelle good-bye in the morning, all I would get was a peck on the cheek. By the time Sasha was born—just as beautiful, and almost as calm as her sister—my wife's anger toward me seemed barely contained. 'You only think about yourself,' she would tell me. 'I never thought I'd have to raise a family alone.' "

Obama acknowledges that it took him a while to figure out why his wife was so angry. In *The Audacity of Hope,* still seeming a little wounded, he points out that he made it a point to pitch in domestically—when he was home, that is—and did not expect her to wait on him or make dinner. "All I asked for in return was a little tenderness," he wrote. "Instead, I found myself subjected to endless negotiations about every detail of managing the house, long lists of things that I needed to do or had forgotten to do, and a generally sour attitude."

Ah yes, the chore list! The sour attitude! The endless negotiations! What working mother of small children has not, in her extremely limited and really pretty nonexistent spare time, written down a list of all the things around the house that she does, and all the things around the house that her husband does, and stared at it in despair, feeling, yes, a little sour, a little inclined to enter into some negotiations, endless ones, if necessary?

The strain on their marriage would complicate his run. During Christmas 1999, Barack and Michelle took their usual trip to Hawaii to visit Barack's grandmother. They usually loved these trips, so relaxed, a winter holiday spent in tropical scenery and a break from the punishingly cold Chicago weather. "We have just some of the most wonderful times when we visit Barack's grandmother in Hawaii," Michelle would later tell *U.S. News & World Report*. "Those are always wonderful times, warm weather, a time to be together and laugh, when everybody's relaxed, no schedules, no nothing, just a lot of good fun together." But according to David Mendell, Michelle at that point was "barely on speaking terms" with her husband. They had truncated the trip to five days because of the campaign, and while they were there, Malia came down with a bad cold, as young children often do after long airplane flights.

Meanwhile, back in Springfield, a politically significant gun control measure, favored by Governor George Ryan, was working its way through the legislature. Obama—whose senate district included neighborhoods where gun violence was an everyday problem—supported the law. But it faced strong opposition and the vote would be close. A special session was called between Christmas and New Year's. Shomon, who had

repeatedly lectured Obama on the political consequences of missing votes, called to urge him to consider
returning early, something that, as Mendell points out,
would "put him in a bad spot with Michelle." He stayed
in Hawaii. The measure came for a vote; it failed, just
three votes short of passage, and Obama was among the
three lawmakers Ryan had counted on who missed the
vote. When he returned to Chicago, he was pilloried. "I
cannot sacrifice the health or well-being of my daughter
for politics," Obama stiffly told reporters, implying, like
many first-time parents, that a toddler's bad cold is tan-
tamount to a life-threatening illness. It's easy to imagine
the chilly atmosphere in the Obama household that
January. The only question, really, is who was madder at
whom.

The rest of the campaign was a disaster; it was snake-
bit from the start. And it was during the Rush challenge
that rumors began circulating that Obama with his biracial heritage was not "black enough." Michelle objected
to the characterization and would staunchly defend him;
she later made a comment to an interviewer defending
his racial bona fides. "I've grown up in this community,
I'm as black as it gets," she told a Chicago public television interviewer. "I was born on the South Side . . . we
weren't rich, you know. I put my blackness up against

anybody's blackness in the state, okay? And Barack is a black man. And he's done more in terms of meeting his commitments and sticking his neck out for this community than many people who criticize him.

"And *I* can say that," she added emphatically, " 'cause I'm black."

In this case, however, Michelle's roots were not enough to help him overcome the perception, among many, that he was an upstart—that he was, in fact, not black enough. Other disasters happened. In October 1999, Bobby Rush's adult son was murdered in a South Side street shooting. Obama, already trailing in the polls, shut down his campaign for a week and could hardly go negative on a father who had just lost his son. In the spring of 2000 he lost by a two-to-one margin, a thorough drubbing and one he did not take well. "He is not a good loser," says Shomon. "He is a very animated winner, and a very quiet, sheepish loser . . . He had a little bit of that killer instinct that Michael Jordan says you need to win in sports or politics."

Mikva met with him and also found him dispirited. "That was the one time he semiseriously thought about giving up politics. He was frustrated; he had been [in the state senate] for four years. The pay is very modest. It seemed that whatever his ambitions were, there wasn't going to be a channel for them." Obama also remembers being discouraged: after his loss to Rush, he told me in an interview, "Some doubts entered my mind as to whether some kid from Hawaii named Barack Obama could succeed in a political venue, where a lot of times voters are relying on very little information and making snap judgments based on somebody's name and whether they've got family ties." In a way, he seemed to have begun believing the line—maybe he *wasn't* black enough. Maybe Chicago would never accept somebody named Obama as one of their own.

Michelle, at this point, wanted him to get out of the business altogether. A bit of a pattern was setting in. "He would always tell his wife, I'm going to give it one shot, and if it doesn't work out, I'm going to go to the private sector," says Shomon. *Just one last time,* he would tell her. Just one more try. Up, or out. After the Bobby Rush debacle, Newton Minow recalls, Obama called and asked to have a talk with him. Minow took him to lunch at the Mid-Day Club. He recalls that Barack had been offered a job as the head of a foundation, which would pay much more than he had been making. "Michelle wanted him to take it," Minow says. "I told him he would have a hundred opportunities." The job offered much-needed financial security, a point Michelle was pushing. This was also a pattern in their marriage—she playing the role of the industrious, paycheck-retrieving ant, he the role of devil-may-care grasshopper. Unafraid of plastic, he had a habit of putting professional expenses on his credit card and neglecting to file for reimbursement. Whenever Shomon got on him about this, Michelle would thank him. Barack's grandmother told the *Tribune*'s Mendell that she was the only one among those who had raised Barack who had any real fiscal sense. She supported her husband and grandson by working in a bank, and was always a financial pragmatist. "I'm sure Michelle would have been happier if I would have emphasized that a little more," she said.

They weren't bankrupt, but they weren't flush. They both had student loans, and Barack had incurred personal debt during the Rush campaign. Even now, in speeches, Michelle talks about the ever-present burden of their student loans, and Barack has written about how, when he tried to attend the 2000 Democratic National Convention, his credit card was maxed out and he was barely able to rent a car.

But Barack wasn't dissuaded, yet. He says that not long after the Rush defeat, he did pass up the chance to run for Illinois attorney general, fearing it would be too hard on the family. By mid-2002, however, he spotted an opening that made the risk seem worthwhile. One of the state's incumbent U.S. senators, Peter Fitzgerald, was foundering in the Senate. Fitzgerald was a Republican. He had defeated Carol Moseley Braun in 1998, in part as a result of allegations, never proven, that she had misused campaign funds. Fitzgerald was a loner and iconoclast and not all that well liked in his own party, and Barack decided that he could take him. "I thought I could beat him," Obama told me in 2007. And so, when he met with Minow, he said, "I want to be a senator."

"You *are* a senator," Minow replied.

"I don't mean a senator in the Illinois senate. I mean a senator in the U.S. Senate," Barack told him. "I think I can do it."

Barack also broke the news to Shomon: The two were driving in southwestern Illinois, on their way to a fellow legislator's annual state picnic. It was September 2002 and the Obamas now had two small children: Natasha, nicknamed Sasha, had been born in 2001, and Malia was four. Shomon pulled over by the side of the road and tried, hard, to talk him out of running, arguing that the impact on Michelle and the girls would be too extreme. "I knew that he personally was someone that has a conscience and feels guilt; and this would not be the right thing for him because of his children, because of his family." Shomon continued, "If you talk to people that really know him that worked for him, they would tell you the personal strife that he goes through because of the fact that he doesn't see his kids enough. It burns a small hole in his heart every night when he is not with them . . . He's a very brilliant and a very driven man, and he's ambitious, [but he also] has a conscience. He felt guilty if he was late coming home. If he got stuck down here in Springfield and had to be in session, he would feel guilty. He would feel guilty if he was being a little lazy and didn't clean up enough around the house." Shomon says that guilt comes in part from Michelle, who makes her views known and does not passively acquiesce. "His wife would call him out on stuff. That's clear."

But Barack was unshakable: "His counterargument [then] was similar to his counterargument always," Shomon says. "We can change politics, we can change the agenda, we can help average people. And I'm not going to be able to help people if I'm stuck in the state senate for twenty years."

Fortunately for Barack, while he was in the state senate Michelle had a revelation: She had to stop being angry and expecting him to change, and focus instead on how she could gain control and extract happiness out of her life. In 2001, she had been recruited by the University of Chicago hospitals, which hired her to serve as a liaison with residents and organizations near the hospital. Like the university, the hospital system had not had a good reputation with its neighbors, and was not seen as a place that served the surrounding African American community well. When she was recruited, she was still breast-feeding Sasha and had no choice but to take the baby with her in a carrier, because she didn't have a babysitter or anybody to help her. At the time, she said, she was thinking about becoming a stay-at-home mom. She had been struggling with "wanting to be a good mother and was on the verge of saying 'I'm not sure what I want to do [professionally], so I'm going to do what I haven't done before and stay home.'"

Instead, she changed her approach to her marriage—accepting the things she could not change, like Barack's nature, and changing the things that she could. "There was an important period of growth in our marriage," she later told O magazine. "He was in the state senate, we had small kids, and it was hard. I was struggling with figuring out how to make it work for me." Michelle had always been hyperorganized and an early riser, and now, she says, she started going to the gym at 4:30 A.M., in part to get in shape but in part to force Barack to deal with the household.

"This was the epiphany," she said. "I am sitting there with a new baby, angry, tired, and out of shape. The baby is up for that 4 o'clock feeding. And my husband is lying there, sleeping." She figured out that if she left, he would have to cope. "I would get home from the gym, and the girls would be up and fed. That was something I had to do for me." She told an interviewer for the *Chicago Tribune* that she realized she could not live her life being resentful; it would wreck her, and it would poison their relationship. "I cannot be crazy, because then I'm a crazy mother and I'm an angry wife." In that interview, she allowed herself the luxury of adding, "What I notice about men, all men, is that their order is me, my family, God is in there somewhere, but me is first. And for women, me is fourth, and that's not healthy."

She also realized that she had to put together a support system. "How do I structure my world so that it works for me and I'm not trying to get him to be what I think he should be?" she would later tell *People*. She hired a housekeeper to do the laundry, cooking, and cleaning, and got her mom to help with babysitting, saying that "it matters less to me that Barack's the one [helping with] babysitting and giving me the time for myself; it's that I'm getting time." She has acknowledged that during his state senate years "there was a lot of tension and stress," but that she realized "I needed to focus on what kept myself sane instead of looking to Barack to give me the answers and to help fulfill me."

And this epiphany was important not just for her but for him. "Obama could not be running for president had he married someone" who could not adjust or withstand the schedule, says Al Kindle. Her breakthrough moment reminded me of a conversation I'd had with Tipper Gore several years ago, when I was reporting a profile of former vice president Al Gore. Before the interview formally started, we were chatting about the pressure of having a husband who is gone a lot doing high-stress public service work; it was not long after 9/11 and my own husband was working in counterterrorism, a job that was urgent, hard, and time-consuming. "You have to understand—it's not going to change," Tipper said, or words to that effect. "You have to create a support network." She knew what she was talking about. If there is a standard profile of the successful political wife—one who is not resentful, or angry, one who doesn't succumb to substance abuse or permit her personality to be subsumed—Tipper Gore might be said to be it. And Michelle, in many ways, does seem to be in the Tipper Gore tradition. Like Tipper, she is warm, well-spoken, sometimes controversial (remember Tipper's campaign against rock music lyrics?), grounded, and friendly, a genuinely devoted wife who is hardy and sensible enough to figure out how to survive.

And it's a good thing Michelle was able to make it work for her: The U.S. Senate campaign would be wearying and even more stressful. During one intense period, Barack Obama would estimate that he had taken *seven days off in eighteen months*. That the Obamas survived at all, as a family, is a testament to Michelle's flexibility and stamina. As Michelle said to me in 2007, every stage of her husband's career has come as a bit of a surprise to her. She's like Charlie Brown and the football, always believing that this time, Lucy won't pull it away. This time, Barack won't run. Or, if he runs and loses, he really will get out. "At every step of the way, I can honestly say—I would say, you know, running for president, there's no way he's gonna do that," she told me in the summer of 2007, six months after he had announced for the presidency. "Why would he do that? That doesn't make any sense." Then, with a laugh: "I'm always the last one to get a clue."

9

At the outset, to be sure, Michelle was opposed to Barack's entering the U.S. Senate race. "The big issue around the Senate for me was, how on earth can we afford it?" Michelle told the *Tribune*'s David Mendell. "I don't like to talk about it, because people forget that his credit card was maxed out. How are we going to get by? Okay, now we're having two households to fund, one here and one in Washington. We have law school debt, tuition to pay for the children. And we're trying to save for college for the girls . . . My thing is, is this just another gamble? It's just killing us. My thing was, this is ridiculous, even if you do win, how are you

227

going to afford this wonderful next step in your life? And he said, 'Well then, I'm going to write a book, a good book.' And I'm thinking, 'Snake eyes there, buddy. Just write a book, yeah, that's right. Yep, yep, yep. And you'll climb the beanstalk and come back down with the golden egg, Jack.' "

According to Obama, he replied, "[P]olitics has been a huge strain on you, but I really think there is a strong possibility that I can win this race. Obviously I have devoted a lot of my life to public service and I think that I can make a huge difference here if I won the U.S. Senate race. I said to her that if you are willing to go with me on this ride and if it doesn't work out, then I will step out of politics." Michelle told Mendell her response was, "Whatever. We'll figure it out. We're not hurting. Go ahead." Then she cracked, "And maybe you'll lose."

Many Democratic contenders for the seat already were massing. Newton Minow recalls that, early on, it was hard to get people to come to fund-raisers. Martha Minow remembers going to one that was sparsely attended, and Michelle, she says, was "elegant and funny, and happy and gracious. She is so smooth. I felt embarrassed that there weren't very many people, and she pooh-poohed it." Michelle also went with Barack to court Penny Pritzker, heiress to the Hyatt hotel fortune and a crucial fund-raising force in Illinois politics. To win her support would be a coup. Penny and her husband, Bryan Traubert, invited the Obamas to their lakefront cottage in Michigan for a weekend, and Pritzker would later say she had been impressed by both of them, their stability and moral commitment. She and her husband, she said, "had a long discussion about Barack and his values and the way he carries and expresses himself, his family and the kind of human beings he and Michelle are—what kind of people they are, as much as lofty political ideas." After the weekend, Pritzker decided to back him; she would eventually become the finance chairman for his presidential campaign.

At these events, it emerged that Barack had a plan for winning, a plan that involved the same strategy that had helped Carol Moseley Braun win the Democratic primary for Senate. In her successful race for the U.S. Senate, Moseley Braun had proved that if a black candidate had at least two white opponents in the Democratic primary, it was possible for the white vote to be split and for a black candidate to win statewide. Barack thought he could do the same thing—split the white vote and run full speed through the middle, attracting the majority of the black vote and, hopefully, some whites.

But in order for this strategy to work, there had to be

only one credible black candidate in the primary race. There was talk that Jesse Jackson Jr. might run for the seat. "You have to talk to the Jackson boys first," Abner Mikva told him, and Obama said, "I know. I'm working on that." Barack, taking advantage of Michelle's family connection, went to lunch with Jackson, who told Obama that he wasn't interested. The problem was, Moseley Braun herself was possibly planning to run. The former U.S. senator, who lived not far away from the Obamas in Hyde Park, was said to be thinking about reclaiming her seat. If she did, his plan would be thwarted. "Our bases overlapped so much—not just that she was African American, but she came out of the progressive wing of the party . . . and our donor bases would have been fairly similar," Obama told me in 2007. "So it would have been difficult, I think, to mobilize the entire coalition that was required for me to run." If she did decide to join the race, he said, "I would probably have stepped out of politics for a while."

All Obama could do was wait. During the second half of 2002, he quietly hired staffers, putting a team together and planning his campaign. Just after the New Year, the family was in Hawaii and Barack was enjoying the beach time and thinking perhaps the race would not work out after all, and that more time with his young family would be pleasant, when his cell phone rang and news reached them that Moseley Braun was running— for president of the United States. That was it. He was in. Barack seized the moment, announcing in early 2003 that he would run.

Four years later, Kwame Raoul, who replaced Barack in the Illinois state senate, recalled that when he asked Obama for advice about how to succeed in the legislature, Barack told him simply, "Stay out of jail." Raoul at first thought it was a joke. Obama was serious. In Chicago, corruption is sufficiently widespread, even, one might say, traditional, that jail is a plausible outcome to a political career, maybe more so now—this was Barack's point—that new ethics laws had been put in place and lawmakers no longer knew, necessarily, what was illegal and what wasn't. But something similar could be said about Barack when he was running for the U.S. Senate. In this race, marital discord and sexual transgressions were so oddly common that all he had to do to win, in a way, was stay out of divorce court. That's an overstatement, of course, but it remains a strange truth that his extraordinary career was enabled, in part, by the fact that he had a more stable marriage than some of his opponents.

There were other factors as well; in a very compressed

period of time, a series of fortunate events would con-
spire to propel Obama not only into political office but
to a level of celebrity that would forever transform his
family's life. One of the first of these occurred in April
2003, when Peter Fitzgerald surprised everyone by announcing he wasn't going to run for reelection. This
was a major development. It meant that there was no
incumbent. Barack was now running for an open seat.
The situation was much more fluid; anything could
happen and anyone, almost, might be able to win. Second, Barack was able to attract the help of David
Axelrod, the premier political consultant in Chicago.
This was an important asset, since his contenders were
formidable and many: At one point, he faced nine
primary candidates.

But his main opposition boiled down to two Democratic opponents: Dan Hynes, the popular state comptroller and favorite of the party establishment; and Blair
Hull, a wealthy stock trader who had sold his company
to Goldman Sachs for $531 million and would be financ-
ing his own campaign. They were both credible candidates, though they did play into Barack's hands by
making it entirely conceivable that the white vote would
split. And in a way, Hull's wealth was also an advantage
for Obama: Under the new McCain-Feingold campaign

finance reform law, a candidate running against a wealthy opponent who was self-financing was allowed to raise six times the normal limit. This meant Obama could raise $12,000 from each donor instead of $2,000. "This was a huge advantage; it just made a huge difference," says Mikva. "I gave him more money than I've ever given anyone in my life." And Obama was getting much better, and more disciplined, about fund-raising.

But Hull was still outspending Obama, and the spending mattered. A poll taken about a month before the primary showed Hull in the lead, with Hynes and Obama trailing. Obama's break came in late February 2004, when Blair Hull's divorce records were unsealed, and it emerged that his ex-wife had accused him of verbal and physical abuse. (He said he struck her shin when she kicked him.) It was a disaster for Hull, and the Obama campaign feared he would drop out of the race, a development that would thwart the split-the-white-vote plan. But Hull stayed in, and he and Hynes continued to struggle against each other, allowing Obama to quietly move forward. Toward the end of the primary season, Obama ran a series of political ads, devised by David Axelrod, whose theme was "Yes, we can." The slogan, presaging his presidential campaign, suggested the general theme of change. More specifically, one of its subtle implications was that a black man could, yes, win statewide. According to Mendell, Obama thought the slogan was simplistic, but Axelrod strongly supported it. Obama used Michelle as a tiebreaker, knowing that she was an accurate and sensitive gauge of the African American community. She thought it was a good message, so he went ahead.

And it turned out that yes, he could. Obama, preaching a message of unity and change, not only did well with African Americans; he did much better with white voters than anyone had thought possible. In March 2004, he won the primary, with 53 percent of the vote. The campaign was incredulous—and ecstatic. Obama won in the most unlikely places, including portions of northwest Chicago, where Harold Washington once had been treated so venomously, and in the so-called collar counties, suburban areas where whites had once fled the encroachment of people like the Robinsons. He was, it now became clear, a true crossover politician, a black man able to attract white voters in significant numbers, an accomplishment, like winning the *Harvard Law Review* presidency, that made him nationally known. William Finnegan profiled him in *The New Yorker* magazine. Bestselling author Scott Turow wrote a piece in *Salon*. And Michelle, as always, kept his head on straight. When the results for the primary were about to come in, Obama went into a service corridor of the Hyatt Regency hotel and started pacing. When an aide told him he had been projected a landslide winner, he gave Michelle a high five—no fist bump yet—and she teased him, doing her best Sally Field imitation. "They like you!" she exclaimed. "They really like you!"

"He's pretty excited," Michelle told a reporter who was struck by Obama's calm, watching him pose for photos on a couch with the girls. "He told me. He's basically a calm guy. It takes a lot to push his buttons. He has incredibly low blood pressure."

It was during this campaign that Obama's political team began testing Michelle's value as a surrogate. They had to cover the entire state, which was a challenge since Barack still had legislative responsibilities. So she started to fill in. At an early February 2004 rally, she implored voters to send a message: "I am tired of just giving the political process over to the privileged. To the wealthy. To people with the right daddy," she said, in what were apparently references to Hull, who was wealthy, and Hynes, who was the son of a powerful Illinois politician. Also that month, she accepted an award on Barack's behalf from the Proviso West Suburban NAACP, saying, "This is an important election for so many reasons.

There are no people of color in the U.S. Senate and very few [in the Senate] are fighting for jobs and health care." By June 2004, with the general election underway, she was hosting fund-raisers on her own.

That same month, Barack got another break when his Republican opponent, Jack Ryan, faced a problem of his own. It was another marital scandal. When his divorce records were unsealed, it emerged that Ryan had allegedly tried to pressure his ex-wife into performing public sex acts at a sex club in Paris. Ryan eventually dropped out, but Michelle would continue stumping for her husband, appearing in Charleston, Illinois, urging voters not to consider the race a "done deal."

Michelle was also absorbing some new truths about politics, and about her husband's talent on the field. While it might appear that Obama had benefited from a spectacular run of luck—and he had—she later pointed out to me that many of these events could have been foreseen if you had the perspicacity to see them. "The thing that gets discounted about Barack is that he's incredibly smart, and not just book smart. He is strategic, and he's a quick study," she said. "He is a good measurer of people. And all of that goes into being able to assess any given situation—whether it's really looking at the chances in a political race, or whether it's calling the outcome of this [Iraq] war. You know, people would like to say that it's luck, but there is a lot that goes into reading the signs that are out there, and understanding what a moment feels like and looks like and how does it all add up." What she came to realize during the Senate race is that the liabilities of a candidate are often known in advance, but not printed or aired. There had been whispering about Hull's divorce records before the primary. David Axelrod, at the beginning of the race, had had meetings with Hull and had asked him if the rumors were true, and Hull's equivocal answer had unnerved him enough that he signed with Obama.

"As the candidate, you know more about the potential stuff than the public does," Michelle said to me, still sounding struck by this realization. "So you go into this race knowing all your opponents' issues, right? You even—the press even knows more than they are willing to say . . . This is why it's strategic—you look at who's running, you know where their backing is, you know whether their house is made of bricks or glass. The things that came to pass were completely known to everybody except the public. These were things that were talked about at the outset . . . To me, the interesting thing about it is that people pretend" they haven't heard the rumors.

This race, then, was Michelle's introduction to the role of political insider. And she would get her introduction to the national stage when, in the summer of 2004, the Democratic Party decided to give Obama some assistance in the general election by inviting him to make a certain speech. In the selection of the keynote speaker for the 2004 Democratic convention, many factors again fell into place for Barack. For one thing, the Kerry campaign made the mistake of declaring there would be no Bush-bashing in speeches, for fear of alienating swing voters. In deciding who should give the traditional keynote address, convention planners were in the unenviable position of trying to find someone who could galvanize a crowd without going negative—stoke up enthusiasm without throwing this partisan crowd the red, anti-Republican meat it craved. Organizers wanted a speaker who would be in the tradition of memorable keynoters of the past: Barbara Jordan, Mario Cuomo, Ann Richards, "people who inspired hope," as the political consultant Donna Brazile put it, "and not only inspired hope, but laid a framework for the party." As Brazile points out, the role of the keynoter is like that of John the Baptist or Paul Revere; it is the keynoter's role to announce the nominee, set the stage, define the message, create energy and anticipation. Convention organizers wanted someone who conveyed newness and diversity, someone who, as John Kerry put it, could impart "a message of inclusiveness and change, a new view about how we can make our politics more relevant to people and, in a sense, just put a little bit of different language in front of folks." Jennifer Granholm, the photogenic new governor of Michigan—and another Harvard Law School grad— was on the shortlist, and so were others, including Obama. His assets were that he was a great speaker, having improved much since his wordy beginnings; he added diversity to the speakers' lineup; and he was a Midwesterner from a major industrial state. Then again, the same qualities were true of Granholm.

The deciding factor was that the Democratic Party needed Obama to win that U.S. Senate seat and wanted to help him with some top-of-the-line national exposure. Though Ryan had now withdrawn, there was talk that some marquee Republican, possibly former Chicago Bears coach Mike Ditka, would enter the Illinois Senate race. The balance in the Senate was 51–48 in favor of Republicans. They needed to put Obama on stage.

When Michelle found out, she called her brother, Craig, who was on the road recruiting for the Brown basketball team but who set up his schedule so that he could watch the speech in his hotel room. The demands on Obama were extraordinary. He was stuck in Springfield, obliged to write his speech between votes and legislative duties, and he was campaigning for the Senate. "He's in the midst of being in Springfield, Illinois," recalled his communications director, Robert Gibbs. "Driving back and forth from Chicago to Springfield to do events up here, every couple of days. He's got the luxury of a little bit of thinking time in the car, [but] largely wrote the thing sitting in a hotel room in Springfield." Obama was working so hard and so feverishly that one morning he called Gibbs very early and said, "What do you think" of the changes?

"What changes?" Gibbs asked. Obama said he was talking about the changes he'd sent in the middle of the night. Up until that point, Gibbs says, he had been in the habit of checking his e-mail at about six-thirty. That's when he realized "a two-thirty A.M. e-mail" would no longer be uncommon.

Obama got the speech written, and the Kerry camp edited it, and there was much backing-and-forthing and then it was the day. The buzz had started, and he already was deluged with interview requests. It was Michelle's job, yet again, to stand there with the bucket of cold water. "He's had some attention in his life, and it's never gone to his head because we were raised with really pretty basic Midwestern values that it's who you are as a person and how you treat others that matters, and it's not the degree you hold or the position you hold," she told the *Chicago Daily Herald*. "All of this is very flattering, but he will not get a big head. We have a 6-year-old and a 3-year-old who couldn't care less about all of this, and he comes home to that every night." Before the speech, Michelle was in the green room with Barack, as were Illinois senator Dick Durbin and his wife. Before he went out, Obama would later write in *The Audacity of Hope*, Michelle told him, "Just don't screw it up, buddy!" As *The New Yorker* would later report, she actually played a bigger role than that. Earlier in the day, Barack had been practicing the speech, and began getting irate because people were giving advice and making comments and suggesting changes. Michelle assuaged his irritation with what came to be called the Look, a kind of nonverbal communication thing they do. "She was listening intently and, without being overly directive, was somebody that he could glance over to, almost a telepathic kind of relationship. He was clearly looking to her for reaction," *The New Yorker* quotes a source as saying. The source described how she calmed him down, and noted that "she was kind of handling both him as well as some of the speech."

When he took the stage, it took Obama a while to warm up and get the crowd in his corner. He began by talking about his mother and father, the diversity of his own heritage, how "in no other country on Earth is my story even possible." He spoke about issues—better government, health coverage, jobs, better care for veterans—and then delivered his famous call for unity and compassion, saying, "We are connected as one people. If there's a child on the South Side of Chicago who can't read, that matters to me, even if it's not my child." Dismissing the idea of "red states for Republicans, blue states for Democrats," he proclaimed that "we are one people, all of us pledging allegiance to the Stars and Stripes, all of us defending the United States of America." In making his stirring call for unity, he invoked his wife's own home neighborhood, making the case for social responsibility and mutual human obligation by reminding citizens that all was not well everywhere in America, and using the streets and projects and schools of her native South Side as an example. Michelle listened as Barack invoked the same vision—change, compassion, solidarity—he had laid out in that church basement. By the end of the speech, which nine million people saw on cable television, along with thousands of delegates and reporters in the convention hall, America had discovered the Barack Obama whom Michelle had always known, creating a whole new set of pressures.

The impact of the speech would forever change their lives. "It's like walking around with Michael Jordan now. It is. And maybe more so," Craig Robinson told me later, marveling at their inescapable celebrity. "People are paying more attention to this than to sports. My sister and Barack are now well-known people—life is completely different for them. You cannot imagine. Like the inability to go anywhere without somebody noticing them. That's the biggest thing. Most people—you can go anywhere and nobody would know who you are, and you go from that to everybody knowing you. It can be overwhelming and creepy and all of those things. It's great and it's not so great in some ways. It is what it is, and I think they're prepared for it." When he told me this in 2007, Craig had recently gotten his children together with Obama's for a family campaign event, mostly so the kids could see their cousins, something that used to happen often before Craig moved away and Obama got so famous and busy. "He and my sister would like their kids to have some semblance of normalcy in a completely abnormal situation."

It was more than a political rise; it was a political levitation. A political teleportation. Obama had been beamed up. He had ascended. Overnight he had become a household name. It's hard to think of a precedent. What political wife has had to adjust to this much intense publicity and fame, this quickly? For Michelle, it meant the man who was her husband now belonged, in a way, to the world. And to the Democratic Party. And to his campaign staff. Everybody wanted a piece of Barack Obama. Everybody wanted Barack Obama to make a speech, wanted Barack Obama to come to their fundraiser. Well before the convention, one of Barack's Senate campaign staffers had planned a multiday RV trip through downstate Illinois, a whistle-stop tour through a part of the state that had been somewhat neglected up to then. According to Shomon, Barack was under the impression that it would be a leisurely trip, a chance to relax and enjoy some family time. Michelle and the girls were coming along, and his idea was that it would consist of ice-cream cones for the girls and downtime for him.

Jeremiah Posedel, the staffer who organized the trip, says it was an effort, too, to bring Michelle in and make her a more visible part of the campaign. Up until then, he says, the campaign had used her sparingly, as the couple tried to figure out how to maintain a family life. But now they wanted to literally bring her on board. "The original goal behind the RV was to introduce the entire family" to voters statewide, says Posedel, now an attorney at McGuireWoods. By then, of course "everybody had seen Barack" and "this was more of an opportunity to introduce his entire family. The idea was that they were going to be in this RV hanging out and playing cards; we show up, and here's the family." It was supposed to be restful, meandering, fun; at one point, he recalls, Barack was even supposed to go fishing. "It didn't turn out that way."

Instead, it was a blur of speeches and rides and dealing with crowds far vaster than expected. Posedel in his zeal had studded the trip with stop after stop; they would visit more than thirty counties and cover 1,600 miles, more than three hundred miles a day, in five days. That's six to eight stops a day, and ten or twelve hours of driving and making appearances. "The point of this was to visit smaller counties in Illinois that you would not necessarily get to at any other time," says communications director Robert Gibbs. "It wasn't like Springfield or Peoria, it was the counties outside those counties that, again, you normally wouldn't get to." And what they quickly began to understand was that the crowds, now, were going to be of an entirely different order of magnitude.

"I remember that first day, we'd had almost no sleep, I flew back at six A.M., mostly because I was like holy shit, a five-day tour, I hope this thing is ready to go, and it was," says Gibbs. "I can remember, the first stop there were like five hundred people in this really small town, and you're like, wow, this is great. I can remember at the end of this day, we did six or seven stops, man, you've really touched something, and then I can remember the biggest affirmation, the next day, this is now Sunday late morning . . . You think to yourself, it's Sunday, we're not going to have the five or six or seven hundred people we had yesterday, we're going back to that hundred and fifty we had [before the convention]. And we turn into this state park, and there are more than a thousand people in this little amphitheater . . . Wow."

From the campaign's point of view, the RV trip was a revelation. From the point of view of Barack and the family, it was cruel and unusual punishment. He—and Michelle—had gone into the trip thinking it would be a nice bonding time, an opportunity to be together with the girls and do a little politicking. "The stress of the trip, and the madness around it, was showing on the ever-affable Michelle," wrote the *Chicago Tribune*'s David

Mendell, who was covering the trip, in his book. "At some moments on the trip, the tension between Michelle and her husband was palpable."

"He was just furious, he thought it was more of a death mission," recalls Dan Shomon, who was not on the trip but heard a lot about it from some of the other campaign staffers who went along. "It was supposed to be the kids traveling around eating ice cream and going to petting zoos. Barack was upset, he needed to spend time with the kids." Instead, Malia and Sasha were whisked away by staffers during the day, and Barack, who often had to get into a campaign vehicle and speed ahead, didn't see his family until the evening. "Barack was really not happy with me during the entire trip," says Posedel, who ended up spending a lot of time in the RV with Michelle. For all her exhaustion and frustration at being separated from her husband, Michelle tried to cheer Posedel up. "Michelle was the only one calming me down, saying 'Don't worry,'" he says. At the end of the trip, Barack thanked Posedel for doing such an energetic job, and, in a comment that has been widely reported, added, "Don't ever fucking do that to me again."

And this was the situation with which Michelle was now dealing; it was everybody's job to get Barack elected, and nobody's job but hers to protect his role as father and husband. She was now, in some ways, at cross-purposes with Obama's dynamic staff, trying to preserve even one day a week in which Barack Obama would belong to the Obama family and not to the Obama campaign. As it happened, the Republicans did not bring in Mike Ditka to run against him, but instead had the bad sense to bring in Alan Keyes, a conservative African American pundit, perennial candidate, and fire-and-brimstone political eccentric who was not a resident of Illinois. There are those who think this was the final star coming into alignment for Obama.

Despite the exhaustion of the downstate tour, Michelle would continue to help. The campaign would employ her as a surrogate, freeing Barack to travel the country, raising his own national profile as he raised money for Democrats in their own races. During her stump speeches, Michelle began to develop one of her themes: the difficulties facing the middle class, people like her mother and her late father. "I am here because I am a taxpayer, a mother, and the daughter of an elderly parent," she had said at a late June event in Charleston, Illinois. "I don't like the direction our country is taking when it comes to working for the middle class." She also would tell the audience why she fell in love with Barack, talking about that time he took her to the church basement and laid out his beliefs. She talked about how before she met him she thought he must be weird—communicating to the audience that it was okay if they initially thought so, too—emphasizing that she abandoned this idea once she got to know him. "I knew he was special and that he connected with the people," she told the crowd. "That is how I fell in love with him." She became a proxy for the voters; the idea was that they would travel the same emotional journey she had, feeling suspicious at first, then perceiving, as she did, his marvelous qualities.

In October 2004, a month before the election, the Associated Press wrote a story that focused on Michelle and the crucial role she was playing in the campaign. "I didn't expect it, but I embrace the responsibility that I think all of us have to be actively engaged in the political process," she said. "I can't sit at home and watch my husband spend 12-hour days and not roll up my sleeves and do what I can to further the cause." Gibbs told the AP that Michelle was "tremendously valuable" to the campaign because she increased its ability to connect with voters one-on-one. "This gives us a chance to be out there and meet twice as many voters," he said. The story also quoted a Republican, former U.S. Senate candidate James Durkin, observing shrewdly that Michelle's high-profile role suggested something about their long-range plans. "It may be the fact that their sights are bigger than Illinois and this is a team that is looking further down the road."

On election day 2004, the family got up and Malia said she was worried her father might lose. "Daddy's not going to lose," Michelle told her. They went as a family to cast their ballots. When they had to stand in a long line, Malia asked Barack, "People can't just walk in?"

"No," he explained. "They have to wait in line. It's a big election."

"Bigger than the last one?" she asked.

After they voted, Malia asked, "Are you going to run for president?"

It was of course the question on everybody's mind. People had started asking him that question the day after the keynote. After Obama won the Senate election, the question would be incessant, almost obligatory. Diane Sawyer asked. Tim Russert asked. Wolf Blitzer asked. The answer was always: Obama would serve out his six-year Senate term. "The first conversation about a presidential campaign was that there was not going to be a presidential campaign," Axelrod told me. Obama agrees: "We had very deliberately tried to tamp down expectations. I didn't do any national interviews until [Hurricane] Katrina. I'd tried to be very deliberate in terms of the work that I did here in the U.S. Senate. I didn't file a lot of symbolic bills—like a universal health-care bill or other legislation that I wasn't in a position to pass because we were in a minority party." And Michelle, she says, believed him. "You know, I'm like—no, no, no. I know he's not going to run for president," she told me in 2007. "I just know that. It doesn't make any sense. Not now."

After Obama won, Michelle had to decide whether to commit to being a senator's wife and move to Washington, maybe join the Senate Spouses' Club, sublimate her life and her career to his new position. She decided to stay in Hyde Park, reasoning that her support network—her mother and her friends—were there, and that Obama was the one who should make the adjustment and weather the airplane flights. Obama would later write about how much he missed his family, saying he had gotten so dependent on Michelle, it was hard for him to buy a shower curtain without her assistance. His national career was under way, but he had paid for it in a very expensive currency, that of domestic ease and routine family happiness. He would call the girls, forlornly, to hear their voices.

Their financial problems finally went away, thanks to

the fact that *Dreams from My Father* was reissued; one of his staff remembers seeing a publicist at the Democratic convention after the keynote, looking ecstatic, knowing that the job of publicizing a book by a person named Barack Obama had suddenly become a whole lot easier. In 2005, with the royalties from the first book and a nearly $2 million advance for future ones, the Obamas were able to buy a $1.6 million mansion in Kenwood, on a historical street in Hyde Park. Michelle was the force behind this; she wanted a "roomy refuge from the public trappings of fame," as Mendell put it. Later, when asked whether their lifestyles had been changed by his Senate win, Michelle said, "Our lifestyles have changed because he wrote a bestselling book. We were able to buy a house; we lived in a condo for the majority of our marriage. We were able to pay off our student loans. For the first time in our lives we are operating outside of debt. That's a new experience for us in our 40s."

They also underwent heightened scrutiny. On the same day that they bought the Kenwood house, the lot next door was purchased by the wife of Antoin "Tony" Rezko, a Chicago developer who at the time was under investigation by federal authorities for influence peddling. Rezko's wife sold them a strip of land for which they paid the market price, enabling them to enlarge their parcel. But it created the appearance of impropriety, raising the possibility that Obama was indebted to Rezko. Obama would call this financial arrangement "bone headed." *New York Times* columnist Maureen Dowd, in a later column, would thump Michelle, the Harvard lawyer, for not pointing out the problematic nature of accepting a favor from a person who is under legal investigation.

Michelle also had to contend with another inevitable aspect of politics: the female competition. The most unappealing men become wildly attractive once they are elected and powerful; in Washington, even "the ugliest men become Adonises," laughs Jo Minow, who lived there when her husband was FCC chairman and witnessed the phenomenon firsthand at dinner parties. Comparisons between Michelle Obama and the late Jackie Onassis are ambiguous praise, considering what Jackie had to put up with in terms of reckless marital infidelity in her role as first lady. But Obama is not, on this front, in the mold of JFK. When Barack was in the state senate and hung out at poker games, he was appalled when married men showed up with women who were not their wives. In 2002, he went to Washington, D.C., for a Congressional Black Caucus meeting, hoping to drum up support and pick up political pointers, and returned horrified to report that the conference was pretty much one long party, during which hotties unabashedly propositioned him and nobody wanted to talk to him about, say, the finer points of fund-raising.

Michelle saw the problem as soon as the convention speech was over. "This is what I have to contend with," she said to Mendell during the RV tour downstate, showing him a political cartoon that said, "Dated Dean, Married Kerry, Lust for Obama." Another time, a friend told Michelle that she'd overheard two women at their health club saying, "Let's go down and watch Barack Obama work out." All of which would be valuable mental and emotional preparation for Michelle. During the presidential race, she would have to confront "I've Got a Crush on Obama," the electronic mash-video that would be endlessly e-mailed, and that would baffle their daughters, who did not see it but absorbed the idea that there was a woman interested in their father and assumed it must be their mother.

It's a real issue and one that would give many wives pause, because not all men, as history has proven, can resist sexual opportunity. But Michelle asserts this is one challenge that does not put her off. "First of all, I can't control someone else's behavior," she told *Ebony*. She said she doesn't worry about "some other woman pushing up on my husband. I never worry about things I can't affect, and with fidelity . . . that is between Barack and me, and if somebody can come between us, we didn't have much to begin with." Valerie Jarrett put it a little more vividly. "He knows that if he messes up, she'll leave him," she told Mendell. "You know, she'll kill him first—and then she'll leave him. And I think there is a subtle element of fear on his part, which is good."

A friend confirmed that Barack also held this view, knowing just how his wife would react to a dalliance. "We would talk about temptation in Springfield," his friend and former colleague State Senator Kim Lightford told *Slate*. "And he would say, 'No, no, no, I would never [cheat]. Michelle would kick my butt. Not only would it not be worth it, but I would not want to have to deal with that.' "

"Michelle is *totally* in control," Lightford added. "She is friendly but very stern and sharp—stern is the only way I know to say it—and she is *very* involved in his decision making."

She would later make it clear, in speeches, what a strain the Senate race had placed on the family, and how, afterward, she hoped that they could coast for a while; push the "easy button," as she called it. She hoped, reasonably, that there might be an interstice of time in which Barack could get used to his new Senate career and life for them as a family could settle down into something resembling a normal schedule. But Barack was so sought after; in addition to his Senate duties, everybody wanted him at their fund-raisers, everybody wanted him to make a speech. And in his nonexistent free time, he also was writing *The Audacity of Hope,* his political manifesto, which would be published in 2006. People wanted Michelle to make speeches, too. The celebrity machine had claimed both of them.

In December 2005, after Barack had been in office for not quite a year, the *Chicago Tribune* did a piece on how things were going for both of them. It led with an anecdote about a time when Barack was supposed to be at a fund-raiser for the Florida Democratic Party, but Michelle told him he had to be at a holiday ballet recital of Malia and Sasha's. "You don't miss it," she said. So he watched the performance, drove to Midway Airport in Chicago, boarded a plane furnished by the Florida Democrats, and while he was in the air, according to the *Tribune,* "two members of his staff pacified nervous party officials who had raised their ticket price to $175 per plate simply because Obama's name was on the marquee." And it quoted an official saying, "I guess he negotiated with his wife and we figured out how to get him here."

That Christmas, Michelle and the kids went ahead to Hawaii and arrived there on December 16 without him. He was stuck in the Senate and would have to follow later. Sitting in his office, Obama said wistfully, "We'd be over the Pacific now." For much of 2005, he had seen the family only on long weekends, and, according to the *Tribune,* "even those were compromised" because of his promises to campaign for Democratic candidates in Virginia and New Jersey. Michelle was unhappy when he went to campaign for New Jersey's Jon Corzine. "It's a tough choice between, 'Do you stay for Malia's basketball game on Sunday or do you go to New Jersey and campaign for Corzine?'" Michelle had said in an interview before she left on vacation, speaking with some sarcasm. "Corzine got it this time around, but it's a constant pull to say, 'Hey guys, you have a family here.'" She had developed the tradition of keeping a family journal so Barack could stay in touch with the girls, just as she would later buy webcams for him and his daughters. But by the end of the year, he was occupied almost exclusively by politics. "The hope is that that is going to change and we're going to go back to our normal schedule of keeping Sundays pretty sacred," Michelle said during the *Tribune* interview, turning away from the reporter and looking directly at Robert Gibbs. Obama did take the girls, costumed as witches, to trick-or-treat for Halloween.

In a question-and-answer session published separately, Michelle was asked by then *Tribune* reporter Jeff Zeleny whether she ever felt like a single mother. "Oh, heck, yeah," she replied. "You know, at times it can be wearing, because you're on 24/7. Part of what we've had to figure out is what kind of support do I need to make my life less hectic? I'd like the support to come from Dad, but when it can't, I just really need the support. It doesn't really matter whether it's him or not as long as our kids are happy and they feel like they are connected to him. So I have to get over the fact that it's not him." Asked how the balance of time had worked, she said, "It's taken a good year to figure out what I, personally, can handle and I think Barack is figuring out the same thing." She did allow that it had been fun going to the red-carpet events with other celebrities, and she was still absorbing the fact that she and Barack were on the A-list now. "You have your element of star-watching, but what is interesting to me is when one of these stars is actually excited to see Barack. It's like, you're kidding, right? They are nervous, too! And I'm like, 'But you're Queen Latifah.' Or Barbara Walters, coming up to me saying, 'I just want to introduce myself to you.' I'm like, I know who you are."

Michelle, in that interview, also explained that a big part of her role in her husband's political career was to "tamp down expectations because they're not realistic." She said she didn't want people to pin all their hopes on Barack Obama, as a kind of one-man-save-the-world machine, because "there is still a lot of hard work that we as a country need to do. They can't look to any one individual."

Crucially, Zeleny asked what the future held for Obama. Michelle replied cautiously. "You can't get ahead of yourself in this thing because you lose focus on your effectiveness," she said. "And that involves family life. When you come home, the dishes have to be done; he has to make the bed and take the kids to school and the kids expect to get through *Harry Potter*." She had expertly deflected the question away from Barack's future to the state of the Obama household. So Zeleny tried again, asking whether she was willing to go along with "whatever the next step is." To this, Michelle said, "I'm not wrapping my arms around more than what we are doing right now. You have to wait and see what happens, what the future holds and what makes sense. Timing is everything."

10

Two major events helped shape the next big decision for the Obama family. The first was the publication, in October 2006, of *The Audacity of Hope: Thoughts on Reclaiming the American Dream*. The book laid out Obama's values and how he had arrived at them, his thoughts on everything from family and faith to race. But it was also an unusually frank assessment of his shortcomings as a family man—as if he were trying to inoculate himself against at least one case that could be made against him as a candidate. It was also, not incidentally, a mea culpa directed at Michelle, as if he were trying to bring her aboard the next adventure with the argument that if he could be this honest about his flaws, he could be trusted to try to fix them.

In the chapter on his family, he talks at length about the strengths he brings to his own family and the philosophy that informs it. "My marriage is intact and my family is provided for," Obama wrote. "I attend parent-teacher conferences and dance recitals, and my daughters bask in my adoration." He described a speech he had given one Father's Day, at Salem Baptist Church on the South Side, which took as its theme the topic of "what it takes to be a full-grown man." In it, he recalls, he "suggested that it was time that men in general and black men in particular put away their excuses for not being there for their families. I reminded the men in the audience that being a father meant more than fathering a child; that even those of us who were physically present in the home are often emotionally absent; that precisely because many of us didn't have fathers in the house we have to redouble our efforts to break the cycle; and that if we want to pass on high expectations to our children, we have to have higher expectations for ourselves." This type of speech—exhorting men, particularly African American men, to step up to their responsibility—would become a theme of his in Father's Day speeches.

But in the book he also turned his scrutiny on himself. "[O]f all the areas of my life, it is in my capacities as a husband and father that I entertain the most doubt." After all, he wrote, "thinking back on what I said, I ask myself sometimes how well I'm living up to my own exhortations." He described a life that keeps him on the road and away from Michelle and the kids for long stretches, and "that exposes Michelle to all sorts of stress." He said the price he has paid for his absences is that he sometimes feels like an interloper when he's home. "There are times when I get the sense that I'm encroaching on her space—that by my absences I may have forfeited certain rights to interfere in the world she has built."

Obama's book tour produced sold-out crowds and regular requests to run for president. Toward the end of it Barack and Michelle went on *Oprah*, an appearance that coincided with their fourteenth wedding anniversary, which, Obama said, they would celebrate over the following weekend because Michelle went to bed so early that there was no way they could celebrate that night. Michelle was asked, again, whether she felt like a single mother.

"You know, you always feel that way," she said honestly. "I mean, when you've got somebody who is traveling so much, that there's a level of that. That's always been the nature of the beast." But she added—diplomatically—that she appreciated what Barack did, and the way he treated her when he was at home. "It's not just the time but it's the intent, right? It's what he does and how he reflects the importance of our relationship when he is there." This is a point that Obama has also made, saying Michelle has impressed it upon him that, while flowers are always nice, what she most wants is his attention, his full presence.

On the show, they also shared two anecdotes from the book. In one, Obama talked about how he called home from the U.S. Senate one day to talk about a legislative triumph regarding arms control, and was informed by Michelle that there were ants in the house and he needed to stop at the drugstore on his way home and buy ant traps.

"I'm thinking, 'Is John McCain stopping by Walgreens to grab ant traps on the way home?'" Obama said.

"If he's not, he should be," Michelle interjected.

The other was about how she tries to get him to participate, at some level, in the organization of the girls' birthday parties, usually assigning him one of the more doable tasks, such as ordering the balloons or pizza. At one point, in a burst of ambition, Obama said, he went so far as to offer to get goody bags, and Michelle told him goody bags were way beyond his level of expertise. Explaining the complexities of goody-bag assembly and distribution, she told him it would be necessary to go to a party store and pick out assorted favors, and, moreover, that it is essential to do separate bags for girls and for boys. "I said, 'You'd walk into that party store and your head would explode,' " she related. "So I was like, 'You just leave the goody bags to me.' " Oprah asked if he was going to run for president, and he demurred. But he wouldn't do so much longer.

The other event that shaped the couple's big decision was a trip they took in the summer of 2006 that led the family to Ethiopia, Chad, Djibouti, South Africa, and Kenya. With a considerable press entourage in tow, Obama spoke out against the violence in Darfur, and, in Kenya, about government corruption. Health officials told Obama that it would be enormously influential if he were to publicly take an HIV test, as a way of normalizing HIV testing and encouraging African men to do the same, thereby, it was hoped, helping alleviate what has become a major health crisis in many African countries. Obama suggested Michelle get tested as well. "Barack thought it would be good for us to do it as a couple," she told a documentary film crew, "because it's really a couples issue, because it doesn't matter, if one half of the couple is tested [but] the other isn't." Gamely, Michelle rolled up her sleeve at a mobile health facility in Kenya and gave blood for the cause of public health. She also toured a massive Kenyan slum with him, describing it afterward as a way to "leverage" their visibility by forcing Kenyan officials to visit the slum and acknowledge its existence.

On this trip, the worship of Obama reached new heights. Citizens lined streets, perched on balconies, sat on outcroppings of building facades, eager and ultimately ecstatic to see a son of Kenya who had risen so far so fast, in the most powerful nation on earth. Adults and children alike chanted his name, and often sang it—*Obamaobamaobamaobama*—until it ceased being a name and became an ululation. There was drumming and dancing everywhere. "It was completely overwhelming, it's hard to describe unless you were there," Michelle told the film crew. "To see hundreds and hundreds and thousands and thousands of people just lining the streets of this very small town, cheering this man, my husband." She seemed stunned by the strangeness of witnessing what her husband—her husband!—had come to signify to the world now, or a portion of it. "It's sort of like—do you *know* him?" she said, one of her trademark feet-on-the-ground jokes. Then she added, "But it was very powerful." To reporters who were there, she also said, "It's hard to interpret what all of this means to me and means to us" as a family.

The trip also highlighted the demands the entire extended Obama family now faced, not just Michelle and Sasha and Malia. When the two of them had visited Kenya in 1992, Barack had taken Michelle to meet his paternal grandmother. "I had to make sure my new wife met the approval of Granny, and she said, 'She's good!'" he told a laughing crowd on the 2006 trip. The much-publicized return visit to his grandmother's homestead was supposed to last more than two hours but, because of chaos and delay, could only last about a half hour. "We really didn't have much time at all to spend with her, and that was a bit of a disappointment for her, having had all this built up only maybe to get 30 minutes to see him and talk to him," Michelle said, clearly able to empathize with what his grandmother was going through.

And it was a powerful trip for Obama. According to David Axelrod, the crowds in Africa "gave him a heightened sense of what he could accomplish." In late October 2006, Tim Russert asked Barack Obama again whether he would run for president in 2008. This time,

Obama acknowledged, "I have thought about it." When the November election returns came in, and it emerged that Democrats had won control of Congress, they sat down in earnest in Axelrod's office and began talking about a run. Michelle, as David Mendell puts it, was a major part of these discussions. Her public comments about feeling like a single mother had been an effective signal; the campaign knew that more comments like that could be damaging, and she needed to be brought on board. So she was, Mendell points out, "as a full partner."

Getting her agreement was paramount. Earlier that year, both Michelle and Barack attended a dinner for Facing History and Ourselves. Martha Minow remembers going over to Barack and asking about his presidential intentions. "I huddled with Barack and said, 'Are you going to run?'" Minow recalls. "And he said, 'There's one answer: It's up to Michelle. Go talk to her.' So I went to Michelle's table, and we were talking about the kids, and I thanked her for all the help she'd [given] with Facing History. And I said, 'So, is Barack going to run?' and she said, 'We're having serious family discussions about it.' She was clearly in the midst of weighing it. I just said, 'It would be so great for the country.' I was very sympathetic about what it would mean for the family." She thinks Michelle's chief hesitation had to do with the toll it would take on the kids. "She was concerned— two young children."

"She's also concerned for his safety," said Jo Minow. "Don't kid yourself."

And she was. During the early days after the keynote speech, David Mendell, who was covering Obama's Senate campaign, had been struck by the people who now would come to listen to his speeches, a few of whom did not look entirely stable. Now that presidential discussions were underway, he mentioned the oddball onlookers to Michelle, wondering if she worried about Barack's safety. "I don't worry about it every day, but it's there. And it's a nonstarter," she said. "So if we take this next step, there would have to be a comprehensive security plan in place . . . It only takes one person and it only takes one incident. I mean, I know history too."

Michelle would later say, of herself, that she goes down "every dark road" before making a decision, and it seems clear that she had. The possibilities included not only something happening to her husband, but the public scrutiny now being given to her. Back in 2004, when they were both little known outside Illinois, media attention given to Michelle consisted of feature reporters asking about her cooking habits ("As far as entertaining, if you want to sit down for a meal, we're coming over to your house") and soliciting a favorite recipe (macaroni-and-cheese casserole) for a warm holiday article. Now the questions were about her salary, her job, her board memberships. In December 2006, *Crain's Chicago Business* wrote a piece highlighting the fact that she served on the board of a company, TreeHouse Foods, that did business with Wal-Mart, which Obama had singled out with criticism for its labor practices. TreeHouse is a supplier to private-label and food service industries. In 2005, the company announced it would close a pickle plant in La Junta, Colorado. The plant was a valued employer in the town, which had a population of just 9,500. More than a hundred and fifty workers lost their jobs, many of them Hispanic—hardly a good advertisement for somebody worried about the erosion of working-class jobs. The mayor of the town, Don Rizzuto, said he wished the Obamas would visit to see what the closure had done to the town. "If she and her husband are the champion of the little guy, it's amazing what they're doing."

"While Mr. Obama bashes Wal-Mart, why does his wife, Michelle, make $45,000 a year serving on the board of a Chicago-area company that pays its executives a very hefty amount of money while laying off mostly minority workers in an economically deprived area, a company whose No. 1 customer is—you guessed it, Wal-Mart?" wondered *Crain's*, pointing out that she was elected to its board of directors in June 2005, not six months after Obama took his position in the Senate. *Crain's* said, based on an interview with her, that Michelle had been asked to join the board after putting out "feelers indicating she'd like to get some corporate management experience." She is quoted saying, "My income is pretty low compared to my peers. You wouldn't ask that question if, like some people in politics, we had trust funds and were rich."

"Michelle and I have to live in the world and pay taxes and pay for our kids and save for retirement" just like other people, Barack Obama told the business journal.

Also that fall, the *Chicago Tribune* wrote a piece, based on released tax returns, pointing out that her salary more than doubled after Barack was sworn in. In March 2005, she had been promoted to vice president for community and external affairs at University of Chicago Hospitals, and got a raise from $121,910 to $316,962. Hospital officials said this was a normal promotion; she had been there for four years, and when they hired her, said Michael Riordan, who was president of the hospital at the time, they had intended to expand her role and deepen the institution's connection to the community. "She is worth her weight in gold, and she is just terrific," Riordan said. A hospital spokesman said that executives had discussed a promotion with her previously, but she had been reluctant to take on more duties during the campaign. Officials pointed out that she had expanded its women and minority vendor program, rejuvenated its volunteer program, and set up a collaborative program with South Side doctors and clinics to steer people away from emergency rooms and into primary care. The latter assignment was a delicate ambassadorial act that only somebody with Michelle's background could pull off. Poor patients are prone to seek routine medical care in hospital emergency rooms, often because they don't have health insurance. In her position, it was Michelle's extremely diplomatic task to steer them away from last-minute emergency care, which is expensive, and into clinics, without making them feel as though they had been rejected or driven away. She has done a good job. Al Kindle recalls being involved in a community health fair whose purpose was to bring health-care services to poorer residents. The fair offered vaccinations for schoolchildren; eye, ear, nose, and throat examinations; and a number of other health-related services. Like many people, he found Michelle to be a crackerjack administrator. "She is a very meticulous, hard-nosed administrator who really knew her business."

Critics would point out that it is expensive vice-presidential administrative positions like hers that help explain why hospital bills are so high. And they would try to make the case that she was exploiting her husband's power. The *Chicago Sun-Times* also wrote about the salary issue, quoting hospital executives saying that some portion of her 2005 salary had been a onetime pension payout and a bonus. In that article, the hospital pointed out that she had expanded a two-person staff to seventeen, increased the number of volunteers, and quadrupled the number of employees volunteering in the community. But the Chicago political consultant Joe Novak was quoted with regard to TreeHouse saying, "She got on the corporate board of someplace where she could make money, and make money quickly. She's cashing in because of her husband." An Obama spokesman said she applied for the TreeHouse post after a friend who consults for companies seeking to increase minorities on their boards told her about the opening. The criticism stung. "I need to be able to take care of myself and my kids," she told author David Mendell. "I have to be in a position that if anything unexpected or unfortunate happens, where are all those people who are being critical of my credentials or my ability to serve on boards, where are they going to be if I have to take care of my kids? There would be great sympathy and outpouring if something were to happen, but I have to maintain some level of professional credibility not only because I enjoy it, but I don't want to be in a position one day where I am vulnerable with my children. I need to be in a position for my kids where, if they lose their father, they don't lose everything."

For all the pain the attention brought her, Michelle allowed the conversation about a presidential run to continue. Shortly before Christmas 2006, Barack met with Newton Minow and Abner Mikva to discuss it. Minow was for going ahead. Initially he had not been, but he had watched Obama in a recent televised speech and felt that he was ready. Plus, this was an open seat, as in the 2004 Senate race. "Michelle's not keen about this," Minow remembers Obama saying. He and Mikva each have three grown daughters. As fathers who had both been in public life, they advised Obama that it made more sense to run when the girls were younger, and would be insulated from the campaign. They also urged him to get protection. "Abner said, 'I know it's expensive, but you've got to hire bodyguards to go with you all the time,'" Newton Minow remembers. Minow says Obama did.

For his part, Mikva remembers that one of Michelle's

aims was to make sure the campaign was plausible; the detail-oriented member of the household wanted to be sure it would be well run, and that her husband had a realistic chance of winning. "It wasn't that she didn't want him to run—clearly he had this burning desire—but she wanted to make sure that it was" well organized, says Mikva. "That was her biggest concern—not that she was trying to stop him, but make sure that if he did it, they had a chance of winning." When Axelrod agreed to put his heart and soul into it, she felt reassured.

Axelrod himself remembers that Michelle's main concern had been pragmatic. "She was interested in whether it was a crazy, harebrained idea. Because she's not into crazy, harebrained ideas." In the end, Axelrod talked her into it, in a series of meetings during which they discussed safety and logistics and strategy and everything else, and he assured her they had a plan as well as a real shot at victory. "Suffusing these discussions was, if we did it, she and he both wanted to make sure it was consistent with who he is and what he thinks, and wouldn't distort that," Axelrod would later say. He pointed out that Michelle wanted to make sure they wouldn't lose themselves in the process. "Michelle has always been in the camp of, 'Let's not forget what we're fighting for.'"

Michelle told me she made sure to think through all

the impediments and dangers they would face—from the financial burdens of a run to its practical implications for the girls, and everything in between. "My comfort zone comes from understanding the plan. How am I going to make my way through the many obstacles that will be there for myself individually, for my children, for us as a family? For me, I have to work those things out, get answers to questions, search my heart. That was the process. It involves all the aspects you will imagine. How do we manage this in terms of time, what happens to my career? How are we going to manage this financially? What most people don't understand—politics is a millionaire's game. It requires you to have resources. Even being in the U.S. Senate you've got to have a home in your home state and in Washington, you have to be able to afford two mortgages. We would have conversations— how are we going to do this? Real practical conversations. Where are we going to live, where would the kids go to school. For me it's all very practical, on-the-ground kinds of concerns. One by one, they were addressed."

And, she said, "Here we are."

She would later imply that it was Barack who had allayed some of these final concerns during their Christmas vacation. "When you're in Hawaii, on a beach," she would tell a crowd in Iowa, "everything looks possible."

11

A<small>T FIRST, PEOPLE WONDERED WHAT HER ROLE</small> would be and whether she was happy with the decision. In January 2007, Obama announced he would form a presidential exploratory committee, and, in an article later that month, *Newsweek* noted that "Michelle was out of sight" even as "many Democrats wondered what she thought of her husband's big leap." In the weeks before the announcement, "Obama seemed to stiffen when asked what his wife thought of a presidential run." But it didn't take her long to become involved. On February 5, 2007, five days before Barack declared his candidacy, she moved to a part-time position at the University of Chicago Hospitals so she could devote more time to the campaign. On February 10, she, Malia, and Sasha were on hand for his official announcement before a crowd of seventeen thousand in Springfield. And she appeared by his side in a *60 Minutes* interview that aired that weekend, showcasing her refreshingly candid humor.

Chatting with interviewer Steve Kroft, she said the girls were fine with the race because it meant they could get a dog. That has pretty much been their main practical concern. They had been angling for a long time; in 2005, they had toured the White House and the chief memory they brought away was that a dog lived there: George Bush's dog, Barney. And now the race had given the girls the bargaining chip they needed. Michelle also described the new leverage she herself had on Obama: She announced she had told him he had to quit smoking if he entered the race. "That was one of my prerequisites for entering into this race is that he couldn't be a smoking president," said Michelle. Kroft pointed out that lots of Americans would now be watching to see if he kept to his nonsmoking vow.

"Absolutely, please, America, watch," Michelle invited. "Keep an eye on him and call me if you see him smoking."

It was Michelle at her best—funny, spontaneous, surprising, girlfriendy, confiding, letting America in on the domestic dynamics of her household, enlisting televisionland in her campaign to help this guy, Barack Obama, her husband, kick the habit. According to her friends, it is this same swift wit she displays in the gym, at lunches, cracking people up—the true child of Fraser Robinson. "My sense is that he is deliberate and thoughtful, and Michelle is much more easygoing, incredibly funny, a little more shoot-from-the-hip," is how a friend and fellow Lab Schools parent describes her. "She is down-to-earth and incredibly funny."

But the interview also highlighted how that spontaneity and candor can land her in controversial territory. When Kroft pointed out that Alma Powell had asked her husband, Colin Powell, not to run for president out of fear of "some crazy person with a gun," Michelle acknowledged the danger but dismissed it. She ventured to say that Barack's vulnerability was the same as that of any black man, no more, no less.

"I don't lose sleep over it," she said. "Because the realities are that as a black man Barack can get shot going to the gas station, you know, so you—you can't—you know, you can't make decisions based on fear and the possibility of what might happen. We just weren't raised that way."

The comment was a little jarring; while it did deflect attention away from Barack's special vulnerability as a candidate, the implication was that every black man is at risk every time he gets out of his car to pump gas. The effect was to suggest that Michelle took a very dim view of the country's racial climate, regarding black men as being vulnerable to physical harm in any public situation. One reporter would describe this as evidence of her "abiding race consciousness."

Nevertheless, Michelle was now taking her first steps as the onstage, in-the-limelight partner of a presidential contender. She started out small, often speaking for a few minutes before introducing her husband. Then in March 2007, she hosted her first solo event—a house party in Iowa at the home of Willie Glanton, Iowa's first black legislator. A month later, in April, she debuted in her first solo fund-raiser, an event in Chicago that was aimed at women, as many of her speaking engagements would be. She brought in about $750,000, according to news reports. From April on, the majority of her appearances would be solo, although the whole family would sometimes take trips to early states. With rare exceptions, her stump speeches were—and have remained—the same: Michelle starts by talking about herself, a girl from the South Side who had a father with a disability who was proud he could afford to send his children to Princeton on a city salary. Audiences heard the familiar refrain, "I'm still that little girl who grew up on the South Side of Chicago," emphasizing her middle-America, working-class roots. As the campaign progressed, and getting out the vote became paramount, audiences would also hear her invoke Fraser Robinson's work as a precinct captain, as Michelle minimized her initial skepticism about politics and talked about learning the importance of voting while sitting in kitchens and listening to her father as he did his precinct work.

Toward the beginning of the primary campaign, when Barack's support among African Americans was still relatively weak and many black voters were supporting Hillary Clinton, or were undecided, the question of whether he was "black enough" also frequently surfaced in her stump speech. These questions had of course been in play for a while now, and rather than let the question linger into his presidential race, Michelle addressed it right off the bat.

"I heard that growing up, 'You talk like a white girl,'" she said in April 2007, her first interview with the *Chicago Tribune* in the presidential race. "There isn't one black person who doesn't understand that dynamic. That debate is about the pain that we still struggle with in this country, and Barack knows that more than any-one." Essentially, she was objecting to the idea that blackness is something that derives from street credibil-ity or poverty or lack of education or how you walk or how you talk. In doing so, she raised what is, for her, an-other crucial theme: "One of the things I hope happens through our involvement in this campaign is that this country and this world sees yet another image of what it means to be black."

And doubtless, this is something she has magnifi-cently accomplished. As Whoopi Goldberg would point out later, during Michelle's television appearance on *The View*, "Any time you see black folks on the news, particu-larly women, they have no teeth, and the teeth that they have have gold around them and they can't put a sen-tence together. You're helping change a perception. I know it sounds funny and silly . . . I just want to say thanks."

Another prominent theme of her speeches was the politics of fear, which she defined as narrowly or as broadly as she required, depending on the audience. It could mean the fear blacks had for the electoral fate of any African American running for president. Sent to South Carolina to court black audiences during the pri-maries, she used the image of plastic on furniture as a metaphor for fear and self-protection. She described it as a legacy of discrimination, of not believing you will be permitted to reach a certain goal, and therefore not trying. In these trips, she was narrowcasting—addressing the black electorate and its concerns, freeing her husband to seem more postracial, or even nonracial in his self-presentation. "What we are dealing with in the black community is just the natural fear of possibility," she told MSNBC in November 2007. "That's the psychology that's going on in our heads and in our souls and I understand it. I know where it comes from, you know, and I think that it's one of the horrible legacies of racism and discrimination and oppression. It keeps people down in their souls in a way, you know, where they sometimes can't move beyond it." But at one point, when she predicted that "black America will wake up and get it," she was criticized for suggesting blacks should automatically vote for Obama because of his race. In the *60 Minutes* interview, Obama himself had said he did not assume black voters would back him out of racial solidarity, and allowed that he had to earn their support, like that of all voters.

Other times, she expanded the definition of fear beyond its expression among blacks, describing a more inchoate version gripping much of America under the

Bush administration. "I don't want to raise my children in a country that's motivated by fear," she said. In Reno in August 2007, she cataloged the fears afflicting the country: "Fear the war, fear terrorists, fear people around the country, fear people who don't look like you, who don't pray to the same God as you." After discussing the flaws of the system, she would offer Barack as an example of a more confident future. "We need a different kind of leadership than we've seen in my lifetime," she said at a New Hampshire event in December 2007. "There's only one person in this race who can do that, and that is my husband." In Vermont, she said, "We are new to politics in terms of just this approach—how we talk, how we look, how we—imagine having a president of the United States who is just two years out of college debt and understands that. Imagine that!"

As this last comment suggests, she also emphasized her husband as a regular guy, a mortal, a person beset by bills and mortgages, a man who is less impressive on the home front than he appears in the klieg lights. As the campaign wore on, she would do this in a very specific attempt to deflect criticism that the Obamas were cultural elitists, talking a lot about her working-class roots, a lot about those student loans, a lot about how they felt connected to working-class hardship despite the fact that thanks to his books, they were now making over a million dollars a year. In 2006, the Obamas brought in $991,296. Obama earned $157,082 from his Senate salary, and Michelle earned $273,618 from the University of Chicago. The rest of their income was royalties, investments, and her TreeHouse compensation.

"I'm always humbled and, quite frankly, surprised by the reaction my husband gets when he goes around the country," she said at a March 2007 event in New York. "Don't get me wrong, I think my husband is a wonderful man with many skills and talents and he can take us to new places. He's a man who's just awesome, but he's still a man." In a kind of have-your-cake-and-eat-it-too delivery, she would contrast the Barack Obama the country sees to the Barack Obama she knows at home, making sure to list his credentials before deflating them.

"There's Barack Obama the phenomenon, Barack Obama the genius, the editor of the *Harvard Law Review,* the constitutional law scholar, the civil rights attorney, the community organizer, the bestselling author, the Grammy winner. This Barack Obama guy's pretty impressive," she said in New York. "Then"—she paused—"there's the Barack Obama that lives in my house."

To laughter, she continued, "That guy's not as impres-

sive. He still has trouble putting the bread up and putting his socks actually in the dirty clothes and he still
doesn't do a better job than our 5-year-old daughter
Sasha making his bed. So you have to forgive me if I'm a
little stunned by this whole Barack Obama thing."
Throughout her speeches, she would weave in personal
stories about his endearing domestic failings, and at the
end of events, voters would often remark upon how Michelle seemed so warm and authentic, so normal.

The approach backfired a little. In April 2007, *New
York Times* columnist Maureen Dowd took aim at this
part of Michelle's delivery, citing those who found her
comments "emasculating" and "casting her husband—
under fire for lacking experience—as an undisciplined
child." Dowd herself would catch fire for this. Her column was regarded by some as feeding the stereotype of
black women as bossy. Michelle brushed off Dowd's
criticism. "OK, well, she obviously doesn't know who I
am, and she doesn't understand. I get way more affirmation, right? I was in a roomful of hugs today."

But after the Dowd incident, Michelle seemed to
tweak that aspect of her speech. Instead of describing
Barack's faults, she would describe the two of them as
opposites who complement each other. Michelle sought
to portray herself as her husband's anchor. Although he

might be a dreamer, she was the realistic half who kept him grounded. "Barack's eyes are focused on the sky— but as his wife, let me assure you that his family is keeping his feet planted firmly on the ground as well," she wrote in a promotional direct-mail piece that appeared in May 2007, which also deployed the ant-trap anecdote.

She also fought hard to counter the notion that Barack lacked political experience. The topic made an appearance in almost every speech she gave after the Illinois announcement; she brought it up at the kickoff fund-raiser, saying, "A leader is more than a set of finite experiences." Only in the world of politics "would insiders dare to look at those accomplishments and dare to have the audacity to say he is not ready," she said, underlining her disdain for politics. She refined that point at a May 2007 campaign event in Winham, New Hampshire, saying, "I know that experience is important but experience without the sort of moral compass is not enough." At a June event in Harlem, she took to listing his résumé, saying, "Name me one other candidate who has organized in the community, name me one other candidate who has been a civil rights attorney."

She would often turn the argument around and direct it back onto those who were questioning Barack's credentials. Sometimes she sounded as if she blamed the country. "He is the real thing," she said at an Iowa event in July. "Because he's ready. It's whether we're ready." Sometimes she blamed Washington. "Barack doesn't have years of experience in Washington, that is true," she said in August 2007 in Nevada. "But my position is we've seen [people with] years in Washington, and they haven't gotten us where we need to be." And sometimes, she appeared to blame discrimination and racial prejudice. "If we lived anywhere else on the planet, a man with the credentials and the commitment and the ability of Barack Obama, we wouldn't have any questions," she told a crowd in Illinois; her comments were quoted in a profile in *Jet*. "He didn't just go to law school, he was the top of the top of the top of the law school—the first black man to achieve that goal. Do you think if any other person had those achievements, they would question him?" In her "anywhere else on the planet" comment, she seems to imply that America is the only country in the world where a man like Barack Obama would meet with any resistance at all. The implication is that every other country is ushering black men with a minimum of political experience into high office. It's a brief remark, but a little at odds with the facts on the ground. And it's in stark contrast to Barack's own observation that "only in America is my story possible." In a way, she seems to be saying the opposite—only in America would Barack Obama be given such a hard time.

This was a running theme of her narrative, the idea that there is something vaguely wrong with contemporary America. Rather than criticize the Republican Party or his Democratic primary opponents, she often went after the electorate itself. "We are still too divided," she said in South Carolina in January 2008. "We are still a nation that is too cynical . . . We're mean." Some of the same sentiment is conveyed when she criticizes the country for not being ready for Obama. "If we're not ready, then it won't matter who is in the Oval Office," she said in Iowa in December 2007, implying that the country needs to change something about itself rather than just change its leader. "Barack can't lead a nation that is not ready to be led." In another: "We are our own evil. We have to be engaged and passionate." To a crowd in Monticello, she said, "You've never seen anyone like us before, and that's a little freaky, isn't it? It's like, 'They're real!' Well, guess what? Real people can be politicians, too. We as a country have grown suspicious of real. We take the fake." *We as a country. We take the fake.* Her argument, often, is not that something is wrong with Barack's opponents, but that something is wrong with us all.

While conservatives prefer to highlight this message as evidence of condescension, and even a lack of patriotism, they fail to point out all the ways Michelle talks about the experiences that unite Americans, which are an occasion for solidarity between her and her audience. Michelle's most vivid and successful speeches tend to be directed at women and focus on work imbalance on the home front. These bring out all her comic, Borscht Belt, take-my-husband-please talents. One of her chief duties as a campaign surrogate was—and remains—courting the female vote, a role that would become even more important after Obama won the primaries and the campaign faced the considerable task of winning back disappointed Hillary Clinton supporters. In a 2007 interview with the *Hyde Park Herald,* she laid out her program, talking about how, as she had gotten older, issues of work and family had taken on a new urgency.

"Now, I am more passionate about issues of family life and balance for women because that is something I am experiencing and struggling with," she said. "We make it hard for families. I wonder every day how nurses do it, how bus drivers do it, how everyday people who are getting up and going to work do it? . . . We have to give them resources. You can't be at the parent-teacher conference at school when you have five personal days and some sick days off at work. I can duck out of work and run around to school. But what about the families who can't?"

This encapsulates what she says in her speeches. After discussing her own life, Michelle uses that as a transition to talk about life in America for working parents, especially working women, arguing that government policies have done little to help them. "We've been told to dream big, but after that you're on your own." Sometimes, she invites her listeners to help one another. "If there was a woman in your life that you have not communicated with because of ego or embarrassment or jealousy or fear of rejection, a sister or a friend or a mother or a child who could or should be a part of your community, I ask you to reach out to that woman today," she exhorted one South Carolina church. To great acclaim, she often shares the toilet truth, saying how, when the going gets tough and the toilet overflows, the men are the ones to get going and the women are the ones juggling their work schedules so as to be there for the plumber.

She waxes both funny and plaintive in describing the plight of the modern mother, accommodating the lapses and inefficiencies of her hapless partner. "Forgive me to the men in the room, but those jobs still fall disproportionately on the laps of women, those jobs like laundry doer, breakfast cooker, discipline handing-outer—and as we see the bills pile up and things not coming together, we have that added responsibility of late-night worrying that so many of us have been faced with, and like many of you I have often stood back and wished for that magical machine that would extend the day," she said at a July 2008 event in the depressed industrial town of Pontiac, Michigan.

It was an event that showed all her theatrical and talk-show-host skills. There, several hundred women, many of them African American, had crammed into the downstairs as well as the balcony of Crofoot, a groovy downtown bar and music club, to eat barbecue sandwiches out of boxes. The speech was part of a listening tour she had been doing urging people to share their struggles. The stage had been transformed into a chat-show venue: There were chairs and a white couch, and twenty-odd people sitting behind her—local dignitaries as well as women ready to testify to their domestic and on-the-job hardships under eight years of Republican rule. Michelle, who was introduced by Michigan Governor Jennifer Granholm, took the stage wearing a dark shift that came down to her knees, showing her bare calves, and matching open-toed dark pumps. At her chest was ornamental beadwork, the only concession she made to adornment. She talked about her central identity as a mother, saying, "There isn't a moment that goes by that I am not thinking about my girls; they are the first thing that I think about when I wake up in the morning, and the last thing I think about when I go to bed." She shared her view that things used to be easier for families, talking, as always, about Fraser Robinson, and how "back then, that single salary could support a family of four, and my mother stayed home and took care of me and my family, because she could." In contrast, she said, the modern mother is torn. "When I'm at work I'm guilty because I am not with my girls, and when I'm with my girls, I'm thinking I should be doing more to help the campaign." She described this as a feeling "that we all live with." She listened to women who poured out a host of troubles, including breast cancer, layoffs, and grandchildren who needed raising. Throughout, she assured them that Barack sympathized. "The people he loves most—the women in his life—he has seen us all struggle with these issues ... Barack carries our stories, our stories as women ... these stories have really shaped who he has become as a man, they've shaped almost every decision he has made in his life, every action he has taken." She assured the crowd that "as president, Barack is going to expand family and medical leave" so that "millions of Americans are able to take some time off when a baby gets sick or an elderly parent needs taking care of. Maybe take a few hours off to attend a child's play. Imagine that!" The crowd responded warmly. "Raise your hands if you or someone you know has been downsized, or offshored, or lost your job in the auto industry," she said, and virtually all hands in the room went up. She made them laugh; when asked a specific policy question, she demurred, saying she tries to avoid getting his policies wrong. "He would be like, 'You said what?'" and "I'm like, 'I said you're going to do this,'" she said, doing a quick theatrical imitation of that conversation.

In her case, of course, the domestic front is unusually hard to manage because of the pressures of her husband's campaign. She freely says that she doesn't believe it is possible to have it all. Certainly, it's not possible for her to be a mother and to campaign for him and to work. So in May 2007, Michelle decided to dial back her workload by 80 percent and would later take a complete leave to campaign full-time. "Michelle had worked so hard to get where she was. I kind of feel bad for her," said her mother, Marian. In the spring of 2007, she also resigned from TreeHouse foods. The *New York Times* wrote an article on her decision to step down, reporting that earlier in the year, when her staff had noticed a coffee-table book about her husband's accomplishments, they made one for Michelle about her own, and she cried when she saw it.

In the online magazine *Salon,* Debra Dickerson, a political commentator who is African American, noted these developments with dismay, deploring the fact that an accomplished and superproductive woman—a woman often described as being as smart as, or smarter than, her husband—was forced to give up her own prospects to further his. "She's traded in her solid gold résumé, high-octane talent and role as vice president of community and external affairs at the University of Chicago Hospitals to be a professional wife and hostess," Dickerson said, worrying that any day now, "Michelle Obama's handlers will have her glued into one of those Sunday go-to-meeting Baptist grandma crown hats while smiling vapidly for hours at a time." Dickerson imagined her having to start every sentence saying "My husband and I," adding, "My heart breaks for her." While she was in a "feminist fury," she didn't blame Michelle. She blamed a system where it's assumed a woman's career is expendable and secondary, and she blamed the black community for assuming that she should make the sacrifice.

"Few could stand up to the pressure she's facing, especially from blacks, to sacrifice herself on the altar of her husband's ambition," she continued. "He could be the first black president, you know!" Dickerson objects to the idea that "women's lives must be subordinate to everyone else's."

But Michelle has never really committed to any one career. She does not have a passionate professional calling, unlike, say, Judith Steinberg Dean, Howard Dean's wife, who in 2004 said she would not give up her medical practice if her husband became president because her own patients needed her. Michelle is a talented administrator, but you don't get the idea that she ended up doing public relations for a hospital system because that's what she always wanted to do. She ended up doing it because it paid well, because she did it well—"I like cultures. I like team-building," she once said—and because it enabled her to help the community by making the hospital more responsive. Social change is her passion, and Barack is now the vehicle for that. Electing him, now, is her job; her job is being a key player in an exciting historical campaign for the presidency of the most powerful nation on earth.

Along the way, there were mistakes. Michelle made some slips, most minor, that were the subject of campaign retractions. In an interview with *Glamour*, she talked about how the girls didn't like to get into bed with her in the morning if Barack was there, because he's too "snorey and stinky." This was widely regarded as too humbling, too uncharitable, as well as being more than most of us wanted to know about anybody, let alone the potential leader of the free world, in the morning. In an interview with *Vanity Fair,* she insisted that this would be Barack's only run at the presidency, America's one chance to elect him as its leader.

"To me, it's now or never," she said. "We're not going to keep running and running and running, because at some point you do get the life beaten out of you. It hasn't been beaten out of us yet. We need to be in there now, while we're still fresh and open and fearless and bold. You lose some of that over time. Barack is not cautious yet; he's ready to change the world, and we need that. So if we're going to be cautious, I'd rather let somebody else do it, because that's a big investment of time, just to do it the same way. There's an inconvenience factor there, and if we're going to uproot our lives, then let's hopefully make a real big dent in what it means to be president of the United States."

She was criticized for remarks like "inconvenience factor," which suggested that seeking the opportunity to live in the White House felt, to her, mostly like a drag on her family time. And this was not a onetime comment; over and over, Michelle makes it clear that this race has been an enormous sacrifice for them as a family. And it has—but not all political wives make a point of this. Lauren Collins, in *The New Yorker,* observed that there is "strategic genius" in the way Michelle makes crowds feel she is doing them a favor by coming out to see them, rather than vice versa. After the *Vanity Fair* comment, Michelle explained that she said "now or never" because she felt they would never again be this close to the lives most people are living.

In truth, her "now or never" attitude seems in character with what she has always told Barack, or at least told herself: Next time, he won't do it. This is the last race! If Barack runs and doesn't win, our lives will return to normal! A remark like that could be seen as a threat to withdraw Barack's excellence if the country doesn't recognize it, or it could be seen as yet another episode of Michelle convincing herself that someday, the man she married will stop running so hard. The woman who describes herself laughingly as "always the last one to get a clue" seems to be telling herself what she has always said: Okay, buster, this is the last race you get to run. Later, she would tell the *Wall Street Journal,* "It wasn't a threat—but to do this again? Put these two girls through this again?"

Along the way there were a few other kerfuffles: At an event in Atlantic, Iowa, in August 2007, Michelle made what was widely perceived as a sly and faintly uncharitable dig at Hillary Clinton. "One of the most important things that we need to know about the next president of the United States is, is he somebody that shares our values, is he somebody that respects family, is he a good and decent person?" she said. "So our view is that if you can't run your own house, you certainly can't run the White House. So we've adjusted our schedule to make sure our girls are first, so when he's traveling around, I do day trips." A *Chicago Sun-Times* columnist reported her comment but left out that final sentence, interpreting "if you can't run your own house" as a subtle reference to Bill Clinton's history of marital infidelity. The campaign objected, clarifying the comment the next day by releasing her full statement. But the quote got a lot of play on blogs and television, which always delight in a possible catfight.

There was another small set-to at an event in September 2007, when Michelle tried to impart how important Iowa was to the campaign. "If Barack doesn't win Iowa, it's just a dream," she said. While several commentators admired her candor, the campaign hastily made it clear that they believed that Obama did have a political future, Iowa or no Iowa.

But despite these brushfires, things, basically, were going well. She had quit her job and taken on this one, and her role, in fact, was significant. Next to David Axelrod, she is Obama's chief adviser, part of a very small inner circle. On February 11, 2008, the *Wall Street Journal* analyzed how MICHELLE OBAMA SOLIDIFIES HER ROLE IN THE ELECTION, leading with an anecdote about how, during a campaign conference call, she broke into the discussion saying, "Barack, feel—don't think!" Many news analyses pointed out that she was so successful at getting primary voters to commit to Obama, she had become known as "the closer." *US News & World Report* wrote about her in "From the Soccer Field to the Stump," observing how real she was, how natural, how she would joke about finishing a speech and going to Target to get toilet paper. (She is such a middle-America big-box shopper that sometimes, her speeches seem like product placement.) And it's true, she does a hilarious job of evoking the strangeness of campaigning and then going home to take care of whoever in her household needs taking care of, a clash of identities any working mother can identify with. "It's sort of like you are Batman," she said in one interview; one minute she's a smashingly well-dressed political speechifier, the next minute she has put away the cape and assumed her

Bruce Wayne identity, wiping runny noses and pouring juice.

OBAMA'S WIFE ADDS HUMAN TOUCH TO HIS APPEAL, crowed the *Financial Times*, admiringly, in mid-February 2008. But that month also brought the day when, campaigning in Wisconsin, Michelle said, "For the first time in my adult life I am proud of my country because it feels like hope is finally making a comeback." Later the same day she made the point again, saying, "For the first time in my adult life I am really proud of my country, and not just because Barack has done well, but because I think people are hungry for change." That time, a television camera was present. The loop would be endlessly played.

12

THE REACTION GREW OVER TIME. CINDY MCCAIN, wife of the presumptive Republican nominee, John McCain, lost no time in saying she had always been proud of her country, and people introducing her in speeches later would remark upon how proud Cindy McCain had always been of America. Michelle backtracked, repeatedly, explaining that she meant she was proud of her country because of the new level of political involvement Barack had inspired in voters. But it gave the conservatives a toehold, a talking point. In May 2008, the Tennessee Republican Party made a video, posted on YouTube, in which sons and daughters of the Volunteer

State professed their patriotism and explained why they had always been proud of America. The Washington State Republican Party would make a similar video. The whisper campaign started: Michelle was a fifth columnist, an internal enemy, a malcontent, an America hater; once embedded in the White House she would . . . what? Hard to know! But it would be bad! Because she wasn't proud of her country!

First Lady Laura Bush later graciously attempted to end this conversation, coming to her rescue by mildly conjecturing that what Michelle had likely meant was that she was "more" proud of her country. But that was like trying to put out a blaze in Malibu in the dry season. It would take more than that to control the flames.

Meanwhile, a number of African American voters did not find her comment surprising or think she had necessarily misspoken. In more than one interview I did for this book, people volunteered that they knew what Michelle Obama was getting at, observing that you can love your country without feeling proud of it. "Love precedes pride," the Reverend Jesse Jackson Sr. pointed out. This was well before Jackson burned his bridges with the Obamas by notoriously commenting that he wanted to castrate Obama because of his speeches urging young black men to be more responsible for their children.

Jackson considered this condescending to African Americans. Weeks before that incident, I had called Jackson to see if he had any reminiscences about Michelle when she was a teenager hanging out in his household. But Jackson wanted to talk about her "really proud" comment, explaining that over the course of history, countless African Americans have felt love for their country without feeling proud of it, citing in particular the way black soldiers who fought in World War II showed patriotism only to experience racism on the battlefield and the home front. Jackson also observed that many parents love their children without always feeling proud of them.

In a separate conversation with Arthur Brazier, the former pastor of the Apostolic Church of God and a longtime South Side religious leader—someone who knew Chicago back when you had to be careful which neighborhood you walked into—Brazier made the same distinction. "Can I make a comment on this?" he said. We had been talking about Chicago history, but he, too, wanted to say something in defense of Michelle's comment. "I understood what Michelle was saying," he pointed out. "People who have not traveled that same road that African Americans traveled could not understand it. But I can understand it because I was drafted in the army in World War II. When I got my notice, I didn't burn my notice or go to Canada, because I love my country. I went to war, but in my uniform I was in a segregated army, totally and completely segregated. And in my uniform, when I was training in the South, I had to ride in the back of the bus. If I wanted to drink water from a drinking fountain, I had to drink from a fountain that said 'Colored.' It was greatly humiliating. But I loved my country. I was awarded two bronze stars. I still loved my country. But I wasn't proud of it. There's a difference."

These comments suggest that in the place where Michelle grew up, it might in fact be unremarkable—a cliché, a trope, a truism—to acknowledge that you loved your country but weren't feeling proud of it at a given moment. It would be a reasonable thing to say. And it could be reasonable to say the same thing now, driving around parts of South Side, witnessing neighborhoods afflicted by drugs and guns and bad public schools, neighborhoods where residents are often blamed for their situation by people who ignore the fact that jobs evaporated but segregation stayed. This sentiment may be best expressed in the Langston Hughes poem "Let America Be America Again," which speaks not just on behalf of blacks, but of all people who have felt disenfranchised despite their faith in the American ideal.

Which sentiment should dominate—hope or despair? That depends on where you are living. Michelle was not permitted to elaborate and had to retract what she had said. It was a conversation America was not prepared to have, and events soon conspired to make sure it didn't happen. In March 2008, ABC News aired a piece by its investigative team on the sermons of Jeremiah Wright, the pastor at Trinity United Church of Christ, of which the Obamas were members. In one 2003 sermon, Wright used the words "God damn America" in a speech about, among other things, incarceration rates of black men. In another, he said that the September 11 terrorists attacks were, in part, the result of American foreign policy, and that America's chickens were "coming home to roost." Other networks followed; Fox aired another sermon in which Wright suggested the U.S. government created the AIDS virus and spread it among black populations. All of the snippets were quickly uploaded onto YouTube.

Up to then, if Americans had heard of Jeremiah Wright at all, most of them thought of him as the pastor who once preached a sermon that gave Obama the uplifting title for *The Audacity of Hope.* Now, people were hearing someone who sounded rabid, crackpot, appalling. Obama distanced himself from the comments, saying he had never heard Wright make his most inflammatory assertions. On March 18, Obama tried to save the relationship during a speech in Philadelphia titled "A More Perfect Union." In it, he discussed the broad theme of race in America and tried to put his pastor's comments into context. In it, he likened Wright's comments to those of an old uncle whom you love even if you do not agree with his wilder statements. He also mentioned his white grandmother, Madelyn Dunham. "I can no more disown him than I can disown the black community," he said, of Wright. "I can no more disown him than I can my white grandmother—a woman who helped raise me, a woman who sacrificed again and again for me, a woman who loves me as much as she loves anything in this world, but a woman who once confessed her fear of black men who passed by her on the street, and who on more than one occasion has uttered racial or ethnic stereotypes that made me cringe. These people are a part of me. And they are a part of America, this country that I love." Wright denounced Obama's speech as politically expedient. Obama chose to break with him entirely, and later quit the church.

This created a slow burn of Internet commentary, in

which Obama's opponents, and some of his supporters, tried to make sense of the fact that Barack Obama—intelligent, probing, postracial Obama—had belonged to that church, sat in those pews. Wright is an adherent of black liberation theology, which employs passionate exhortation in seeking to address racial inequality, and which in some forms likens African Americans to the true, oppressed Christians, and white people to Christ's oppressors. How to reconcile this puzzling affiliation? It seemed so unlike Obama, cool and reasonable as he is. So those seeking an explanation looked to . . . Michelle.

The anti-Obama web contingent immediately set out trying to connect the dots, tracing what they felt sure must be an unbroken line between Michelle and Wright and other purportedly anti-American influences on Obama. "From what we've heard from Mrs. Obama, she was paying close attention to the Reverend Wright, eating up his fiery words and probably enthusiastically nodding agreement as he blamed whitey for inventing AIDS to kill blacks as Barack dozed beside her, wondering when the Reverend Wright was going to shut up" is one example of the ensuing commentary. And none other than Dinesh D'Souza wrote a web post asking, "Could Obama's wife be largely responsible for the candidate's damaging association with crackpot race-baiters like the Reverend Jeremiah Wright?" D'Souza even took this opportunity to speak out against affirmative action at Princeton dating back to the eighties.

And it wasn't just right-wing opponents. In May, the contrarian Christopher Hitchens wrote his column for the online magazine *Slate* dismissing Wright as a "conceited old fanatic" and pointedly wondering whether Michelle Obama was the fellow traveler. "Even if he pulls off a mathematical nomination victory, he has completely lost the first, fine, careless rapture of a post-racial and post-resentment political movement and mired us again in all the old rubbish that predates Dr. King. What a sad thing to behold. And how come? I think we can exclude any covert sympathy on Obama's part for Wright's views or style," Hitchens ventured, conjecturing that Michelle was the resenter and the covert sympathizer. After all, he pointed out, she wrote her thesis about race. And cited Stokely Carmichael. "This obvious question is becoming inescapable, and there is an inexcusable unwillingness among reporters to be the one to ask it," Hitchens wrote, preachily, to his colleagues.

Looking closely at Hitchens's analysis, one senses the grief of an intellectual who doesn't want to let go of his pure admiration for the intellect and character of somebody like Obama, and who turns, therefore, to his wife. Race aside, there is something infuriatingly sexist about all of this commentary. It reeks of Eve and the apple, Pandora and the box, the fallen woman luring her loving and besotted man down the road to sin and temptation. If a smart man does something stupid, cherchez la femme!

In fact, the evidence overwhelmingly suggests that it was Obama's idea to sign up with Wright. Michelle would later confirm this in an interview with Melinda Henneberger, who interviewed her for *Reader's Digest*. Wright said the same thing in an interview in 2007. Talking to the *Hyde Park Herald* for an all-Obama issue, Wright explained it this way: "He kept coming back to talk and started worshiping with us and then he joined."

Doubtless, Obama did so for many of the same reasons most Americans join churches: to worship; to be part of a community of worshipers; to see and be seen; to make contacts. Obama has noted that even when he was a community organizer, South Side pastors told him he needed to join a church, not only to save his soul but to establish his bona fides. And they were right. For black politicians, to begin a speech by praising God is "the black secret handshake," says Debra Dickerson. "It's like saying, 'Joe sent me.'" And so he explored other churches but kept circling back to Trinity and to Wright, who for all his theatrics is highly respected not only as an intellectual but as an effective leader in Chicago. He built the church into a powerhouse with some nine thousand members, and was one of the first South Side preachers to talk openly about AIDS in the black community. The church is well known for its social programs serving the poor. It's easy to see how somebody as brainy as Obama would feel more comfortable with a socially active pastor preaching a politicized form of religion. And for a newcomer bent on proving he's black enough, what better church to join than one with an Afrocentric bookstore and a plaque in its inner hallway saying "Unashamedly black and unapologetically Christian"?

That it was a well-connected congregation is the other reason Obama joined. As noted in *The New Yorker,* the person who pointed him in that direction was Obama's Hyde Park alderman, Toni Preckwinkle, who told Obama that Trinity would be a good place to worship. "It's a church that would provide you with lots of social connections and prominent parishioners," she said. "It's a good place for a politician to be a member." In other words, Obama chose his church for the same reason many do—among other things, to rub shoulders with people who could be helpful to him.

By May, opinion of Michelle was diverging. Polls showed she had both higher negatives and higher positives than Cindy McCain. Of course, Cindy McCain had not attracted nearly the amount of controversy, despite an admitted past addiction to prescription medicine, which at one point prompted her to steal drugs from a charity she was involved with. Any number of news outlets published pieces that spring asking whether Michelle was a liability or an asset, and the answer, always, was both. By now, Obama himself had begun reacting to the criticism she was absorbing: "Lay off my wife," he warned during an appearance on *Good Morning America*.

Even as Obama was clinching the nomination, Michelle, who had made the sacrifice and okayed his run, was taking more hits, in a way, than he was. In April, for instance, the *National Review* put her on the cover under the headline MRS. GRIEVANCE. On the Internet, a malicious campaign was underway to foment the rumor that a tape existed in which Michelle had used the racial epithet *whitey*. The charge was pushed by a blogger, rogue even by the standards of the Internet, who had no evidence and never produced any. Most other bloggers refused to touch the claim with a ten-foot pole, but it burbled nastily up to the surface and a reporter asked Obama about it. The campaign, which had resolved to react quickly to slurs, created an antismear Web site whose first item of business was to say that "no such tape exists."

But according to *Time* magazine's Karen Tumulty, before that denial was posted Michelle had to submit to vetting by the campaign itself. When the rumor first surfaced, Valerie Jarrett asked her if there was truth to it, and now that the charge had intensified, Michelle's chief of staff at the time, Melissa Winter, interviewed her at some length. Michelle denied ever saying it, pointing out that people of her generation didn't even use that word. According to *Time,* she was "shocked and frustrated" that she had to undergo such questioning from the campaign. In Montana, in June, Michelle would allude to the controversies by urging a crowd in Billings, "Don't trust bloggers or someone else's opinion, because people lie."

But despite the fact that it was retracted, the rumor was now in the mainstream media. Eugene Lowe, former dean of students at Princeton, now a high-ranking official at Northwestern, picked up a newspaper with a picture of her on the cover and said to himself, Well, there we go again. "I look at that, and I say, this is just the latest episode in a long history. No matter what was said, now the suggestion has been made, even if it's subsequently corrected, making the suggestion . . . is enough to achieve the desired result."

Ultimately, however, the detractors overplayed their hand. In June, when Barack had enough committed delegates to secure the Democratic nomination, making him the first African American presidential nominee of a major political party in U.S. history, Michelle gave him an affectionate fist bump as she congratulated him before a speech in St. Paul. It was played and replayed, and much of America was introduced to the gesture. A commentator on Fox described it as a "terrorist fist jab." Around the same time, Fox, in its crawl at the bottom of the screen, referred to Michelle as Obama's "baby mama," as if this accomplished woman and committed parent were no more than a ghetto girlfriend. In an act clearly of desperation, the Obamas' wildest detractors were trying to introduce the idea that if the Democratic nominee were to win, the White House would become hip-hop central, transformed by street culture. Even Maureen Dowd couldn't stand it anymore and took to defending her.

The charges were ridiculous, absurd. And yet they didn't keep Michelle from developing her own fan club. She is an unbelievable draw at fund-raisers. "Sign my Bible! Can you sign my Bible?" shrieked a woman in

Rhode Island. "She's not like a plastic talking head the way that some of them can be," said one fan, forty-one-year-old Kimberley Sorrell. And in the waning days of the primary, her clout in the campaign had become such that she was phoning superdelegates to get them to commit to Obama. By then she was headlining fundraisers on a regular basis; in Fort Myers, Florida, in late July, she starred in "what's thought to be Southwest Florida's largest Democratic event in modern times," wrote the *News-Press,* attracting six hundred listeners to hear a twenty-one-minute speech. Afterward, one admirer exclaimed, "She's so eloquent, and you can tell she speaks from the heart. She has the gift of making you feel like an old friend."

Still, the campaign was careful, wary. In a way, commentator Debra Dickerson's prediction came true. While it hadn't yet put her in a church-lady hat, the campaign began to seriously limit Michelle's accessibility, steering her into interviews with friendly media vehicles such as *Us Weekly,* which titled its cover story "Why Barack Loves Her." Interviews were given to *People* and *Access Hollywood,* emphasizing her parenting and domestic life, but interviews were also denied to others. During her trip to Pontiac, Michigan, the campaign called up the editor of Twist, a women-oriented supplement of the *Detroit Free Press,* seeking an interview. The editor wrote a gusher in which she concluded, "I felt like I was talking to my girlfriend." This, doubtless, was exactly the coverage they wanted.

She continued speaking at fund-raisers and rallies; her speeches became shorter, and they tended not to be so rhetorical or negative. She talked, still, about the hurdles facing the working class, but she did not go on at such length about the *they* that had put obstacles in her, or Barack's, way. She talked of course about how she had met Barack, joked about their household, assured people she would be listening to their concerns about work and family. She met with military families about the problems of returning veterans, a topic that combines her real expertise in family life and health care. But one of the points in her speeches she did not abandon is the image of that little girl in South Carolina, who symbolizes, for her, discouragement and neglect. Remember the little girl in South Carolina? "She knows that she's probably already five steps behind in schools that are underfunded, without the resources to prepare her" is how Michelle Obama described her in one speech.

"She knows that if she or her family gets sick, she doesn't have access to a primary care doctor. She's going to be sitting in some ER for hours on end. She knows that her parents' work situation is hit or miss. They don't know what's going to happen day to day. She knows that. But you know what she also knows? That she's so much better than this nation's limited expectations of her. And all she has is hope."

She didn't stop talking about the little girl. She talked about her at the Jan Schakowsky fund-raiser in May. She talked about her in North Carolina, Rhode Island, Texas, and California. That girl. That little girl in South Carolina. She cannot leave that girl behind because she continues to identify with her. She is still a little girl the world didn't expect much of. "You know how I know so much about that little girl?" she has said so many times. "Because she's me. I was not supposed to be here."

And yet here she is: A woman who has grown up to be really quite establishmentarian, when you get down to it, personally conservative in many ways, outgoing, friendly, comfortable around people—black, white, other. She is outspoken, likable, grounded. She may indeed be quick to find fault—with bosses, with America, whatever—but she is also warm and loyal and, truth be told, not much of a rabble-rouser. As first lady, she will be an interesting and occasionally lively one. "I'm taking some cues," she said slyly on *The View,* before the election, talking about Laura Bush's comment defending her and how grateful she was for it, how she wrote Mrs. Bush a letter but couldn't quite figure out how to address her. She was paying attention, studying up, preparing. Because that's what she is: a preparer.

It's a skill—along with being a quick study and conscientious list-maker—that she will need to draw on. Following her husband's victory in November 2008, she was vaulted into an extraordinarily public role, one for which she had had less time to prepare than almost any first spouse you can think of. Most first ladies in recent memory have had time to get used to the public gaze and the stresses it imposes, often by spending years in a governor's mansion. Not Michelle, who just five or six years ago was a private citizen, the wife of a small-time politician hardly known outside Chicago. Now she is one of the most famous women in the world, the object of fascination to people in Washington and Paris and Nairobi and Santiago, not just first lady but the first African American first lady—an immensely significant title, one that she and her family are still getting their heads around. Now, every stitch of clothing she wears, every parenting decision she makes, every word she utters is judged and probed and broadcast. The job of first lady is constraining. You have all the scrutiny, and little of the power. Hillary Clinton was perceived as too activist, Laura Bush as a bit too subdued. "It is so hard to project out realistically what life will be for me as a woman, for me as a mother when Barack becomes president," Michelle Obama told *Good Morning America*. "It's hard to know. What I do know is that given the many skills that I have on so many different levels, I will be what I have to be at the time. And it really will depend on what the country needs, what my family needs, what Barack needs. So I want to remain flexible enough so whatever is needed of me, that's what I will do."

Because their daughters are still so young, Michelle has made it clear that as first lady she will spend a great deal of time mothering them, trying to give Sasha and Malia Obama a sense of normalcy and privacy, taking them to birthday parties, buying those goody bags, supervising homework, organizing lessons, shepherding their transition into a new school and a new community. Hence her pronouncement, soon after the election, that as first lady she sees herself as "mom in chief."

"Working mom in chief" would have been a better description, however. What was probably most surprising to observers, during the first weeks of the Obama administration, was how little time Michelle spent choosing china and hanging clothes in closets—or even resting—and how swiftly she moved to assemble a formidable team of her own, one that includes policy advisers like her Harvard Law classmate Jocelyn Frye, who was brought in from the National Partnership for Women & Families and has a strong résumé on issues like workplace discrimination. Her friend Desiree Rogers came from Chicago to take the job of White House social secretary; together she and Michelle plan to make the White House more accessible and open, a social destination not only for politicians and the cultural A-list, but for ordinary citizens. One of her first acts as first lady was to speak on behalf of the Lilly Ledbetter Fair Pay Act, which makes it easier for women and minorities to sue for pay discrimination. Following that, she began high-profile visits to government agencies to promote her husband's stimulus plan, say "thank you" to civil servants, and bask in their reciprocal admiration.

Her plans clearly extend beyond supporting her husband's message. As part of what is shaping up to be an ambitious and active agenda of her own, she plans to spearhead a national service program, encouraging young people into volunteerism, as she did more than a decade ago at Public Allies. She also plans to focus on the burdens on military families. She will travel around the country listening to working parents and reporting back to her husband and his staff. These conversations could well lead to new flex-time and family-leave laws for the rest of us. But they won't change Michelle's life: A White House marriage can never be a model for a new kind of power division in the American family. When your husband is commander in chief, you can never count on his coming home early. On the other hand, now that the Obama family is spending most of its time under the same roof for the first time in years, they at last can at least realize that long-ago goal of eating dinner together. Most nights.

She clearly remains one of her husband's closest advisers and will continue to have a say in those policy issues that interest her.

It's likely there will be some discussions in the First Bedroom about, say, affirmative action, perhaps new attention paid to America's inner cities. When was the last time you heard a presidential conversation about the plight of the urban poor? It's telling that the two federal agencies Michelle visited first were the U.S. Department of Housing and Urban Development and the U.S. Department of Education, both of which have a profound impact on the lives and well-being of adults and children in urban areas such as her native South Side.

Among many things, her presence in the White

House will be, like her presence in the campaign, a powerful catalyst to an American conversation about race. We know just from this campaign that it's not an easy conversation to have. At one point, a blogger for the website *Daily Kos* posted a lurid, Photoshopped illustration showing Michelle Obama being lynched, and the image was so horrifying that the blog had to take it down. Illustrator Barry Blitt's attempt to satirize the notion of the two of them as terrorist extremists on the cover of *The New Yorker* had the same problem: The image was so powerful that some people took it literally. The content overpowered the joke.

If we needed to be reminded how uncomfortable it is to converse about race, this campaign has provided plenty of fresh examples. Michelle's attempt at starting that conversation may have been imperfect, but then again, her very presence at Obama's side as the descendant of slaves is forcing us to have it. She could have said nothing at all, and her life story would still raise questions about how far we have come in our tolerance and how far we have to go. In the end, it may be that Michelle Obama's reluctant political journey will have a more lasting impact on our dreams of equality, our hopes and our audacity, than her husband's headlong reach for the White House.

acknowledgments

This book would have been impossible to write without the help of any number of people. I would especially like to thank my friends Margaret Talbot and Nell Minow for their warm and crucial support. Lisa Sockett helped more than she knows. I am indebted to Don Rose for explicating his city, and to Stephan Garnett for the tour of Chicago's South Side. Al Kindle, thank you for the ride. For the hospitality and good will of Newton, Jo, and Martha Minow, I am so thankful. David Mendell took a break from his own reporting to help with mine. At the *Washington Post,* Lynda Robinson, Tom Shroder, and Kevin Merida were ever-ready with support and guidance. Linda Davidson and Michel duCille helped with photos. And Alice Crites and Madonna Lebling, who assisted with research, proved as always that they can find anything and anybody.

I am so grateful to my terrific editor, Priscilla Painton, an endless source of wisdom and reassurance. Dan Cabrera helped in many ways. Jay Colton did a masterful job gathering photos, and Jonathan Evans kept the production moving seamlessly. I would also like to thank Emily Yoffe, Sally Bedell Smith, Emily Bazelon, David Plotz, Hanna Rosin, Gary Johnson, Mary Hutchings Reed, Jacob Weisberg, Mark Grishaber, Elizabeth Antus, Andrew Prevot, Jack Shafer, Louis Bayard, Sharon Zamore, Jill Wijangco, Michael Jamison, John McCarron, Alex Apatoff, Marcel Pacatte, Brad Flora, Jordan Buller, and Molly Seltzer. And of course I thank my agent, Todd Shuster.

I would also like to thank Stephens and Leigh Mundy and other family members for the support and for inviting my children to their home. As always, I thank my husband, Mark Bradley, and our children, Anna and Robin, who took a lively interest in the project.

I would like to single out for thanks Leah Nylen. She started as a research assistant and became a valued ally. Her tenacity, resourcefulness, skill, and capacity for work were sustaining. I would also like to thank all those who provided interviews. Doing so was a public service, and this book benefited from every one of them.

notes

prologue

1   *On a seasonally chilly*: The description of Fraser Robinson III's job is from records provided by the city of Chicago's Department of Human Resources.

2   *In the coastal community*: Details on Georgetown County were provided by Walter Edgar, Director of the Institute for Southern Studies at the University of South Carolina, July 24, 2008. The first Fraser Robinson's military registration says that he was a kiln laborer for the Atlantic Coast Lumber Company and had lost his left arm.

3   *Some members of the Robinson*: An estimate of when Fraser Robinson II moved to Chicago is based on his marriage license, which says he married in Cook County in 1934.

3   *The Great Migration was*: This description of the Great Migration and its impact on Chicago draws on comments by Don Rose and also was sourced by the online Encyclopedia of Chicago, compiled by the Chicago History Museum and available at www.encyclopedia.chicagohistory.org. See the entries "South Side" by Dominic A.

Pacyga, "Great Migration" by James Grossman, and "African Americans" by Christopher Manning.

11 *She once remarked*: Debra Pickett, "My Parents Weren't College-Educated Folks, So They Didn't Have a Notion of What We Should Want," *Chicago Sun-Times*, September 19, 2004.

11 *Michelle Obama estimated*: Monica Langley, "Michelle Obama Solidifies Her Role in the Election," *The Wall Street Journal*, February 11, 2008.

13 *"Who is Barack Obama"*: Scott Helman, "Michelle Obama Revels in Family Role," *The Boston Globe*, October 28, 2007.

14 *"If he cares half as much"*: Jennifer Loven, "Obama and Family Spend Fourth of July in Montana," Associated Press, July 4, 2008.

14 *"He was raised in"*: Mary Mitchell, "A Girl from the South Side Talks," *Chicago Sun-Times*, August 5, 2007.

14 *"Maybe one day, he"*: Jodi Kantor and Jeff Zeleny, "Michelle Obama Adds New Role to Balancing Act," *The New York Times*, May 18, 2007.

15 *"The only thing I'm telling"*: Suzanne Bell, "Michelle Obama Speaks at Illinois State U.," *The Daily Vidette*, October 26, 2004.

15 *"[he] was a smart guy"*: M. Charles Bakst, "Brown Coach Robinson a Strong Voice for Brother-in-Law Obama," *The Providence Journal*, May 20, 2007.

17 *"that veil of impossibility"*: Richard Wolffe, "Inside Obama's Dream Machine," *Newsweek*, January 14, 2008.

20 *"The life that I am talking about"*: Robin Abcarian, "Michelle Obama in Spotlight's Glare," *Los Angeles Times*, February 21, 2008.

21 *"You know why I know"*: Kristen Gelineau, "Michelle Obama: A Would-Be First Lady Drifts into Rock-Star Territory, Tentatively," Associated Press, March 29, 2008.

326 notes

21 *In April 2008, in Indiana*: Caren Bohan, "Obama's Wife Joins Push to Court U.S. Working Class," Reuters, May 1, 2008.

22 *"Who in their right mind"*: Mitchell, "A Girl from the South Side Talks."

22 *One commentator astutely pointed out*: Megan Garber, "The Sisterhood of the Traveling Pantyhose," *Columbia Journalism Review* online, June 19, 2008, http://www.cjr.org/campaign_desk/the_sisterhood_of_the_travelin.php.

23 *"I will walk anyone"*: Michael Powell and Jodi Kantor, "After Attacks, Michelle Obama Looks for a New Introduction," *The New York Times*, June 18, 2008.

25 *Unlike her husband, who*: David Mendell, *Obama: From Promise to Power* (New York: HarperCollins, 2008), 62. During Barack Obama's "solitary spell" at Columbia University, he read voraciously.

26 *"in the black experience"*: Eugene Y. Lowe, interviewed by author, June 13, 2008.

27 *"African Americans have far more"*: Ronald Walters, interviewed by author, May 28, 2008.

29 *"I really thought his election"*: Meg Hirshberg, interviewed by author, June 8, 2007.

one

32 *"Deep down inside, I'm"*: Gelineau, "Would-be First Lady Drifts."

33 *In fact, Barack Obama*: Barack Obama, *Dreams from My Father: A Story of Race and Inheritance* (New York: Three Rivers Press, 2004), 144–47.

35 *Fraser Robinson was a volunteer*: Scott Helman, "Holding Down the Obama Family Fort," *The Boston Globe*, March 30, 2008.

36 *The precinct captain kept*: John Stroger, quoted in Milton L. Rakove's oral history of the Daley years, *We Don't Want Nobody Nobody Sent* (Bloomington: Indiana University Press, 1979), 175–78. James Taylor, quoted on p. 163.

38 *"massive incremental conspiracy"*: Don Rose, interviewed by author, May 29, 2008.

38 *"Containing the Negro was"*: Mike Royko, *Boss: Richard J. Daley of Chicago* (New York: Dutton, 1971), 132.

38 *"Blacks could walk through"*: Royko, *Boss*, 135.

39 *"As a rule, South Side"*: Royko, *Boss*, 135.

39 *The way Daley preserved*: Don Rose, "Chicago Politics from Daley-to-Daley: Stumbling Toward Reform," *Illinois Political Science Review*, Spring 1995, vol. 1, no. 1, 13–21.

40 *"Negroes were warned"*: Royko, *Boss*, 134.

41 *"To get a city job"*: Author interview with Rose.

41 *"We had some volunteers"*: Cliff Kelley, interviewed by author, July 26, 2008.

41 *"He was [almost certainly]"*: Leon Despres, interviewed by author, June 18, 2008.

42 *"My father had M.S."*: Pete Thamel, "Coach with a Link to Obama Has Hope for Brown's Future," *The New York Times*, February 16, 2007. Barack Obama describes Fraser Robinson's death in *The Audacity of Hope: Thoughts on Reclaiming the American Dream* (New York: Three Rivers Press, 2006), 332.

43 *"Some of [Michelle's] subconscious"*: Al Kindle, interviewed by author, May 30, 2007.

44 *"We as a family"*: Craig Robinson, interviewed by author, June 20, 2007.

two

45   *Around 1970, according to:* Michelle Obama once remarked that
      her family moved into the house on Euclid Avenue when
      she was a year old, but Marian Robinson's voting registra-
      tion says they moved in 1970 from South Park. Either
      way, it seems likely that six or seven is the age when she
      would have become aware of neighborhood dynamics.

47   *One of Michelle's friends:* Rosalind Rossi, "Obama's Anchor,"
      Chicago Sun-Times, January 21, 2007.

47   *"Both my kids were":* Harriette Cole, "From a Mother's
      Eyes," *Ebony,* September 2008.

49   *Back when Chicago was:* Details on South Shore are drawn
      from conversations with Abner Mikva and Don Rose,
      from the Encyclopedia of Chicago's entry "South Shore"
      by Wallace Best, and from the *Local Community Fact Book:
      Chicago Metropolitan Area: Based on the 1970 and 1980 Censuses,* ed-
      ited by the Chicago Fact Book Consortium (Chicago:
      Chicago Review Press, 1984), 116–18.

50   *"Chicago still works better":* Abner Mikva, interviewed by au-
      thor, May 20, 2008.

51   *"All my life—I was born":* Arthur Brazier, interviewed by au-
      thor, June 10, 2008.

51   *"There were racial boundaries":* Byron Brazier, interviewed by
      author, June 10, 2008.

51   *"I can remember when":* Stephan Garnett, interviewed by au-
      thor, June 17, 2008.

52   *"We wanted to bring up":* Sel Yackley, "South Shore—Integra-
      tion Since 1955," *Chicago Tribune,* April 9, 1967.

54   *"Whites and Negroes in South Shore":* "Interracial Home Visits
      Will Begin Dec. 12," *South Shore Scene,* December 1965.

56   *"If you'll show me":* Steve Kerch, "South Shore: Country Club
      Symbolizes Rebirth of Neighborhood," *Chicago Tribune,*
      November 25, 1984.

57 *Her brother, Craig, would*: Bill Reynolds, "Yes, He's Much More than Obama's Brother-in-Law," *The Providence Journal*, February 10, 2008.

58 *"That always seemed so unfair"*: Bakst, "Brown Coach Robinson."

58 *"When you grow up"*: Peter Slevin, "Her Heart's in the Race," *The Washington Post*, November 28, 2007.

58 *"The academic part came"*: Desmond Conner, "Coach Has Own Campaign," *Hartford Courant*, February 28, 2008.

58 *"smart, he was hardworking"*: Bakst, "Brown Coach Robinson."

58 *"It's difficult to miss"*: Jesse Jackson Sr., interviewed by author, June 12, 2008.

59 *In 1968, the area*: Author interview with Kindle.

59 *Stephan Garnett recalls attending*: Author interview with Garnett.

60 *"My mom and dad were"*: Terrance Thompson, interviewed by author, June 18, 2008.

61 *Earma Thompson remembers*: Earma Thompson, interviewed by author, June 18, 2008.

62 *"Basically everybody else here"*: Ola Credit, interviewed by author, June 18, 2008.

62 *"Oftentimes blacks moved"*: Author interview with Jesse Jackson.

63 *"My kids were glad to"*: Sammie Jackson, interviewed by author, June 18, 2008.

63 *"When you grow up"*: Author interview with Garnett.

64 *"We learned from the best"*: Christi Parsons, Bruce Japsen, and Bob Secter, "Barack's Rock," *Chicago Tribune*, April 22, 2007.

64 *"lots of aunts, uncles"*: Pickett, "My Parents Weren't College-Educated Folks."

64 *"very personable, and down"*: Johnie Kolheim, interviewed by author, May 8, 2008.

65   "I always say Michelle": Cassandra West, "Her Plan Went Awry, But Michelle Obama Doesn't Mind," *Chicago Tribune,* September 1, 2004.

65   "She always had poise": Author interview with Credit.

66   "If the TV broke": This quote, and the details about board games and summer vacations, are from Lauren Collins, "The Other Obama: Michelle Obama and the Politics of Candor," *The New Yorker,* March 10, 2008, 88; Barack Obama compares Michelle's family to the one on *Leave It to Beaver* in *The Audacity of Hope,* 330; Michelle's comment is in Wolffe, "Barack's Rock," *Newsweek,* February 25, 2008.

67   "You're not raised on": Author interview with Garnett.

69   "What I learned growing up": Pickett, "My Parents Weren't College-Educated Folks."

69   "We have become a nation": Collins, "The Other Obama."

72   "The summer of 1963": Author interview with Rose.

three

76   "It was just spontaneous": Christy McNulty Niezgodzki, interviewed by author, June 3, 2008.

79   "My parents weren't college-educated folks": Pickett, "My Parents Weren't College-Educated Folks."

79   "When she applied and": Dagny Bloland, interviewed by author, May 29, 2008.

81   The term and the changes: Author interview with Brazier.

81   "It was a school that": Author interview with Kindle.

85   "It was racially diverse": Robert Mayfield, interviewed by author, June 4, 2008.

87   "Although it was racially diverse": Michelle Ealey Toliver, interviewed by author, June 3, 2008.

88   "She stayed away from": Ava Griffin, interviewed by author, June 16, 2008.

89   *"Michelle's always been very vocal"*: Collins, "The Other Obama."

89   *"She badgered"*: Holly Yeager, "The Heart and Mind of Michelle Obama," *O, The Oprah Magazine*, November 2007.

89   *"Just pretend you don't"*: Collins, "The Other Obama."

89   *"It was clear that"*: Author interview with Jackson.

90   *Her mother laughs about*: Rebecca Johnson, "The Natural," *Vogue*, September 2007.

91   *"She was disappointed"*: Wolffe, "Barack's Rock."

91   *"Not many people believed"*: Theresa Fambro Hooks, "Teesee's Town," *Chicago Defender*, November 16, 2006.

92   *"Every step of the way"*: Mark Steyn, "Mrs. Obama's America," *National Review*, April 21, 2008.

93   *"No one talked to"*: Charla Brautigam, "The Secrets of Success," *Herald News*, October 14, 2004.

94   *"If you pick your"*: Thamel, "Coach with a Link to Obama."

94   *"No disrespect to the"*: Conner, "Coach Has Own Campaign."

94   *"I was overwhelmed by"*: Reynolds, "Yes, He's Much More than Obama's Brother-in-Law."

95   *"I'm so embarrassed to"*: Thamel, "Coach with a Link to Obama."

95   *"I knew him, and"*: Wolffe, "Barack's Rock."

four

98   *In 1936, Bruce M. Wright*: James Axtell, *The Making of Princeton University: From Woodrow Wilson to the Present* (Princeton: Princeton University Press, 2006), 144, *n*78.

102   *"People do not learn"*: Axtell, *Princeton University*, 307, cites this quote by Supreme Court Justice Lewis Powell, and points out that it was influenced by an essay by William Bowen published in the *Princeton Alumni Weekly* in 1977, and that Bowen attributes the idea to Eugene Y. Lowe.

103   *In 1972, the same*: "Princeton President Fights Charges by Conservative Alumni," Associated Press, January 18, 1985. Axtell discusses CAP in *Princeton University*, 216–18.

103   *"These were people who"*: William Bowen, interviewed by author, June 5, 2008.

105   *In the fall of 1985, CAP*: David D. Kirkpatrick, "From Alito's Past, a Window on Conservatives at Princeton," *The New York Times*, November 27, 2005.

106   *One of her new roommates*: Brian Feagans, "Color of Memory Suddenly Grows Vivid," *Atlanta Journal-Constitution*, April 13, 2008.

106   *"Mom just blew a gasket"*: Powell and Kantor, "After Attacks, Michelle Obama."

107   *"Michelle early on began"*: Sally Jacobs, "Learning to Be Michelle Obama," *The Boston Globe*, June 15, 2008.

109   *Students of color*: Author interview with Eugene Y. Lowe.

110   *"We all learned painfully"*: Author interview with Bowen.

111   *"I suppose it seemed"*: Robin Givhan, interviewed by author, May 21, 2008.

111   *"We weren't sure whether"*: Wolffe, "Barack's Rock."

113   *"Definitely you got the"*: Lisa Rawlings, interviewed by author, June 15, 2008.

114   *"She was then, and"*: Czerny Brasuell, interviewed by author, June 23, 2008.

116   *"My sister and I"*: Author interview with Craig Robinson.

121   *"It was awkward"*: Sharon Fairley, interviewed by author, May 8, 2008.

121   *"I always felt like"*: Author interview with Givhan.

123   *According to Marvin Bressler*: Powell and Kantor, "After Attacks, Michelle Obama."

123   *Howard Taylor, a former*: Taylor and Charles Ogletree are quoted in Jacobs, "Learning to Be Michelle Obama."

124   *Crystal Nix Hines*: Powell and Kantor, "After Attacks, Michelle Obama."

124   *"I would not characterize"*: Author interview with Brasuell.

five

127   *"She was never overtly political"*: Peggy Kuo, interviewed by author, June 7, 2008.

129   *"There was a lot of academic"*: Neil Quinter, interviewed by author, June 11, 2008.

130   *"extremely nice and affable"*: Mark Blocker, interviewed by author, May 27, 2008.

133   *"There was a little bit"*: Dave Jones, interviewed by author, June 10, 2008.

134   *"It was the most fun"*: Ronald Torbert, interviewed by author, June 16, 2008.

six

139   *Though he describes himself*: Stephen Carlson, interviewed by author, June 11, 2008.

143   *The marketing group*: Brian Sullivan, interviewed by author, May 2, 2008.

144   *"It was the most fun"*: Mary Carragher, interviewed by author, May 30, 2008.

145   *"I loved her"*: Mary Hutchings Reed, interviewed by author, May 30, 2008.

145   *"Michelle—you didn't want"*: Andrew Goldstein, interviewed by author, May 30, 2008.

146   *At least one person*: Quincy White, interviewed by author, June 12, 2008.

148   *"That doesn't surprise me"*: Abner Mikva, interviewed by author, June 19, 2008.

149 *"If what you're doing"*: Thamel, "Coach with a Link to Obama."

150 *"nerdy, strange, off-putting"*: Scott Fornek, "He Swept Me Off My feet," *Chicago Sun-Times,* October 3, 2007.

150 *"He sounded too good"*: Mendell, *Obama: From Promise to Power,* 93–94.

151 *"She would meet guys"*: Author interview with Craig Robinson.

151 *"the only two black"*: West, "Her Plan Went Awry"

151 *"I remember one of the members"*: Author interview with Carlson.

151 *"I had made this proclamation"*: West, "Her Plan Went Awry."

152 *"I think they were a little embarrassed"*: Newton Minow, interviewed by author, May 9, 2008.

152 *"You can only imagine"*: Author interview with Carragher.

153 *"as if, deep inside"*: Obama, *Audacity of Hope,* 329.

155 *"It makes the case"*: Mendell, *Obama,* 102.

155 *"I am thrilled"*: Kim McLarin, "The Real Prize," The Root. com, http://www.theroot.com/id/44409.

155 *Debra Dickerson has pointed*: Debra Dickerson, interviewed by author, June 2007.

157 *"This is the thing"*: Kalari Girtley and Brian Wellner, "Michelle Obama Is Hyde Park's Career Mom," *Hyde Park Herald,* February 14, 2007.

158 *"He was very, very low key"*: Stefano Esposito, "Two People Who Love Each Other," *Chicago Sun-Times,* July 13, 2008.

158 *Craig likes to tell*: Author interview with Craig Robinson.

158 *"From the start, Michelle"*: Esposito, "Two People Who Love Each Other."

159 *"I am sure that from"*: Martha Minow, interviewed by author, May 9, 2008.

159 *"We had many debates"*: Sarah Brown, "Obama '85 Masters Balancing Act," *The Daily Princetonian,* December 7, 2005.

160   *But even as Michelle*: Author interview with Carragher.

161   *"As we were dating, we"*: Michelle Obama, interviewed by author, July 18, 2007.

161   *"transparently and lovably ambitious"*: Robert Putnam, interviewed by author, June 2007.

161   *"I think he saw himself"*: Author interview with Newton Minow.

161   *Craig also likes*: Author interview with Craig Robinson.

162   *"He probably should have"*: Author interview with Michelle Obama.

162   *"She knew what she"*: Leslie Bennetts, "First Lady in Waiting," *Vanity Fair* online, December 27, 2008, http://www.vanityfair.com/politics/features/2007/12/michelle_obama200712.

162   *"History is littered with"*: Author interview with Kindle.

162   *Michelle tells a funny story*: Fornek, "He Swept Me Off My Feet."

164   *Newton Minow recounts*: Author interview with Minow.

165   *He, too, had agonized*: Obama, *Audacity of Hope*, 328.

166   *"I looked out at my"*: Powell and Kantor, "After Attacks, Michelle Obama."

166   *"Can I go to the family"*: Pickett, "My Parents Weren't College-Educated Folks."

166   *"I didn't see a whole"*: Wolffe, "Barack's Rock."

166   *"I do understand"*: Author interview with Reed.

167   *"At the beginning it's"*: Author interview with Carragher.

168   *"We left corporate America"*: Byron York, "Michelle's Struggle," *National Review*, February 9, 2008.

169   *"We don't need a world"*: Abcarian, "Michelle Obama in Spotlight's Glare."

169   *"When you're given the gift"*: Scott MacKay and Mark Arsenault, "Campaign 2008—Making Obama's Case," *The Providence Journal*, February 21, 2008.

170   *"I'm perfectly happy doing"*: Author interview with Carlson.

seven

172 *During his first term*: Anecdotes provided by Don Rose.

173 *It became clear to*: Judson Miner, interviewed by author, June 2007.

173 *"I was, like many people"*: Barack Obama, interviewed by author, July 2007.

174 *"You've got to have a grasp"*: Author interview with Michelle Obama.

176 *Miner says that during*: Author interview with Miner.

177 *"I offered her a job"*: Wolffe, "Barack's Rock."

177 *"Certainly, it would be something"*: Don Rose, interviewed by author, August 1, 2008.

178 *Obama was also worried*: Mendell, *Obama*, 103.

178 *"My fiancé wants to know"*: Parsons et al., "Barack's Rock."

178 *"Barack hasn't relied deeply on me"*: Parsons et al., "Barack's Rock."

179 *"Fundamentally we work well"*: Girtley and Wellner, "Michelle Obama."

179 *"There are a lot of successful people"*: Karen Springen and Jonathan Darman, "Ground Support," *Newsweek*, January 29, 2007.

181 *"These are folks"*: Marilyn Katz, interviewed by author, June 10, 2008.

183 *"A lot of people are uncomfortable"*: Parsons et al., "Barack's Rock."

184 *Barack was on the founding*: Parsons et al., "Barack's Rock."

185 *"I wear jeans and I'm the director"*: Carol Kleiman, "Xers Don't Fit the Stereotypes," *Chicago Tribune*, April 9, 1995.

185 *"There was an intensity to her"*: Julian Posada, interviewed by author, June 19, 2008.

187 *Michelle "had incredibly high expectations"*: Yeager, "The Heart and Mind of Michelle Obama."

188 *"The most powerful thing"*: Parsons et al., "Barack's Rock."

188 *"It was too touchy-feely"*: Suzanne Perry, "Fired Up and Ready to Grow," *The Chronicle of Philanthropy*, April 17, 2008.

189 *"You kind of know"*: Jobi Petersen, interviewed by author, June 23, 2008.

191 *In the* National Review: Steyn, "Mrs. Obama's America."

193 *"We have so much more"*: Sandra Sobieraj Westfall, "Michelle Obama: 'This Is Who I Am,' " *People*, June 18, 2007.

194 *She took Michelle to lunch*: Jo Minow, interviewed by author, May 9, 2008.

195 *"He is not Mr. Door Opener"*: Girtley and Wellner, "Michelle Obama."

195 *"He worships her"*: Author interview with Martha Minow.

195 *Michelle—the boss—has*: Deanna Bellandi, "Michelle Obama Likes to Razz Her Husband," Associated Press, May 29, 2007.

196 *"He had no money"*: Girtley and Wellner, "Michelle Obama."

eight

199 *Obama came to his*: Ryan Lizza, "Making It," *The New Yorker*, July 21, 2008.

199 *Michelle told me*: Author interview with Michelle Obama.

199 *"She thought he was so"*: Melinda Henneberger, "The Obama Marriage," *Slate*, October 26, 2007.

200 *"You know, Barack is"*: Author interview with Michelle Obama.

201 *"concentrated and persistent joblessness"*: William Julius Wilson, *When Work Disappears: The World of the New Urban Poor* (New York: Knopf, 1996), 3–24.

203 *"I have a ton of bright friends"*: Girtley and Wellner, "Michelle Obama."

205 *"She came—she sat"*: Author interview with Minow.

206 "At first she was": Author interview with Mikva.

208 so avid to hire him: Jason Zengerle, "Con Law," *The New Republic*, July 30, 2008.

208 "I would often spend": Obama, *Audacity of Hope*, 338.

208 During this period, Michelle: Kevin O'Leary, "Why Barack Loves Her," *Us Weekly*, June 30, 2008.

208 "the kind of dinner": Kantor and Zeleny, "Michelle Obama Adds New Role."

209 "There are times when": Mendell, *Obama*, 104.

209 "He didn't want to be": Mendell, 140.

210 "He had no idea": Joyce Feuer, "Typical First-Time Dad," *Hyde Park Herald*, February 14, 2007.

210 "for three magical months": Obama, *Audacity of Hope*, 339.

211 "Our kids are used": Girtley and Wellner, "Michelle Obama."

212 "we'd had some intense discussion": Author interview with Martha Minow.

213 "aloof Ivy League": Mendell, *Obama*, 121.

213 "I wasn't prepared to": Author interview with Barack Obama.

214 "I was a little bit": Author interview with Mikva.

214 "It was no secret": Author interview with Kindle.

214 "My failure to clean": Obama, *Audacity of Hope*, 340

216 "We have just some": Liz Halloran, "Q&A: Michelle Obama; From the Soccer Field to the Stump," *U.S. News & World Report*, February 11, 2008.

216 "barely on speaking terms": Mendell, *Obama*, 135.

216 Shomon, who had repeatedly: Mendell, 136–69.

218 "He is not a good": Dan Shomon, interviewed by author, June 2007.

218 "That was the one time": Author interview with Mikva.

219 "Some doubts entered": Author interview with Obama.

219 "He would always tell": Author interview with Shomon.

219 "Michelle wanted him to": Author interview with Minow.

220 "I'm sure Michelle": Mendell, *Obama*, 145.

220 *Barack has written about*: Obama, *Audacity of Hope*, 355.
220 *He says that not*: Mendell, *Obama*, 150.
221 "*I thought I could*": Author interview with Barack Obama.
221 "*You are a senator*": Author interview with Minow.
221 "*I knew that he*": Author interview with Shomon.
223 *She had been struggling*: West, "Her Plan Went Awry."
223 "*There was an important period*": Holly Yeager, "The Heart and Mind of Michelle Obama."
224 "*I cannot be crazy*": West, "Her Plan Went Awry."
224 "*How do I structure*": Sandra Sobieraj Westfall, "Michelle Obama," *People*, June 18, 2007.
224 "*there was a lot of*": Judy Keen, "Candid and Unscripted, Campaigning Her Way," *USA Today*, May 11, 2007.
225 "*Obama could not be*": Author interview with Kindle.
226 *During one intense period*: Slevin, "Her Heart's in the Race."
226 "*At every step of*": Author interview with Michelle Obama.

nine

227 "*The big issue around*": Mendell, *Obama*, 151.
228 "*[P]olitics has been*": Mendell, *Obama*, 152.
228 "*elegant and funny, and*": Author interview with Martha Minow.
228 *Michelle also went with*: Mendell, *Obama*, 155.
230 "*You have to talk*": Jo Becker and Christopher Drew, "Pragmatic Politics, Forged on the South Side," *The New York Times*, May 11, 2008.
230 "*Our bases overlapped*": Author interview with Barack Obama.
230 *Just after the New Year*: Mendell, *Obama*, 161.
231 *Four years later, Kwame*: Kwame Raoul, "Stay Out of Jail," *Hyde Park Herald*, February 14, 2007.
233 "*This was a huge advantage*": Author interview with Mikva.
234 *Obama used Michelle as*: Mendell, *Obama*, 230.

235   *"They like you!"*: Eric Zorn, "Victory Party Puts Tiny Crack in Obama Calm," *Chicago Tribune,* March 18, 2004.

235   *"He's pretty excited"*: Zorn, "Victory Party."

235   *"I am tired of just"*: Lauren W. Whittington, "Final Days for Fightin' Illini," *Roll Call,* March 9, 2004.

236   *"The thing that gets discounted"*: Author interview with Michelle Obama.

237   *There had been whispering*: Mendell, *Obama,* 171.

237   *"As the candidate"*: Author interview with Michelle Obama.

238   *"people who inspired hope"*: Donna Brazile, interviewed by author, June 2007.

239   *"a message of inclusiveness"*: John Kerry, interviewed by author, July 2007.

240   *"He's in the midst"*: Robert Gibbs, interviewed by author, June 14, 2007.

241   *"He's had some attention"*: Eric Krol, "Obama Tries to Keep Cool as Star Rises," *Chicago Daily Herald,* July 27, 2004.

241   *"Just don't screw it up"*: Obama, *Audacity of Hope,* 359.

241   *"She was listening intently"*: Collins, "The Other Obama."

243   *"It's like walking around"*: Author interview with Craig Robinson.

244   *Jeremiah Posedel, the staffer*: Jeremiah Posedel, interviewed by author, August 1, 2008.

245   *"The point of this"*: Author interview with Gibbs.

246   *"The stress of the trip"*: Mendell, *Obama,* 293.

247   *"He was just furious"*: Author interview with Shomon.

249   *"I didn't expect it"*: Christopher Wills, "Obama's Wife Takes Big Role in Campaign," Associated Press, October 23, 2004.

250   *"Daddy's not going to"*: Christopher Benson, "Barack and Michelle Obama Begin Their Storied Journey," *Savoy,* February 2005.

250   *"The first conversation"*: David Axelrod, interviewed by author, June 2007.

250   "We had very deliberately": Author interview with Barack Obama.

251   "You know, I'm like": Author interview with Michelle Obama.

251   Obama would later write: Obama, Audacity of Hope, 72.

252   "roomy refuge from": Mendell, Obama, 383.

252   "Our lifestyles have changed": Girtley and Wellner, "Michelle Obama."

253   New York Times columnist: Maureen Dowd, "She's Not Buttering Him Up," The New York Times, April 25, 2007.

253   "the ugliest men become": Author interview with Jo Minow.

254   "This is what I have": Mendell, Obama, 293.

254   Another time, a friend: Mendell, 259.

254   "First of all, I": Joy Bennett Kinnon, "Michelle Obama: Not Just the Senator's Wife," Ebony, March 2006.

255   "He knows that if": Mendell, Obama, 259.

255   "We would talk about": Henneberger, "The Obama Marriage."

256   "You don't miss it": Jeff Zeleny, "The First Time Around," Chicago Tribune, December 25, 2005.

258   "Oh, heck, yeah": Jeff Zeleny, "Q&A with Michelle Obama," Chicago Tribune, December 25, 2005.

ten

261   "My marriage is intact": Obama, Audacity of Hope, 346–48.

266   "It's hard to interpret": Jeff Zeleny, "Kenyans' Welcome Is Heavy with Hope," Chicago Tribune, August 27, 2006.

266   "gave him a heightened": Author interview with Axelrod.

267   "as a full partner": Mendell, Obama, 380.

267   "I huddled with Barack": Author interview with Martha Minow.

268   "She's also concerned": Author interview with Jo Minow.

268   "I don't worry about": Mendell, Obama, 382.

268 *"As far as entertaining"*: Maura Webber Sadovi, "Family Recipe," *Chicago Sun-Times*, December 22, 2004.

269 *In December 2006, Crain's*: Greg Hinz, "Off Message: Sen. Obama Sees No Hypocrisy in His Wife's Post at a Firm That Does Business with Wal-Mart," *Crain's Chicago Business*, December 11, 2006.

270 *Also that fall, the*: Mike Dorning, "Employer: Michelle Obama's Raise Well-Earned," *Chicago Tribune*, September 27, 2006.

272 *"She is a very meticulous"*: Author interview with Kindle.

272 *The Chicago Sun-Times*: Rosalind Rossi, "Obama's Anchor."

272 *"I need to be able"*: Mendell, *Obama*, 382.

273 *"Michelle's not keen"*: Author interview with Minow.

274 *"It wasn't that she"*: Author interview with Mikva.

274 *"She was interested"*: Gwen Ifill, "Beside Barack," *Essence*, September 2007.

274 *"Suffusing these discussions"*: Wolffe, "Barack's Rock."

275 *"My comfort zone comes"*: Author interview with Michelle Obama.

275 *"When you're in Hawaii"*: Rachel Gallegos, "Obama's Wife Says U.S. Must Be Ready for Change," *Iowa City Press-Citizen*, December 21, 2007.

eleven

276 *"Michelle was out of sight"*: Springen and Darman, "Ground Support."

279 *"abiding race consciousness"*: Jonathan Tilove, "Balancing Act," *Post-Standard*, March 4, 2007.

280 *"I heard that growing up"*: Parsons et al., "Barack's Rock."

283 *"I don't want to raise"*: Chris Fusco and Lynn Sweet, "Feels Good to be Home," *Chicago Sun-Times*, February 12, 2007.

283 *"Fear the war, fear"*: Guy Clifton, "Michelle Obama Illuminate's Husband's Vision," *Reno Gazette-Journal*, August 10, 2007.

283 *"There's only one person"*: Joe Astrouki, "Michelle Obama Backs Husband's Nomination," *The Equinox*, December 13, 2007.

283 *"We are new to"*: Paul H. Heintz, "Wife Touts Obama's Achievements," *Brattleboro Reformer*, December 6, 2007.

284 *"I'm always humbled"*: Zita Allen, "Barack-star in the Big Apple," *New York Amsterdam News*, March 15, 2007.

285 *The approach backfired*: Dowd, "She's not Buttering Him Up."

285 *Michelle brushed off*: Keen, "Candid and Unscripted."

286 *"A leader is more"*: Lynn Sweet, "Facing the Experience Question," *Chicago Sun-Times*, February 15, 2007.

286 *"I know that experience"*: Beverley Wang, "Michelle Obama Campaigns for Husband," Associated Press, May 7, 2007.

286 *"Name me one other"*: Tanangachi Mfuni, "Michelle Obama in Harlem," *New York Amsterdam News*, June 28, 2007.

287 *"He is the real thing"*: Margaret Talev, "Michelle Obama Says 'He's Ready,'" McClatchy Newspapers, July 8, 2007.

287 *"Barack doesn't have years"*: Clifton, "Michelle Obama Illuminates."

287 *"If we lived anywhere else"*: Dana Slagle, "Michelle Obama Juggles Marriage, Motherhood and Work on the Campaign Trail," *Jet*, September 10, 2007.

288 *"We are still too"*: Craig Gilbert, "Race Enters the Race," *Milwaukee Journal Sentinel*, January 22, 2008.

288 *"If we're not ready"*: Gallegos, "Obama's Wife Says U.S. Must Be Ready."

288 *"We are our own evil"*: Rebecca Traister, "Michelle Obama Gets Real," *Salon*, November 28, 2007.

288 *"You've never seen"*: Traister, "Michelle Obama."

289 *"Now, I am more passionate"*: Girtley and Wellner, "Michelle Obama."

290 *"If there was a woman"*: Yeager, "The Heart and Mind of Michelle Obama."

293 *"Michelle had worked so"*: Westfall, "Michelle Obama."

294 *when her staff had noticed*: Kantor and Zeleny, "Michelle Obama Adds New Role."

294 *"She's traded in her solid"*: Debra Dickerson, "Michelle Obama's Sacrifice," *Salon*, May 21, 2007.

295 *"I like cultures."*: West, "Her Plan Went Awry."

296 *"To me, it's now"*: Bennetts, "First Lady in Waiting."

297 *"strategic genius"*: Collins, "The Other Obama."

297 *"It wasn't a threat"*: Langley, "Michelle Obama Solidifies Her Role."

298 *"One of the most"*: Jennifer Hunter, "A Swipe at the Clintons?" *Chicago Sun-Times*, August 23, 2007.

298 *"If Barack doesn't"*: Nedra Pickler, "Obama Hopes to Surprise Clinton in Iowa," Associated Press, October 5, 2007.

299 *"Barack, feel—don't"*: Langley, "Michelle Obama Solidifies Her Role."

299 *"It's sort of like"*: Mary Mitchell, "Makeup's Too Much Work," *Chicago Sun-Times*, August 7, 2007.

twelve

303 *"Can I make a comment?"*; Author interview with Brazier.

307 *"From what we've"*: Michael Reagan, "Rev. Wright's Pupil," FrontPage Magazine, May 12, 2008, http://www.frontpagemag.com/Articles/Read.aspx?GUID=BC7F1FF0-E964-4C5C-B72B-EED8EBA9C0D8.

307 *"Could Obama's wife be"*: Dinesh D'Souza, "Michelle Obama's Inferiority Complex," Townhall.com June 30, 2008, http://townhall.com/columnists/DineshDSouza/2008/06/30/michelle_obamas_inferiority_complex.

308 *In May, the contrarian*: Christopher Hitchens, "Are We Getting Two for One?" *Slate*, May 5, 2008.

309 *Michelle would later*: Melinda Henneberger, interviewed by *Reader's Digest*, October 2008.

309 *"He kept coming back"*: Erin Meyer, "Where Obama Developed His Audacity of Hope," *Hyde Park Herald*, February 14, 2007.

309 *"the black secret handshake"*: Author interview with Dickerson.

310 *"It's a church that"*: Lizza, "Making It."

312 *But according to Time*: Karen Tumulty, "Can Obama Shred the Rumors?" *Time*, June 23, 2008.

312 *"Don't trust bloggers"*: Howard Kurtz, "History in Slow Motion," *The Washington Post*, June 4, 2008.

313 *Even Maureen Dowd*: Maureen Dowd, "Mincing Up Michelle," *The New York Times*, June 11, 2008.

313 *"Sign my Bible!"*: Geleneau, "Would-Be First Lady Drifts."

314 *During her trip to Pontiac*: Laura varon Brown, "Michelle Obama Shares with Twist in Exclusive," *Detroit Free Press*, July 19, 2008.

about the author

Liza Mundy is a staff writer at the *Washington Post*, where for more than ten years she has covered politics, popular culture, and women's issues. She is a regular contributor to the online magazine *Slate* and participates in their women's blog *XX Factor*. She has also written for *Lingua Franca*, *Redbook*, *Mother Jones*, *Washington City Paper*, and *Washington Monthly*. She lives in Arlington, Virginia, with her husband, Mark Bradley, and their two children, Anna and Robin.